RELIGION IN WESTERN CULTURE:

Selected Issues

Frank E. Eakin, Jr.
University of Richmond

University Press
of America™

To my parents

Gotthold Ephraim Lessing, an eighteenth-century German dramatist, wrote during a period when most European Jews were still confined to the ghettos. Through his writing he waged a personal struggle against religious bigotry and intolerance, as indicated by his play, Nathan the Wise (1779). In a conversation between Friar Bonafides and Nathan, a Jew, the Friar was captivated by Nathan's character:

FRIAR: O Nathan, Nathan! You're a Christian soul!
         By God, a better Christian never lived!
NATHAN: And well for us! For what makes me for you a
         Christian, makes yourself for me a Jew![1]

CONTENTS

PREFACE

This volume is the outgrowth of both an undergraduate introductory course and a seminar in a graduate humanities program. An unfulfilled need for a text which combined basic data relative to the Judeo-Christian tradition and investigated some implications of that tradition within western cultural experience prompted the writing of the manuscript.

Definitive treatment of the subject matter is neither intended nor claimed. My intention has been to give sufficient background information with paradigmatic application so that the reader can pursue his own course in similar cultural manifestations. The text has been designed, therefore, to guide the novice into selected areas of investigation relative to the Judeo-Christian tradition. The instructor should assist the reader's examination of particular areas of concern within a classroom context. Apart from a class setting, however, a student should be able to gain direction for further study through the Notes and the Selected Bibliography. While explanatory notes have been kept to a minimum, it will be clear that bibliographical materials abound in the areas addressed in the text. This book must be seen only as a beginning, therefore, as one seeks understanding of the expression of religion within western culture.

The reader should recognize that the writer stands within the Judeo-Christian tradition. As a Christian, however, I acknowledge and affirm my relationship and indebtedness to the Jewish faith. Judaism is recognized as a fulfilling faith for those who stand within that tradition, as a vehicle which speaks meaningfully regarding man's relationship to God and man. One lives with the hope that perhaps the age is past when most Christians would sense a "divine" compunction either "to save" the Jew from perdition or to hold him accountable for his historic act of "deicide." Jews and Christians are brothers in a faith pilgrimage, with both affirming that Yahweh is God (1 Kings 18:39; Deuteronomy 6:4; and Mark 12:29). My intention has been that the book's content might be informed by this perspective.

I am indebted to the Division of Christian Education of the National Council of the Churches of Christ in the United States of America for permission to use extensively quotations from the Revised Standard Version of the Bible, copyrighted 1946 (New Testament) and 1952 (Old Testament), 1971, 1973. The word LORD indicates translation of the proper name of Israel's God, Yahweh.

Indebtedness for information goes far beyond the bounds of acknowledgment. Differing authors whom I have read have contributed directly to the manuscript, as indicated by the Notes; and indirectly they have contributed as personal positions have been formulated. Permission to use specific materials is by courtesy of the sources indicated: excerpts from Jonathan Livingston Seagull by Richard Bach from Macmillan Publishing Co., Inc. (Text: Copyright 1970 by Richard D. Bach); the dialogue from Gotthold Ephraim Lessing's play, Nathan the Wise, by Frederick Ungar Publishing Co., Inc.; Harcourt Brace Jovanovich granted permission to use material from Mircea Eliade's The Sacred and the Profane; excerpts from Roland de Corneille's Christians and Jews is by courtesy of Harper & Row, Publishers, Inc.; and excerpts from JB by Archibald MacLeish by Houghton Mifflin Company, copyright 1956, 1957, and 1958 by Archibald MacLeish.

Given the sensitivities of our day, one tries diligently to avoid sexist connotations. Nonetheless, ease of expression frequently makes the use of "he" or "man" preferable. The reader can discern where a masculine antecedent is intended, but generally where "he" and "man" are used they convey generic sense. I ask the reader's indulgence in recognizing that no sexist connotations are intended!

The library personnel of both the University of Richmond and Union Theological Seminary in Richmond have been most cooperative and helpful while this manuscript has been in preparation. This assistance is gratefully acknowledged.

The Committee on Faculty Research at the University of Richmond has supported generously my effort. During the 1972-1973 session, a research grant made possible the purchase of some needed materials. A summer research fellowship for the summer of 1974 relieved me of teaching duties that I might devote my full attention to writing the manuscript. My appreciation is extended to my colleagues and to the University of Richmond for this tangible expression of support.

One's indebtedness to students can never be fully appreciated. Through lectures, discussions, and some distributed materials differing groups of students have been exposed to most of the materials. Characteristically they have helped to sharpen focus and clarify issues.

In like fashion, numerous individuals have read various portions of the manuscript. From their suggestions I have profited immeasurably. Needless to say, however, only I can be accountable for the manuscript in its completed form.

Mrs. Jane Crum, Department of Religion secretary,

has been extremely helpful in typing from handwritten copy the first draft of the entire manuscript. Her patience in deciphering what often appeared to be impossible script is greatly appreciated.

My wife, Frances, consistently supports my professional activities. She encourages my engagement in projects such as this, and she has tolerated in good spirit my obsession to see this particular manuscript completed. In addition, she has frequently served as a sounding board for the development of new concepts or for the refinement of the more popularly known, encouraging me by both her interest and reactions. While words are an inadequate expression, her encouragement and assistance are warmly appreciated. One can never express sufficiently appreciation for this kind of continuing support.

My wife joins me in dedicating this book to my parents, Frank Edwin Eakin and Vera Taylor Eakin. It was from them that I received my initial introduction to the Judeo-Christian tradition. From them the love of learning was implanted, and to them I continue to be indebted for their encouragement and support as my post-secondary education was undertaken. This book serves only as a token of my appreciation for, indebtedness to, and continuing esteem for them.

INTRODUCTION

In the final third of the twentieth century, the influences and interdependencies of east and west upon each other make unthinkable extended isolationism on the part of either. Politics, global economics, population control, food provision, and religious expression are but some of the more obvious influences and interdependencies. Oriental impact is clear in western society, and the east equally manifests western lifestyle.

In spite of pervasive cross-fertilization, the principal western religious tradition remains the Judeo-Christian. It would be a mistake, however, to conclude that, since the Judeo-Christian tradition dominates, it has developed monolithically. One needs only to observe the differing denominational expression within both Judaism and Christianity to verify the absence of singular perspective among its devotees.

To understand religion in western culture, we take as investigational base the Judeo-Christian tradition, seeking to glimpse both what it was and what it has become. This tradition undergirds many aspects of western thought and is the base of its primary religious institutional expression. This tradition has both been transmitted by and has shaped significantly western culture.

Edward Cell stated that "'Culture' may be defined as the way of life of a people and includes their language, art, literature, religion, philosophy, science, technology, education, ethics, law, and political system."[1] The advantage of this definition is its breadth, for it indicates the inclusive nature of

culture. Two points need to be emphasized, however,
from the perspective of religion and culture. First,
we recognize the dual-edged nature of religion's sword--
it both determines cultural expression and serves as an
indicator of cultural development. Second, we recognize
that a volume of limited scope cannot treat exhaustively
religion in western culture. We are limited to dealing
with some selected aspects of religion and western culture.

A part of our difficulty centers in space-time
limitations which preclude our examining approximately
3000 years of Hebrew history and almost 2000 years of
Christian history. Both faith communities have under-
gone significant changes since their inception, both
reacting to and absorbing from their environment. Not
inconsequential in this process, of course, has been
the interaction of the two communities themselves.
Unfortunately, we cannot look in depth at these historical developments, instructive and interesting as they
would be. We must selectively view our concerns as
these are derived both from antiquity and modernity,
always seeking to deal faithfully with the materials.

Christianity's history exudes these historical
problems, for perspectives have been altered in significant fashion as the faith community developed. Once
Christianity spilled into Europe from the Levant, where
it had originated, western history assumed a new dimension. A cultural encounter was set in motion which
would alter significantly Christianity from its Jewish
roots and bring it both into conflict and conformity
with the thought pattern characteristic of the Greco-
Roman world.

Several examples will suffice. In Hebrew thought
man was viewed in his wholeness. He was a psychosomatic

unit. Wherever there was life there was body and spirit, and the concept of soul as envisioned by the Greek was foreign to Hebrew thought. Had Christianity remained true to its Hebrew heritage, therefore, this same sense of unity would have prevailed. Instead, Christianity was absorbed into a Greek thought pattern which divided man into body and soul (or body, spirit, and soul). The thought even went so far as to reckon the body as the "prison house" of the soul and man's prime aspiration to be escape from this "prison house." It is in this context that Christianity came to speak of "saving souls," a concept totally foreign to Christianity's Hebraic roots. Jesus' ministry displays a Hebraic foundation, for only this illuminates the mighty act tradition. Since man is a unit, you cannot deal with "physical" or "spiritual" problems in isolation. The total man must be the object of scrutiny.

Or look at another example. What do Christians call the worship chamber? A sanctuary! It is as though worship were a refuge, a place of withdrawal from the hurts and pains of the world. According to Biblical understanding, however, in Hebrew and Christian thought one meets and expresses love toward God through the encounter with one's neighbors. Worship is authentic, therefore, not as it feeds our need for salving our wounds but as it forces us out of the cocoon of complacency and makes us meet our fellow with his hurt and need! Sanctuary hardly conveys this!

Christopher Dawson, in his excellent book, Religion and the Rise of Western Culture, described religion as the key to history.[2] Focusing on the Middle Ages, he noted religion's integrating and binding nature which had successfully withstood the waxing and waning of national powers. He suggested that a study of culture demonstrated "an intimate relation between its religious faith and its social achievement."[3] This relationship may be either positive or negative, in terms of its effect on human life; but nonetheless few individuals would question that a relationship exists.

Dawson directed little attention to the Judeo-component of the Judeo-Christian tradition. He focused on the Christian church and emphasized its importance for unifying western culture: "Apart from this single exceptional case [the Carolingian Empire], there has never been any unitary organization of western culture apart from that of the Christian Church, which provided an effective principle of social unity."[4]

While it has been the church which has exercised this phenomenal influence, we should not lose sight of the church's Hebrew heritage. The church's earliest thought pattern was Hebraic, although its rapid Hellenization permitted such aberrations as the division of man to which reference has earlier been made, the rise of monasticism, and the ultimate wedding of religious and political authority within western culture.

Modern western society is immeasurably more complex and cosmopolitan than that of our fathers and grandfathers. In spite of this, individual and community religious values continue to be influenced and/or shaped by the dominant Judeo-Christian tradition. Individual determination is not to be denied, but how seriously does an individual generally consider the options of Islam or Buddhism, for example, when born and raised in western culture? To what extent is religious affirmation truly individual response? Is it really more to be credited to societal conditioning?

Unfortunately, because of traditional training most find it difficult to view objectively religious values and understandings. One problem focuses on the nature of religion. As prelude to a study of religion in western culture, therefore, it is necessary to clarify the concept of religion, the subject of inquiry in Chapter I.

Another obstacle to objectivity in religious values and understandings revolves around attitudes toward the Bible, the primary literary deposit of the Judeo-Christian tradition. Many react to the Bible either with excessive allegiance or with total rejection. Regardless of the pole, such attitudes result from a misconception of the Bible--how it was formulated and transmitted, and what its significance is for the community and the individual today. If we are to understand religious perspectives in western culture, therefore, we must seek some clarification of the Bible. This we pursue in Chapter II. Also, as further aid for understanding the Bible, the impact of the historical-critical methodology is investigated in Chapter III.

Chapters IV and V focus selectively on the historical and conceptual development of Yahwism-Judaism and Christianity. Both Judaism and Christianity are historical faith structures, and an understanding of these communities must incorporate historical development.

Chapter VI portrays selectively the Jewish-Christian relationship from the beginning of the Christian movement to the present. Some of the main problems which have plagued the path of constructive Jewish-Christian dialogue will be discussed.

Chapter VII investigates some of the manifestations of religion within western culture. Specifically, the doctrinal, ritual, mythical, and social expressions are discussed.

The final Chapters focus on some specifics of religion's influence upon western culture. Chapter VIII concentrates on the impact of religious perspectives upon actions within society, emphasizing the problems associated with making ethical decisions and the phenomenon of civil religion. How the individual reacts to his environment has interested writers of every age, and in Chapter IX this perennial theme is investigated. A survey of spokesmen ranging from Biblical to contemporary writers will contribute to this study.

Only one other factor should be noted. It is necessary for the investigator of religion and western culture to be as objective as possible in searching for understanding. No one lacks conditioning influences, but one may seek consciously to subjugate prejudices and to pursue openness.

I

WHAT IS RELIGION?

Religion is as much a part of western lifestyle as
the automobile and the skyscraper. In spite of religion's
everyday manifestations in language, literature, the arts,
ethical systems, and legal and political structures, religion is nonetheless difficult to define. As a working
definition is sought, the following suggestions are proposed:

Religion . . .
  is affirmation or acceptance of an ultimate commit-
      ment by an individual and/or community.
  affects the totality of lifestyle: beliefs, emotions,
      and actions.
  encourages meaningful relationship(s) with a tran-
      scendent presence and/or man.
  assists the individual's integration into his exis-
      tential situation.
  enables the finding of meaning by an individual and/
      or community in/for his/their existence.

These suggestions propose a definition which is
broad, which will include as many thought patterns as
possible. Initially it indicates that the individual and/
or community either affirms or accepts an ultimate commit-
ment--the former more an active, the latter more a passive
expression. The ultimate commitment connotes that which

the individual/community takes with absolute seriousness, that which could not be rejected and the sense of ultimacy survive. At the same time, it is the ultimate commitment which shapes the life either of the individual or the community, providing for relationships, integration, and meaning.

The practice of religion is both subjective and corporate. Because of its subjective aspect, religion is expressed in radically different ways. Conversely, by virtue of its corporate associations, there is always a pull toward conformity. The individual inclination toward distinctiveness through personal expression is thereby counterbalanced by community demands for uniformity. In the Judeo-Christian tradition, the individual-community tension is intensified since it is commonly accepted that a meaningful belief-action relationship may be experienced only within the nurturing life of the institutionalized movement.

In traditional Judeo-Christian religious circles, it is assumed that transcendent presence means God; but that which is taken with ultimate seriousness may or may not be understood as divine. The suggestions for definition indicate that religion's ultimate commitment serves to encourage meaningful relationship(s) with a transcendent presence and/or man. Paul Tillich, in Christianity and the Encounter of the World Religions, stated:

Religion is the state of being grasped by an ultimate concern, a concern which qualifies all other concerns as preliminary and which itself contains the answer to the question of the meaning of our life. Therefore, this concern is unconditionally serious and shows a willingness to sacrifice any finite concern which is in conflict with it. The predominant religious name for the content of

2

such concern is God--a god or gods.[1]

Perceiving religion in this broad perspective, many cultural expressions which have not usually been acknowledged religious have religious overtones. A number of "isms"--as Socialism, Communism, Humanism, and Existentialism--may be viewed in terms of their religious import.

Where transcendent presence is not identified with deity, some notion of hierarchal value(s) will generally be acknowledged. There is in religious structure, therefore--whether affirmed or accepted, whether individual or community--that which gives direction, purpose, goal, meaning.

Within an individual's life, religion cannot be restricted to one portion of existence. Religion is not just emotion, nor is it reserved solely for the intellect. Embedded in the suggestions for definition is the idea that the ultimate commitment must affect the totality of lifestyle--beliefs, emotions, and actions. Short of such encompassing involvement, the expression should not be designated religious. Much more than the sense of transcendent presence, it is this trilogy-umbrella which is crucial in determining whether a cultural expression should be designated religious.

In addition, our definition suggestions state that religion pertains to the question of relationships. In both Judaism and Christianity, this has implied a relationship to God making itself known in the devotee's reaction to his neighbor (see Amos 5:1-24 and 1 John 4). Both the definition suggestions and the quotation from Paul Tillich raised the possibility, however, that perhaps deity is not essential in the understanding of religion. One recognizes many persons of otherwise traditional religious orientation who find increasingly difficult the acceptance

3

of an all-powerful, transcendent, and yet immanent deity presence. These individuals, within both Judaism and Christianity, frequently take seriously the role of the synagogue or the church within society. Such seriousness of purpose argues for a broader definition of religion, such as expressed by Tillich, a definition permitting both theistic and non-theistic concerns in a study of western culture and religious influences. Theistic or not, however, it might be argued that the faith structure acknowledged by the individual must bring the person into meaningful relationship with his neighbor, with neighbor being interpreted in its broadest possible sense.

It has been suggested also that religion assists the individual's integration into his existential situation. Socially and psychologically our lives are spent relating to various publics. Individually, we react to our existential situations quite differently. Some are crushed beneath this burden; others conceal inadequacies through various facades; while some appear to cope effectively with their existential situation. While the premise that religion is only the individual's social-psychological crutch appears inadequate, a person's faith commitment should enable him to meld more meaningfully into his existential situation. Religion, however understood, should enable the individual to bind together constructively the disjointed pieces of the puzzle called life.

The final definition suggestion states that religion enables the finding of meaning. Regardless of one's optimism, life continually presents obstacles and paradoxes which encourage viewing life as meaningless uncertainty. Jeremiah verbalized this concern: "Why does the way of the wicked prosper?" (Jeremiah 12:1). This concern, however, was not limited to antiquity; for modern man still searches with Koheleth[2] for the key giving

4

meaning to a meaningless existence. As Job found his answer in personal submission and affirmation (Job 42: 1-6), so man in western culture has traditionally sought the key to meaning in submission and affirmation. Recognizing the dangers associated with such a quest, nonetheless history records many individuals who have been personally victorious in this search. Some find this meaning within community, while others discover fulfillment in individual, isolated fashion. The primary point, however, is that religious commitment should assist the finding of meaning.

Religion in Etymological Perspective

An etymological investigation of the word "religion" assists as we search for a working definition of religion.[3] Assistance comes primarily from probable Latin derivations, since it is from the Latin that English derived. At the outset, note also that "religion" was not used in the New Testament until the latest writings and Biblical Hebrew has no word which is translated as "religion." Two Latin words, however, provide possible derivations.

Relegere conveys the ideas of "to gather together," "to review," and "to reread," among other translations. Associations of "attentiveness" and "studiousness" could derive from relegere. From this base, several possible manifestations of religion emerge.

A relegere-religion might express itself in an individual's intense desire for understanding which is accompanied by zealous motivation for study. This expression cannot ignore the overall impact of religion on the inclusive needs of the individual--beliefs, emotions, and actions. Much of the traditional expression of Judaism and Christianity might be captured under this rubric.

5

A relegere-religion, however, might also be oriented toward the more intellectual/academic grasp of life. Such a religion might be essentially a philosophical system to which the individual is committed in intellectual quest and lifestyle. Some of the manifestations of "Godless" Judaism would demonstrate this thrust, as might also a Christian structure whose sole emphasis was ethics.

Particularly within the Roman Catholic Church a third possible manifestation of relegere-religion has been developed, monastic lifestyle. As a Christian phenomenon, monasticism emerged in the third century and became a fixed characteristic of the Catholic Church by the fifth century.[4] While the movement has assuredly had its redeeming qualities in terms of academic zeal and mission activity, Kenneth Scott Latourette expressed a concern shared by many, namely that the prime emphasis of the monk "was his own salvation, not that of others."[5]

Religare is the other Latin word most often suggested for the derivation of "religion." Religare conveys the meanings of "to tie up," "to bind back," or "to moor" (as a ship). A religare-religion bespeaks the individual's commitment which integrates existence so that life becomes meaningful and coherent. Like the central shrine around which pre-monarchical Israel gathered,[6] so the religious affirmation serves to tie together the individual's existence. This is the understanding most often affirmed both in academic and dictionary treatment as the more probable derivative choice.

Religion: Problematic Terminology

Etymology notwithstanding, "religion" is problematic in that negative connotations have attached to the word. In 1961 James Muilenburg published The Way of Israel.[7]

While the content of the book is excellent and highly recommended for the individual who would understand "Biblical Faith and Ethics" (the book's subtitle), the title itself is our primary interest. It conveys helpfully the emphasis of the Hebrew faith. According to Acts 9:2, Jesus' earliest followers, devout Jews heralding the arrival of the Messiah, were designated those "belonging to the Way." These individuals affirmed a dynamic, meaningful relationship with Yahweh, the God of Israel. This relationship accepted man's dependency upon God, as the creature "leaned upon" his Creator in recognition of the Creator's ultimacy in existence.[8] This was not "religion" in the sense that the word is traditionally used in western culture.

"Religion" is first used in late New Testament writings, roughly near the turn of the first Christian century. The young Christian movement now found itself in difficulty on two important fronts.

On the one hand, a gradual separation from Judaism was initiated early in the life of the church, particularly as the church expanded beyond the borders of Palestine into dominantly Greek areas. Resulting from this expansion, the constituency of the church became more Greek than Jew. This development was essentially accomplished by the end of the first Christian century, and the two communities reached such an impasse that it appeared likely that their re-unification was forever precluded.

On the other hand, Christianity's estrangement from Judaism resulted in concomitant problems with the Roman Empire. Rome was characteristically tolerant toward religious expressions so long as they were (1) ancient established structures, (2) tolerant of other viewpoints, and (3) supportive of the highly revered Pax Romanae.

7

Thus the reaction to Christianity, once the ties to Judaism were severed, was inevitable--Christianity was a new religion; had a "one-way" focus denying tolerance; and, as we see in Paul's travels recorded in the Acts of the Apostles, the Pax Romanae was evidently frequently disturbed. This led to persecutions during the reign of the Emperor Domitian (A.D. 81-96), when, for the first time, Christians were persecuted because they refused to disavow the name "Christian."

In such a conflict-persecution situation most institutions seek to preserve themselves by digging deeper their trenches, making firmer and clearer their requirements, crystalizing their focus. This happened in the life of the late first-century (or early second-century) church through several of its writings. A good example of this crystalization process is seen in the following:

If anyone thinks he is religious, and does not bridle his tongue but deceives his heart, this man's religion is vain. Religion that is pure and undefiled before God and the Father is this: to visit orphans and widows in their affliction, and to keep oneself unstained from the world (James 1:26-27).

On the positive side, this passage clarifies that genuine faith expresses itself in the individual's relations with his fellow, that true faith can never be restricted to devotional exercises. While applauding this viewpoint, the faith was essentially reduced to an approved pattern of behavior. If this be not sufficiently negative, there is strong withdrawal-from-the-world emphasis in the view that one must "keep oneself unstained from the world." The following statement expresses the detrimental effect of introducing such an understanding:

8

The introduction of the general concept of "religion" into the late NT writings meant the weakening, if not the abandonment of the revelation character of Christianity. "Religion," now meaning the Christian religion, becomes a system of doctrine, an organization, an approved pattern of behavior and form of worship.[9]

While not involving the specific word "religion," a criticism parallel to that expressed toward Christianity might be leveled against Judaism. Judaism similarly continued the transition from the dynamic "word" to scriptural authority.[10] The word "religion," therefore, is only symptomatic of the problem but its clearest symbol, namely the danger of vesting in any individual, group of individuals, written corpus of materials, or oral tradition an ultimate and unalterable authority for determining acceptable action (namely, orthodoxy). Any such vestment must be counter-balanced by scrupulous safeguards which assure both the freedom of the individual and the non-abusive exercise of authority.

Another example of the entrenched and static thought of late first- or early second-century Christianity is seen in 1 Timothy 3:1-6:19. Among other things, the requirements are stated for holders of ecclesiastical office: "Now a bishop must . . . Deacons likewise must be . . . Command and teach these things . . . ." How different this was from the charismatic appointment of the early judges, the prophets, or for that matter from Peter's defense of Jesus' followers at Pentecost (Acts 2). The progression is unfortunately easy from the spontaneity and dynamic quality of existential encounter to the staid, static transmission of a sacred tradition which must be preserved at all costs! As we shall see, this was a part of the Judeo-Christian problem against which

Sigmund Freud so violently reacted. Not only should he
have done so, but so too should those who seek today to
affirm that tradition. An individual's most authentic
act may come at the point of rejecting ideas which have
become tradition encrusted, if those ideas are recognized
to be inconsistent with the realistic thrust of one's
ultimate commitment.

A problem for Christianity has been its refusal or
inability to deal on the layman's level with the crucial
problems of understanding the New Testament text, particularly the Gospels. As will be discussed further in
Chapters II and V, it is impossible to determine assuredly the authentic word of Jesus in the Gospels. Not
desiring to make a complex problem appear simple, one
criterion might be that the more authentically the saying
strikes of first-century Judaism the more probable is its
being a genuine word. Jesus was born and died a Jew,
and Christianity is a post-Jesus phenomenon established
by his followers who affirmed "Jesus is the Christ." In
this light, the following saying attributed to Jesus indeed sounds authentic:

And one of the scribes came up and heard them disputing
with one another, and seeing that he answered them well,
asked him, "Which commandment is the first of all?"
Jesus answered, "The first is, 'Hear, O Israel: The Lord
our God, the Lord is one; and you shall love the Lord
your God with all your heart, and with all your soul,
and with all your mind, and with all your strength.' The
second is this, 'You shall love your neighbor as yourself.' There is no other commandment greater than these"
(Mark 12:28-31).

These responses were not original with Jesus but were

drawn directly from the Jewish tradition. The initial
response derives from Deuteronomy 6:4-5, with only a
single inclusion, "with all your mind," an indication of
Hellenistic influence upon first-century Judaism.[11] The
response relative to loving your neighbor stems from
Leviticus 19:18. This juxtaposition of ideas clearly
indicates the dual emphasis upon love of God and neighbor
which characterized the faith of Israel. The writer of
1 John, while a Christian, was pointing those "belonging
to the Way" to a proper Jewish orientation for their
faith when he asserted:

Beloved, let us love one another; for love is of God,
and he who loves is born of God and knows God. He who
does not love does not know God; for God is love . . .
We love, because he first loved us. If any one says,
"I love God," and hates his brother, he is a liar; for
he who does not love his brother whom he has seen, cannot love God whom he has not seen. And this commandment
we have from him, that he who loves God should love his
brother also (1 John 4:7-8, 19-21).

Little of interpretive note could be added to this passage that would make clearer the author's expression.
It seems difficult, however, to envision the Johannine
thought apart from a firm foundation in the prophetic
tradition:

"With what shall I come before the LORD,
    and bow myself before God on high? . . ."
He has showed you, O man, what is good;
    and what does the LORD require of you
but to do justice, and to love kindness,
    and to walk humbly with your God? (Micah 6:6a, 8)

11

Or again, the eighth-century prophet, Hosea, a contemporary to Micah, speaks:

For I desire steadfast love more than sacrifice,
    the knowledge of God more than burnt offerings (Hosea
      6:6).[12]

From these emphases in Israel's faith, it was natural that early Christian teaching such as that expressed in 1 John 4 should develop.

Recognizing the vitality of Israel's faith witnessed in the law and the prophets as well as the dynamic quality characteristic of the sayings attributed to Jesus and to spokesmen within the early Christian tradition, the unfortunate development of "religion" in the late New Testament writings and the loss of dynamic quality in much of Judaism becomes the more apparent. "Religion" was covered with negative overtones, with the basic idea being that "religion" was something done during periods of withdrawal from the world.[13] One even withdrew into the sanctuary to be religious! While "religion" appears to be the best semantic vehicle for conveying the whole array of emotion-belief-action concerns characteristic of faith's expression in western culture, one uses the word with full recognition of the associated problems historically.

Social and Institutional Expressions

In western culture, religion finds expression in numerous ways. Two of these are social and institutional manifestations. A brief comment on these cultural expressions gives further insight into religion.

Socially, the Judeo-Christian faith manifests itself

12

in diverse ways. The pendulum swings from the tent-meeting revival in the small rural community to the educational institution or the health center supported by a religious body, from the church- or synagogue-supported bingo game to the religiously-supported counseling agency. In terms of lifestyle, the range extends from the simple life of the beloved country minister to the much more complex existence of the bishop presiding over many subordinates or the tzaddik who acts as spiritual leader for a Hasidic community.

Religion's social manifestations sometimes have negative impact. Whenever a structure interacts with society, there is the possibility of sham. The tent meeting may bring a charlatan to town, or "professional religious degrees" may be purchased, or a clergyman may become sexually involved with a parishioner--all of which results from the fact that the social manifestation of religion necessitates human involvement and humans are not always motivated by the highest aspirations. The results of human societal involvement cannot be programmed. The individual seeking to understand religion must be mindful of its multiple social manifestations in western culture.

Perhaps the most common manifestation of religion in our culture is the institutional structure. Too often Judaism is identified with the synagogue or Christianity with the church. One must recognize, however, that Judaism/Christianity is more than the faith's manifestation in a single body of devotees. Both Christianity and Judaism have rich heritages, and it is a travesty to either tradition to equate any single church or synagogue with Christianity or Judaism respectively. For example, one may point to a particular church that is

racist socially and illiterate theologically. Surely
one could not conclude from such limited evidence that
Christianity should be so characterized!

Accepting the fact that such churches and synagogues
exist, however, what negative effect does this have on
the devotee? In The Future of an Illusion, Sigmund Freud
addressed a related problem. Freud was concerned particularly about the impact of prejudicial religious training upon youth and their developmental process. He noted
the remarkable difference observable between a mentally
active, inquisitive child and a passive, accepting adult.
He was convinced that religious education was responsible
for at least a part of this atrophy occurring between
childhood and adulthood, for he was certain that apart
from implanted thought a child would not normally begin
to think about God and related ideas. He could not conclude that a child, who was not introduced at an early
age to religious indoctrination, might not ultimately
develop in precisely the same fashion as the indoctri-
nated child. He was certain, however, that society did
not give the child unhampered time for mental development.
He noted that religious indoctrination is a part of the
child's early training, and thus "by the time the child's
intellect awakens, the doctrines of religion have already
become unassailable."[14]

Freud was correct in noting that considerable attention has traditionally been directed to the child's religious training in much of western culture. The various
religious traditions within the Judeo-Christian umbrella
stress childhood education, although some more than others.
It is acknowledged that at least one clue to maintaining
the child within the fold of the faithful once the child
reaches adult status is the early training which makes
increasingly difficult the adult's wavering from the

commitment once made.

Supreme Court decisions forbidding the reading of scripture and the offering of prayers within public school classrooms address also the problem noted by Freud. Rather than being anti-religious, such a decision protects the parent/child against the child's being so conditioned that the child cannot make intelligent personal decisions at a later age regarding religious matters.

It is true that Freud had a low opinion of man, that he was reacting against perversion of the Judeo-Christian faith, and that he formulated questionable assumptions regarding man and his religious inclinations. These arguments do not cancel out the facts that Freud was reacting to observed experience and, more importantly, that we experientially are confronted by similar data.

Perhaps the most telling of Freud's argument is his conviction that religious indoctrination prevents an individual's questioning his religious experience, thereby precluding the possibility of individual, responsible choice/decision. This situation continues to characterize much of traditional Christianity and Judaism, whether parental, Biblical, or institutional authority be used as the instrument for implanting and upholding the traditions of the faith. It is puzzling why religious believers have frequently permitted the affirmed faith to become so restrictive and binding a garment.

Surveying the faith of ancient Israel, the prophet Amos (approximately 750 B.C.) criticized those practices and institutions which characterized Israel's worship:

I hate, I despise your feasts,
     and I take no delight in your solemn assemblies.
Even though you offer me your burnt offerings and cereal

offerings,
   I will not accept them,
and the peace offerings of your fatted beasts
   I will not look upon.
Take away from me the noise of your songs;
   to the melody of your harps I will not listen.
But let justice roll down like waters,
   and righteousness like an ever-flowing stream (Amos
     5:21-24).

Amos spoke against the structure of the ritual establishment, appealing for justice to be the bench mark of
Israel's faith. His criticism and caustic remarks were
not welcomed (Amos 7:12-13), but at least he could express his concerns. At one point, however, Amos had a
vital advantage which we do not share--there was not in
his day an established body of literature designated as
scripture, a corpus to which all of the faithful must
give unerring allegiance! One must not imply that canonical scriptures convey only negative connotations; but
certainly in the name of orthodoxy history records many
incidents of enforced thought agreement, strange and
unloving acts, and general restriction of thought.

    To the contrary, Jesus lived when the traditions
of the law and the prophets were firmly set by centuries
of use.[15] Even with this restriction on his thought,
he did not hesitate to question the "acceptable" religious
thought and action of his day. At times he reacted very
traditionally, as when he is recorded to have stated:

Think not that I have come to abolish the law and the
prophets; I have come not to abolish them but to fulfil
them. For truly, I say to you, till heaven and earth
pass away, not an iota, not a dot, will pass from the

law until all is accomplished (Matthew 5:17-18).

Nonetheless, at another point in Matthew's compilation
of the "Sermon on the Mount," Jesus is portrayed icono-
clastically as setting himself against the revered "law
of Moses":

You have heard that it was said to the men of old, "You
shall not kill; and whoever kills shall be liable to
judgment." But I say to you that every one who is angry
with his brother shall be liable to judgment . . .
(Matthew 5:21-22a).

Similar "But I say to you" statements follow as regards
adultery (Matthew 5:27-30), divorce (Matthew 5:31-32),
swearing (Matthew 5:33-37), retaliation (Matthew 5:38-42),
and the demand of love for one's enemies (Matthew 5:43-
48). While the Pharisaical attitudes of the first century, with which Jesus is depicted as being so frequently
in opposition, sometimes indicated tradition's self-
serving and demeaning nature, the presence of Jesus and
his words give witness to the continuing possibility of
questioning and innovative interpretation. Unfortunately,
Jesus' death signaled the response of the static community of faith to such zeal. Should it come as a great
shock, therefore, that Judaism and Christianity often
have permitted themselves to become the servants, indeed
the victims, of their own traditions?[16]
     The meaning of religion in western culture is clar-
ified by the institutional forms in which the religion(s)
expresses itself. One must not identify the institution
(whether this be corporate body, service structure, canonical scriptures, etc.), however, with religion. This is
not a valid assumption. Institutions give clues regarding

the commitments of the faith community, indicators which
are important, however, in evaluating and understanding
the relationship of a given religious expression to its
culture.

Conclusion

This examination of some selected areas of religion's
impact upon and expression within western culture has begun with an attempt to define "religion." It is imperative that the concept's parameters be understood by the
investigator, and the position here presented has argued
for a definition as inclusive as possible. Judaism and
Christianity in western culture are practiced within a
pluralistic society. Increasingly, we are being sensitized to the diversity within these traditions and of the
traditions' encounter with religions which are based on
presuppositions different from those characteristic of
Judaism and Christianity. If one is to be a contributing
member of such a pluralistic society while affirming a
faith posture within the Judeo-Christian tradition, such
breadth of understanding must be recognized.

We have concluded broadly that religion must speak
to the questions of relationships, integration, and meaning. Overarching these three concerns is our earlier
understanding that any religious expression, be it theistic or non-theistic, must relate to the entirety of
man's existence--his beliefs, emotions, and actions.
How much more one might assert of minimal expectation
and gain consensus is difficult to assess, but these
criteria are sufficient to embark us on our investigative
pilgrimage.

Finally, then, we express the definition suggestions
as a working definition:

Religion is affirmation or acceptance on the part of an individual and/or community of an ultimate commitment which affects the totality of lifestyle (beliefs, emotions, and actions), which ultimate commitment serves to encourage meaningful relationship(s) with a transcendent presence and/or man, to assist the individual's integration into his existential situation, and to enable the individual and/or community to find meaning in/for his/their existence.

II

THE HEBREW-CHRISTIAN SCRIPTURES:
ORIGIN AND TRANSMISSION

Within western culture it is perhaps impossible for
an individual to view the Bible objectively. For some a
rigid Biblical fundamentalism was associated with childhood training, resulting in a life of revolt against this
background.[1] For others a Biblicist perspective dominates
so thoroughly that the individual cannot be understood
apart from this orientation. Even if one has not been
affected in such polar fashion, nonetheless the pattern
of western culture has been determined in numerous ways
by the Biblical mind. This statement is true whether
we refer to institutions dealing with such concerns as
health (hospitals, nursing homes, etc.), education (col-
leges, universities, seminaries, etc.) and welfare (as
orphanages and homes for the elderly), or whether we look
to those numerous allusions to the Bible which have in-
filtrated our language: "the patience of Job," "saved
by the skin of his teeth," "the law of the Medes and the
Persians," "the handwriting on the wall," as well as many
others.

The Question of Authority
Scripture's authoritarian position prevails because
of the attitude toward the material by persons of Judeo-
Christian orientation. The authority of the scriptures

is granted rather than inherent. This should not sur-
prise, since every religious community must have its
ultimate authority, its final court of appeal. While
the Roman Catholic Church takes scripture seriously, the
Catholic's ultimate appeal has been the Pope. Even this
authority, however, is understood to have a Biblical base.

The Synoptic Gospels (Matthew-Mark-Luke) follow a
similar pattern in portraying Jesus' ministry. They depict a Galilean ministry which is followed by a brief
period of withdrawal in the area of Caesarea-Philippi.
From this retreat Jesus made his way to Jerusalem and
there spent his final days.

In the Caesarea-Philippi withdrawal, however, the
Gospel of Matthew records a statement by Jesus not recorded by the other Gospels. Speaking in response to
Peter's affirmation, "you are the Christ, the Son of the
living God" (Matthew 16:16), Jesus is recorded to have
said:

Blessed are you, Simon Bar-Jona! For flesh and blood
has not revealed this to you, but my Father who is in
heaven. And I tell you, you are Peter, and on this rock
I will build my church, and the powers of death shall not
prevail against it. I will give you the keys of the kingdom of heaven, and whatever you bind on earth shall be
bound in heaven, and whatever you loose on earth shall be
loosed in heaven (Matthew 16:17-19).

The Roman Catholic Church has interpreted this passage to
mean that Jesus vested in Peter a unique power and authority. It is understood that this investiture has been
transmitted within the Papacy and correctly resides in
the designated Pope.[2] The stability of the authoritarian
Papacy depends upon the acceptance of this passage by the

faithful. Currently, however, a changed attitude toward
scripture is making untenable such a view of the Papacy
for many people. Numerous examples might be cited of
Roman Catholic priests renouncing their vows of celibacy
for marriage. Many Roman Catholic families use various
birth control measures in open defiance of the Papal edict
regarding birth control in order to limit the size of
family. It is difficult to maintain that the Pope continues to have the same type of authority, at least in
the United States, as was true even a generation ago.

This questioning of authority is not unique within
the Roman Catholic structure. For Judaism and Protestant
Christianity, the primary authority has been vested in the
scriptures. The Bible has been the source of ultimate
recourse, but perhaps this authority symbol has degen-
erated even more markedly than the Roman Catholic authority symbol. A person, such as the Pope, can always maintain a distance between himself and his would-be detrac-
tors, a distance which may also have the effect with many
devotees of enhancing the untouchable holiness of his
person. This obviously is not the situation for the
Jewish-Protestant Christian Biblical authority, for once
that authority symbol was translated into the vernacular
of the people it was thereby potentially opened to the
eye and reason of scrutiny.[3] Once literary-critical
evaluative procedures developed, it was inevitable that
the Biblical text would be subjected to such a process.
It was also inevitable that any vestige of holy aura
forbidding man's careful analysis of the authority source
would be dismissed. Thus we recognize that in most Jewish
and Protestant Christian circles the Bible no longer conveys that sacred aura so unquestionably accepted one or
two generations earlier[4]--an air of questioning has replaced the earlier air of acceptance.

It is the impact of Biblical criticism which has altered the view of the Bible so drastically and with such radical impact on Judaism and Christianity.[5] Biblical criticism could not advance very far, however, were it not for the availability of the vernacular scriptures. We turn our attention, therefore, to some of the relevant data regarding the process of scriptural transmission. We do so partially to call attention to the long process of transmission and partially to note some of the difficulties involved. We do so also, however, because once a person has recognized the way the scriptures evolved, were transmitted, and ultimately were accorded canonical status, it is difficult ever again to look upon scripture as possessing that divinely handed-down sacred aura.

The Evolution, Transmission, and Canonization of the Scriptures

Two key words--revelation and inspiration--need to be clarified. Revelation has to do with the process of communicating divine truth. When one attempts description of the process, disagreements emerge. May revelation be conveyed through the realm of nature itself, more of a natural revelation open to all, or is revelation restricted to a more special type of communication which comes directly from God to the specially chosen person? Resolution of this problem is not germane to our interests, although the reader should be aware that differing positions are taken by scholars on this issue.

The greater issue rests in understanding inspiration, basically the idea of influence exerted upon persons so that their writings have special authority. The nature of that influence and the degree of the authority are the pressing problems. Many differing positions along the spectrum are supported, but one position in particular must be singled out as unacceptable. This is the view generally designated as plenary inspiration. This position asserts that the writings are essentially a verbatim dictation by deity, which if carried to the extreme means that man becomes only a moot instrument with the deity assuming the task of authorship. Such a view also holds that the written product must thereby be infallible, without error of any sort.

Plenary inspiration is unacceptable because it is an insult both to God and to man. As one reads the Biblical text, errors are found therein. For example, Joshua 7:1-8:29 records the Israelite conquest of the city of Ai, yet archaeologists indicate that Ai was not even an occupied city in Joshua's day. In Genesis 21:34, Abraham is noted to have spent considerable time in "the land of the Philistines," yet the Philistines did not enter Canaan until approximately 1150 B.C., roughly a half millennium following the period usually associated with Abraham. In Genesis 1 and elsewhere the Bible assumes a three-tiered cosmological understanding, but any modern school child knows that this is a primitive cosmological concept unacceptable for contemporary man. The Israelite often expressed strong prejudice against the Canaanite, which is one of the central thrusts in Genesis 9:18-27. Is one to take historical error, limited scientific knowledge, and human prejudice as indication of divine dictation or as clear sign that man himself is the author and interpreter of the materials? Obviously the latter is preferable, for it is only in this choice that one avoids a problematic view of God and a demeaning portrayal of man. Only in this perspective does man become a meaningful, self-determining agent rather than a puppet. And if the Biblical record is clear on any point, it is that man was created to be a free agent capable of choice and determination.

Thus much depends on our basic attitude toward the Bible, how we would describe the volume as a literary product. The Bible is man's understanding of his encounter with God. In such a view the integrity of both God and man are preserved. Only in such a view is the record consistent with its evolution, transmission, and ultimate canonical status.

The manuscripts which eventually were combined to form the Hebrew scriptures were written during the millennium roughly from 1200 B.C. until 150 B.C. There are perhaps some vestiges of earlier material, for example Exodus 15:21 (the "Miriam couplet") is generally judged one of the oldest poetic couplets in the Hebrew scriptures, perhaps even the record of an eyewitness to the Hebrew encounter with the sea. As shall be discussed below, however, the oldest large block of material is the Yahwist source, which is dated approximately 950 B.C.

As regards those books which comprise the New Testament, these materials were generated over a much briefer time span, roughly the century from A.D. 50 to 150, with the latter date being assuredly an outside date. One would expect that the thought structure expressed in material which developed over a century to be less diverse than that evolving over a millennium. Nonetheless, one does not find a monolithic thought structure in the New Testament, as witnessed for example in the differing evaluation of God's reaction to the Jews in Matthew 7:22-23, 8:11-12, 25:10-12 (paralleled in Luke 13:22-30) as compared to Paul's evaluation in Romans 9-11. Or again view the distinctiveness of the nativity accounts of Matthew 1-2 and Luke 1-2[6] as compared to the pre-existence ideas expressed by the Fourth Evangelist

(John 1:1-18) and by Paul (Philippians 2:5-11). This differentiation in thought pattern could be illustrated many times over, but the primary point is the recognition that in both the Hebrew and Greek scriptures there are a multitude of viewpoints expressed. While this recognition does not discourage the search for the thread(s) which bind(s) together the scripture, nonetheless such a recognition helps to prevent an overly simplistic view of the scriptures.

We have indicated the dates during which the Hebrew and Greek[7] manuscripts were formed, and now several notations helpful to reading the translated manuscripts follow:

1. There is not extant today one single copy of any original manuscript, what is usually designated an "original autograph." This is true whether one speaks of entire books or only of portions of books. For no book or portion of the Bible do we possess an original manuscript. This obviously renders as rather misguided references to "reading the original," or similar assertions.

2. None of the scriptures, either the Hebrew or the Greek, were written as sacred scripture. This is a position which certain writings came to possess over a lengthy period of time, be that position determined by association with a certain ritual occasion (the book of Esther and the festival of Purim), with a misguided view of authorship (as the letters of 1 and 2 Timothy), or simply a general sense of the law of use, however that be applied--the Psalms as the "hymnbook of the Second Temple" or the "Model Prayer" of Matthew 6:9-15 (parallel in Luke 11: 2-4) as a part of the worship format of the early church. Recognizing that neither the Hebrew nor the Greek writings were penned to be scripture should again sharpen our perspective on the ultimately accepted canonical scripture.

26

3. Chapter and verse divisions in the Biblical books are artificial divisions inserted by Stephen Langton, the Archbishop of Canterbury, in the year 1228. Clearly mistakes were made regarding the best point for dividing chapters and verses (note the division of Genesis 2:4). The modern reader should be attuned to this possibility, recognizing his literary-critical responsibility in the study of the materials.

4. Approximately 1600 Irish Archbishop Ussher published a monograph which discussed the chronology of the Bible. It was in Ussher's treatise that the date of creation was set at 4004 B.C. Shortly after the monograph's publication, an enterprising publisher of the King James Bible determined to include Ussher's chronological schema in his publication by inserting the dating at the top of each page in inter-columnar fashion. While one does not find this dating in modern translations, the impact of the dating schema which stood alongside the "sacred word" on the page and came thereby to share its "sacred aura" is witnessed in the science-versus-religion problems, most notably that of evolution.

5. Errors were inevitably made in the translation-transmission process. Contemporary interpreters must seek through various literary critical tools to deal with these errors. At the same time, one must acknowledge that, in spite of the general reliability of contemporary translations of the Bible, there are errors which have become sacred to some religious communities.

A prime example of this problem is found in Isaiah 7:1-17. Tiglath-Pileser III of Assyria was preparing to march on the Mediterranean coastal region to bring the area under the aegis of his control. To meet that threat, a union of Mediterranean nations was formed, among the coalition nations being Israel under King Pekah and Syria

under King Rezin. For reasons unexplained King Ahaz of
Judah had not joined. Thus in 735 B.C. Judah was issued
an invitation-ultimatum to become a part of the defense
force, probably because the coalition leaders did not
wish to risk being forced to fight on two fronts, with
Assyria attacking from the northeast and Judah from the
south. King Ahaz refused to enter, raising the possibility of the coalition's laying siege to Jerusalem.
Recognizing this imminent threat, King Ahaz went to the
reservoir servicing Jerusalem to assure himself that the
city would have sufficient water to withstand the siege.
While at the reservoir, he was approached by Isaiah; and
the following conversation took place:

Again the LORD spoke to Ahaz, "Ask a sign of the LORD
your God; let it be deep as Sheol or high as heaven."
But Ahaz said, "I will not ask, and I will not put the
LORD to the test." And he said, "Hear then, O house of
David! Is it too little for you to weary men, that you
weary my God also?
Verse 14   Therefore the LORD himself will give you a sign.
            Behold, a young woman shall conceive and bear
            a son, and shall call his name Immanuel.
He shall eat curds and honey when he knows how to refuse
the evil and choose the good. For before the child knows
how to refuse the evil and choose the good, the land before whose two kings you are in dread will be deserted.
The LORD will bring upon you and upon your people and
upon your father's house such days as have not come since
the day that Ephraim departed from Judah--the king of
Assyria" (Isaiah 7:10-17).

Verse 14 has been isolated since it is this verse which
presents the major problem. One familiar with the King

James translation recognizes a major change made in the Revised Standard Version, namely the use of the translation "young woman" rather than "virgin."

In the Hebrew, the word used is almah, which means a young woman of marriageable age but conveys no judgment regarding virginity. There was a Hebrew word, bethulah, properly translated as "virgin" (for example, Rebekah is so designated in Genesis 24:16); but this is not the word used in Isaiah 7:14. The problem stems from the Septuagint where the word almah was rendered by the Greek parthenos, properly translated as "virgin." When English texts were first translated, more was known about Greek than Hebrew; and the translators depended significantly on the Greek translation, the Septuagint. Thus the confusion found its way into English readings, a confusion compounded because of the Septuagintal use by the writer of Matthew's Gospel in 1:23:

Behold, a virgin shall conceive and bear a son, and his name shall be called Emmanuel.

The Septuagint was the scripture of the early Christian church, and the vast majority of quotations from the Jewish scriptures found in the Christian scriptures were derived from the Septuagint. The author of this Gospel obviously searched the Septuagint for passages giving substantiation to his affirmation about Jesus of Nazareth, and Isaiah 7:14 met his need.

The translators have partially dealt with the problem by properly translating almah, but the verse could be better rendered by translating the verbal forms in the present tense. The verse better states:

Behold, a young woman is now pregnant and is about to

give birth and the child shall be called Immanuel.

Why should the child be called Immanuel? As a sign rather than an actor-participant or messiah figure, the child shall be recognized as a sign of Immanuel, i.e. "God with us," in two basic ways. Hosea, a contemporary of Isaiah, spoke also in the context of the Assyrian menace, warning of the following treatment of small children and pregnant women by the Assyrian forces:

Samaria shall bear her guilt,
    because she has rebelled against her God;
they shall fall by the sword,
        their little ones shall be dashed in pieces,
        and their pregnant women ripped open (Hosea 13:16).

How was the child a sign? Since the ultimate threat was Assyria, the birth of the child itself should be taken as a sign of "God with us." Second, Isaiah said to watch the growth of the child. By the time the child matures sufficiently to choose between good and evil, the two nations (Syria and Israel) would no longer be a threat--Yahweh would protect them!

Obviously Isaiah's message must have imminent fulfillment if it were to assist Ahaz. Isaiah was assuredly not saying to Ahaz, "Don't worry Ahaz! In just seven and one half centuries a child will be born who will make right this terrible threat!" This idea, seen in the context of the statement, is patently absurd!

If this passage does not refer to Jesus of Nazareth, then to whom? One cannot say with certainty, but differing scholars support varying possibilities. Some note that Isaiah might refer to a child to be born into the royal house. Surely such a child was in the direst danger

30

imaginable.[8] Other scholars note a child of Isaiah, Mahershalalhashbaz, mentioned for the first time in the following chapter (8:1). Is the reference to the child about to be borne by the wife of Isaiah, the only prophet to refer to his wife as "the prophetess" (8:3)?[9] Or did Isaiah simply see a woman obviously pregnant who had come to the reservoir to draw water and he used the woman as a type of object lesson for King Ahaz? One cannot say with certitude who the child intended by Isaiah was, only that the author of Matthew's Gospel has misappropriated the verse from Isaiah.

One would not desire misunderstanding at this point. There are passages in the Hebrew scriptures authentically pointing toward the messiah's coming. Just as certainly, however, Isaiah 7:14 was not one of those references. The church must be willing to investigate such use honestly and openly in the light of Biblical criticism, and this returns us to our original presupposition--this is one of those errors assuming a type of sacred association in the Christian community, and such passages are extremely difficult to correct because emotion rather than reason often dominates.

Earlier "canon" was used, a word which originally meant a "reed" or "cane" and which later was used in the sense of "measuring rod." In the latter sense the connotation of "rule" or "standard" developed. When referring to the canon of either the Jewish or Christian community, therefore, one refers to those writings which have been declared authoritative by the community of faith, and ultimately, especially for the Christian scriptures, through the mechanism of formal council pronouncement.

For the Hebrew scriptures, the process of canonization was primarily informal. By virtue of use and established tradition, we know that no major changes occurred in the Torah[10] after 400 B.C. While no formal closure was enacted, the Torah was informally established.

The second portion of the Hebrew canon is designated the Prophets and consists of the Former Prophets (the books of Joshua, Judges, Samuel, and Kings[11]) and the Latter Prophets (Isaiah, Jeremiah, Ezekiel, and the Book of the Twelve[12]). In the same way that the Torah was closed informally, so too the Prophets was closed by approximately 200 B.C.

The third portion of the Hebrew scripture is called the Writings. This section incorporates those writings not earlier mentioned--Psalms, Job, Proverbs, Ruth, Song of Songs, Ecclesiastes, Lamentations, Esther, Daniel, Ezra, Nehemiah, and Chronicles. About A.D. 90, at Jamnia in Palestine, it was formally determined which of the numerous writings available would be included. Basically it was agreed that all material included must be written in Hebrew, which automatically precluded the inclusion of many circulating Greek writings, although a few passages in Aramaic did find admittance.

Several factors led to the establishment of the Jewish canon. By A.D. 90 many of the Christian writings were circulating. Most, if not all of these, were written by Jewish Christians. How many, if any, spoke with any authority for the Jewish community? In addition, from approximately 200 B.C. until A.D. 200, a type of writing emerged and flourished known as apocalyptic literature. This literature arose during political and religious per-secution and sought to convey a message of hope and com-fort to the persecuted community. To do so, however, the message was purposefully cryptic, couched in symbolism and imagery hopefully meaningful to the persecuted commu-nity but unintelligible to the persecutors. This liter-ature was obviously open to misinterpretation and misuse.

How many of these writings spoke with any authority for Judaism? Finally, in A.D. 70 Rome destroyed the Jerusalem Temple as a result of the Jewish revolt which began in A.D. 66. With the destruction of the Temple and the resultant removal of a locus for the priestly office, there was a need for a clear understanding of those writings which would be designated and accepted as authoritative by the community.

Thus it was that at Jamnia in A.D. 90 essentially the seal of approval was given to the earlier informal canonization of the Torah and the Prophets. Decisions were made regarding the Writings, and thus the canon of sacred scripture was officially closed for the Hebrew people and has never since been reopened for later inclusions.

The Greek translation of the Hebrew scriptures, the Septuagint, was translated in Alexandria, Egypt, beginning about 275 to 250 B.C. and continuing for the next several centuries until all of the Hebrew scriptures were translated. These translators significantly influenced the placement of certain Biblical books not only in this Greek translation but also in later English translations, for early English translators used the Septuagint more than the Hebrew manuscript both for translation and arrangement purposes. The Septuagintal translators rearranged some of the later derived books which are deposited in the final section of the Hebrew canon, the Writings, so that they were placed in proximity to the earlier writings with which they were associated. Chronicles, Ezra, and Nehemiah were moved from the Writings to follow Samuel and Kings, Ruth to follow Judges, and the apocalyptic book of Daniel was inserted into the Latter Prophets between Ezekiel and the Book of the Twelve. This realignment of the materials unfortunately caused

33

some of the materials to be misread, most especially has this been true of the book of Daniel. As a result, Daniel has often been treated as a book of prophecy. The understanding of the Hebrew scriptures would be enhanced were the publishers of English translations to place the materials in the same order as found in the Hebrew Bible. The Hebrew arrangement both keeps writings of like nature in close relationship and assists the reader by giving clues to the chronological formulation of the materials. For example, Daniel and Chronicles' being found in the final section, the Writings, indicates that these are among the latest written materials. Because of changing historical conditions, this awareness is helpful to the interpreter. Misplacing the materials causes confusion (see "The Canon of Hebrew Scripture," pages 293-295).

For the Christian scriptures, the process of canonization extended over a period of three and one-half centuries. There was considerable dispute within various sections of the church as to which writings were authoritative, with particularly the following writings being seriously questioned: 2 Peter, 2-3 John, Jude, Hebrews, James, and Revelation. In the so-called Muratorian Canon, dated about A.D. 200, the church at Rome listed twenty writings, with these seven writings being omitted. The first extant listing of the twenty-seven writings eventually included in the Christian scriptures came from the pen of Athanasius, the Bishop of Alexandria, who in A.D. 367 sent an Easter letter to those under his jurisdiction. In this Easter letter he suggested the writings which he thought should be considered authoritative, listing the selections as currently in the canon. It took three church councils, however, to settle finally the much debated question, the Councils of Laodicea (A.D. 363), Hippo (A.D. 393), and Carthage (A.D. 397).

34

Finally the question of canonicity had been resolved, only to be raised again approximately a millennium later by the Protestant Reformation, particularly by Martin Luther. Luther's study of the scriptures led him to question the authenticity of Hebrews, caused him to designate James an "epistle of straw," and precipitated his rejection of both Jude and Revelation. As a result of activities associated with the Reformation, the Roman Catholic Church convened the Council of Trent in A.D. 1545 (met sporadically 1545-1563), at which Council the canonicity of the twenty-seven books was re-affirmed. Serious question regarding canonicity, either in terms of exclusions or later inclusions, has not been raised since that time.

As with the Hebrew scriptures, certain criteria governed the selection of writings. Again, the importance of use cannot be overstated in determining not only what would be preserved but also the manner in which it would be preserved. In addition, it was mandatory that the writing relate either to Jesus directly or have to do with the propagation of the faith. It was also necessary that the writing be derived either from an apostle or from one who stood in direct descent from an apostle. Needless to say, in an age when literary-critical tools were unknown, mistakes could be and were made in this latter category.

Again, as with the Hebrew scriptures, some very specific factors precipitated the establishment of an official canon on the part of the church. First, the early church lived in the expectation of the imminent return of Jesus with the resultant establishment of the Kingdom of God. This expectation did not materialize, and, as a result, many of the eyewitnesses to Jesus' ministry had either died or were quite old. Long before the close of the first Christian century, therefore, there arose the imperative to preserve in literary form the words and deeds of Jesus in Gospel accounts. Qualitative choices between the various writings inevitably followed this literary activity.

Second, many doctrinal disputes arose within the church. The trinitarian formulation and the Christological debates, ranging from the second through the sixth centuries, influenced the desire for scriptural stability.

Third, in the church the words of Jesus and the apostles were becoming increasingly important. This emphasis had the practical result of exalting certain documents over others in the esteem of the church.

Fourth, as the conflict between Judaism and Christianity intensified, many in the church desired a sacred literature which would clearly separate the church from the synagogue. The common use of the Hebrew scriptures, even in Greek translation, no longer sufficed.

Fifth, as with Judaism, it became increasingly necessary to set up a mechanism for separating those writings considered to be "orthodox" from that vast body of literature developing in the church. Again, apocalyptic literature was circulating widely.

All of these factors, plus others, directed the church toward canonization. For both the Hebrew and the Greek scriptures, this process has prevented a proliferation of writings of potentially dubious value. At the same time, canonization creates a rather staid, static situation, one in which continuing creativity and a dynamic spirit is hardly encouraged.

Recognizing that canons for Hebrew and Greek scriptures do exist, an important consideration for the English-speaking individual of western culture is the process by which English translations came into being. To this question and its necessary background data, we now turn our attention.

The scriptures were translated into other languages

long before they were translated into English--Syriac,
the Hebrew into Greek, Latin, etc. Remembering that we
possess no original autographs, these early translations
have been important both in preserving the scriptures
and in assisting modern scholarship to pursue its critical
task of formulating a Biblical text as near as possible
to the original.

Our oldest Hebrew manuscripts date at the earliest
from approximately 100 B.C. These manuscripts are the
Dead Sea Scrolls, which have been discovered in the caves
surrounding the Dead Sea in the years following the initial discoveries in 1947. With the exception of the book
of Esther, every book of the Hebrew scriptues is represented either in whole or in part in the Scrolls. For
the New Testament Greek manuscripts, our earliest sub-
stantive manuscripts date from the fourth Christian century. Significantly, for both the Hebrew and Greek
manuscripts, ample time had transpired between the events
and their recording for multiple changes and alterations
to the manuscripts, whether or not these were purposeful.
Sometimes a scribe altered a reading which he judged to be
in error. Copying mistakes were also frequently transmitted. The possibility of human error was the greater
since the scribe frequently transcribed as materials were
read to him by a second individual. A comparison of manuscripts clearly portrays their differences.

During the fourth Christian century, St. Jerome
determined to translate the scriptures into Latin. His
interest focused on both the Jewish scriptures and those
writings uniquely associated with the Christian community.
In order to accomplish his task, he journeyed to Palestine
where he taught himself Hebrew. The end result was the
Vulgate translation, the Latin translation that became
normative for the Christian church throughout the medieval

period and has remained the basis for Roman Catholic Church scriptures.

Turning our attention now specifically to English translations, it was during the latter years of the fourteenth century that the first English translations were associated with John Wyclif.[13] While he actually died in 1384, two incomplete English translations, dated 1380 and 1397, are associated with him. He actively worked on the 1380 translation, and after his death his followers continued his efforts and brought out the 1397 translation. Both of these were essentially translations of the Vulgate into English.

In 1453 a discovery to have monumental significance for Biblical translation occurred, the printing press. This made possible the dissemination of the written word more rapidly and more accurately. The Bible as translated into German was first printed in 1466, and in 1470 the first English translation was printed. Before 1500 ninety-two editions of the Latin Bible came from the press. The Vulgate, however, was the first book printed in its entirety.

William Tyndale (1492?-1536), an Englishman educated at Oxford, played a significant role in the English-text transmission process. He recognized the necessity of utilizing the earliest available Hebrew and Greek manuscripts. As a result of Tyndale's work, an English translation of the New Testament appeared in 1525 and the Pentateuch and some other portions of the Hebrew scriptures were translated in 1529. On the darker side of the church's history, because of his translation work Tyndale was tried and condemned as a heretic in 1536. He was strangled and his body then burned at the stake. This movement toward making the vernacular text available could not be reversed, however.

In 1535, under the auspices of Miles Coverdale, the first complete English translation of the Bible appeared. Significant as the first complete translation, this work did not exemplify the creative spirit of Tyndale. Coverdale's translation was based upon earlier Latin translations, upon Tyndale's work, and upon earlier translation work by Martin Luther (1483-1546, German) and Ulrich Zwingli (1484-1531, Swiss) in the German language. English translation efforts were beginning to fall within the purview of the "Establishment," however, as indicated by Coverdale's translation being dedicated to King Henry VIII of England.

In 1539 the "Great Bible" appeared, having been commissioned by Sir Thomas Cromwell, Secretary to King Henry VIII. This also was not an original translation, the work being done under the direction of Miles Coverdale and based on the earlier work of Tyndale, as well as Coverdale's own earlier efforts.

Demand for the "Great Bible" created a shortage which, in 1563-1564, precipitated Archbishop Parker's commissioning of a slight revision of the "Great Bible." Nine of the designated revisers were Bishops, thus the version appearing in 1568 is usually designated the Bishops' Bible. Some textual corrections were made on the basis of available Hebrew and Greek manuscripts, but this was assuredly not the prime intention of the "revision."

The Roman Catholic Church having been outlawed in England in 1560, some Roman Catholic scholars fled England and went to France. As a result of their translation efforts, which focused upon a rather literal translation into English of the Latin Vulgate, the "Rheims and Douay Version" of the Bible appeared, the New Testament being printed at Rheims in 1582 and the Old Testament at Douay in 1609-1610. The Rheims and Douay Version remained the

normative text of the Roman Catholic Church until revised
by Bishop Challoner, Vicar Apostolic of the London Dis-
trict, in 1750. This revision of the Rheims-Douay text,
with slight revisions periodically, has remained the
accepted Roman Catholic text. In 1941, under the request
and supervision of the Episcopal Committee of the Con-
fraternity of Christian Doctrine, a new version was published which was both a revision of Bishop Challoner's
earlier work and an attempt to provide a more faithful
translation of the Vulgate. Thus, even to the present
day, Roman Catholic faithfulness to the Vulgate is clearly
evidenced.[14]

In 1604, largely because of Puritan opposition to
the "Prayer Book" which utilized the scriptures of the
"Great Bible," King James I of England commissioned
fifty-four individuals to prepare a new translation.
Although the best available Hebrew and Greek manuscripts
were used, nonetheless the translators were commissioned
to use the Bishops' Bible and to alter the translation
of same as little as possible. The King James Bible,
which appeared in 1611, was neither commissioned nor intended to be original translation work. Nonetheless, it
was this translation which became the Authorized Version
of the English-speaking peoples and retained that primal
position for at least two and a half centuries. Popularly
it still retains that status for many today.

Efforts at revision of the King James Bible were
mounted during the 1850's, resulting in England in the
publication of the Revised Version of the New Testament
in 1881 and the Old Testament and the Apocrypha in 1885
and 1895 respectively. The American Standard Version
appeared in 1901 and incorporated some variant readings
preferred by American scholars involved in this revision
process.

The International Council of Religious Education acquired the copyright to the American Standard Version in 1928; and, after some study, in 1937 a revision of the 1901 publication was authorized. It was clear that the revisers were to utilize the best available Hebrew and Greek manuscripts and to translate in the best English idiom possible. The result was the publication of the Revised Standard Version of the New Testament in 1946, the Old Testament in 1952, and the Apocrypha in 1957. Of primary importance to our concern, however, is the expressed commission to utilize the best available Hebrew and Greek manuscripts. This same assertion is true for the New English Bible, of which the New Testament appeared in 1961 and the Old Testament in 1970.

Quite obviously this discussion has included only some of the major steps in the process by which the English Bible was derived. Many other translations and revisions might be included, as well as paraphrases of the scriptures which really are a totally different literary genre.

The following is a diagrammatic presentation which visually incorporates the skeleton of the foregoing discussion:

Selected Translation and Transmission Events

Hebrew Manuscripts
(1200-150 B.C.)

(Septuagint)
(275-100 B.C.)

Greek Manuscripts
(A.D. 50-150)

No original autographs

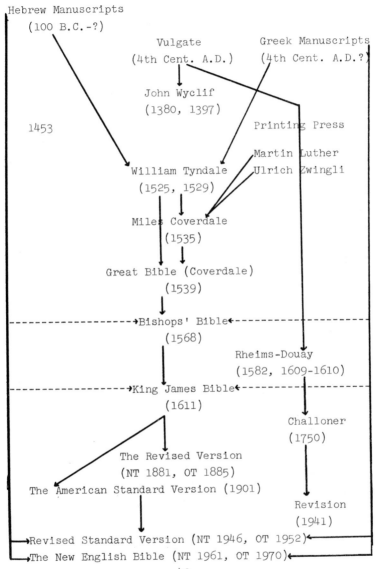

Hebrew Manuscripts
(100 B.C.-?)

Vulgate
(4th Cent. A.D.)

Greek Manuscripts
(4th Cent. A.D.?)

John Wyclif
(1380, 1397)

1453

Printing Press

Martin Luther
Ulrich Zwingli

William Tyndale
(1525, 1529)

Miles Coverdale
(1535)

Great Bible (Coverdale)
(1539)

Bishops' Bible
(1568)

Rheims-Douay
(1582, 1609-1610)

King James Bible
(1611)

Challoner
(1750)

The Revised Version
(NT 1881, OT 1885)

The American Standard Version (1901)

Revision
(1941)

Revised Standard Version (NT 1946, OT 1952)
The New English Bible (NT 1961, OT 1970)

Conclusion

It is vitally important that an individual understand the derivation and development of the Hebrew-Christian scriptures. Only this understanding can prevent an undue exaltation of the scriptures on the one hand and make possible the opening of scripture's meanings through the use of critical, analytical tools on the other. The misguided zeal of the literalist is thereby revealed, as is the immature rejection of scripture by one who would seek thereby to demonstrate intellectual superiority.

It is also important, however, for the interpreter to recognize that the material canonized by both the church and the synagogue was viewed holistically by the faith communities. Canonization was a prescientific process, one that occurred long before the development of the literary-critical approach to scripture. Transmitted traditions regarding authorship, for example, were simply accepted. But even more importantly, a body of material, as for example the Hebrew account of the exodus event (Exodus 3-24) or the Christian record of the sermon on the mount (Matthew 5-7), was accepted unquestionably as a unit of tradition. The modern interpreter, if some of the most profound implications of the canonized text are to be understood, must recognize the internal integrity of the tradition, a recognition that must precede analytical evaluation of literary units to determine component parts.

The Judeo-Christian community must recognize that sacredness can never be attached to a book, the Bible, for this is merely the worship of a book. The Bible should be read to discover the One whom the written word seeks to convey, in spite of human errors, finitude, and prejudice. Veneration is directed toward the end, not the means to the end, toward the One who is conveyed, not

43

the vehicle for the conveyance.

We return, therefore, to the view of the Bible earlier affirmed, namely that the Bible should be interpreted as man's understanding of his encounter with God. With this perspective we are freed to investigate, to search for truth. Only in this light is justice done to God, to man, and to the Bible.

III

THE BIBLICAL TEXT: ENCOUNTER WITH MODERNITY

In Chapter II the Biblical text has been investigated
in terms of its evolutionary development, transmission,
and eventual canonization by the Jewish and Christian communities. This approach has emphasized both the multiple
human hands active in formulating Biblical materials and
the Bible's being the product of majority opinion. In
the past no less than the present, consensus agreement on
questions of ultimate authority was impossible to obtain;
and many dissatisfied and disenchanted individuals lie in
the wake of the Biblical text so highly esteemed today.

This historically developed esteem, however, contrib-
utes to the contemporary interpreter's problem. Individuals have struggled and died for their beliefs regarding
the Biblical text. Sometimes these beliefs would be en-
dorsed by this writer, but occasionally they would be rejected adamantly as ill-grounded. That notwithstanding,
these strongly held beliefs have caused convictional
polarities to develop around the Biblical text.

To approach the scriptures in a fashion that is both
adequately grounded in historical understanding and yet
preserves the distinctiveness of the material from the
faith communities' perspectives is always difficult. It
is partially fear or insecurity that causes many individuals to react so negatively to the historical-critical
literary study of the Biblical text, but among the options

this appears to be the most viable approach if the integrity of both the text and the interpreter is to be preserved.

Recognizing the evolution of the text, the Bible's being a divinely dictated and therefore inerrant document must be rejected. To interpret this humanly developed text, one can no more refuse the use of critical tools than would be possible in the study of William Shakespeare's writings. Denying the Biblical text every avenue of clarification is a negation of the Bible's importance. Thus, it is the Biblicist who does the great injustice to the Biblical text, not the individual who seeks understanding. To refuse the application of tools used in the study of other literary-historical documents is a type of religious schizophrenia.

It is perhaps helpful to recognize that our interpretive approach to the Biblical text must correspond to that used in a critical study of the Koran. Admittedly what the Koran means to the Muslim and the non-Muslim from a faith perspective differs, and faith's perspective colors what the Jew or Christian finds in the Biblical text. A faith commitment can never be permitted, however, to preclude the use openly and freely of all available interpretive approaches. The search for truth can never be clouded by affirmation, regardless of the area in which that truth be sought--medicine, science, law, religion, or any other discipline.

Biblical Criticism

The tool most often used to interpret the Jewish-Christian scriptures is Biblical criticism. We turn now to understand what the phenomenon is and something of its development.

Early Christianity and post-Biblical Judaism viewed

the scriptures in essentially identical fashion. Both accepted the scriptures of Judaism as their basis for faith; and, as described in Chapter II, only over a lengthy period of time did the Christian scriptures evolve and assume primacy over the earlier Hebrew scriptures. For both Judaism and Christianity, the scriptures were interpreted literally and traditions associated with authorship were accepted without question.

The situation just described is the expected, for these were a prescientific people. Such a people would not question the authorship of the Pentateuch by Moses, of the Psalter by David, of the Wisdom writings by Solomon, or the traditionally ascribed authorship of the various Gospels. The emergence of scientific methodology, however, was inevitably going to effect such assertions.

The Renaissance, from the fourteenth through the seventeenth centuries, coupled with the Protestant Reformation, basically a sixteenth-century phenomenon, altered practically every earlier preconception of man. A radical shift was set in motion from essentially a theistic to a humanistic modality of interpretation.

While science was set on its irreversible course through the Renaissance era, Reformation events momentarily precluded parallel advances in religious understanding. Because everything traditional was being questioned, the early post-Reformation establishement church, the Roman Catholic Church, was ultra-orthodox. This attitude made it practically impossible for ecclesiastical leaders to use fully their powers of reason in scriptural studies. One could not interpret the scripture in the rational fashion utilized in the scientific study of the cosmos and continue to remain a participant in good standing within the church.

This situation largely forced the emergence of

Biblical criticism outside of ecclesiastical circles.
While earlier examples might be cited, an early and significant figure was Jean Astruc (1684-1766), Royal Surgeon
to King Louis XV of France and Medical Professor at the
University of Paris. His scientific background caused
him to focus upon inconsistencies within the early chapters
of the book of Genesis. Why were there several designations for God if all of this material were written by one
person? Why were some events narrated more than once?
Why did the writing style differ in various sections?
Such questions led Astruc to the publication of an anonymous monograph in 1753 where he expressed his conclusions
regarding sources brought together to form the Pentateuch.
While he was rather orthodox in asserting that it was Moses
who brought together these diverse sources, the emerging
questioning mood was the primary factor.

Earlier individuals had also questioned Mosaic authorship of the Pentateuch--Grotius (1583-1645), Thomas Hobbes
(1588-1679), and Baruch Spinoza (1632-1677), the latter of
whom was banned from the synagogue in Holland because of
his writing. We look ahead, however, to Johann G. Eichhorn
(1752-1827), who from 1780-1783 published a three-volume
introduction to the Old Testament. Kendrick Grobel, com-
menting on Eichhorn's introduction, stated:

. . . Eichhorn's enduring merit is that he, more than
any other, naturalized within Protestant theological investigation the humanistic insight that the OT, like any other
literature, may and must be freely scrutinized, free from
tradition, dogma, and institutional authority.[1]

This emphasis in Eichhorn's introduction still embodies
what the Biblical critic seeks to accomplish.

Any attempt to define Biblical criticism will inevi-

tably be incomplete when scrutinized. The following will
serve, however, as a working definition:

Biblical criticism is the investigation of Biblical literature for the purpose of recovering as nearly as possible the original text, discerning the intended meanings,
and answering various literary-historical questions.

Within Biblical criticism, there are two primary
divisions of study, although there are numerous methodological applications of Biblical criticism deriving from
these two branches. One focus of Biblical criticism is
usually designated lower criticism, the other higher
criticism. These terms do not indicate qualitative differential; both point to vitally important roles in
Biblical criticism.

Lower criticism is frequently designated textual
criticism and seeks to recover as nearly as possible the
original text of a Biblical writing. This acknowledges
that we possess no original autographs and that there are
many manuscript evidences for almost every canonical writing, with these manuscripts often having significant textual differences. By weighing the evidence the textual
critic seeks to reconstruct as nearly as possible the
original text. Reading the Revised Standard Version of
the Bible or the New English Bible, one sees the results
of the textual critic's efforts. Since this is such a
highly specialized linguistic and analytic task, only the
highly trained and skilled are competent to make judgments.

Higher criticism might be designated literary criticism. This branch of Biblical criticism seeks to deal with
issues such as sources, style, structure, and the relationship of documents to one another. In the Oxford Annotated
Bible, an excellent study Bible which utilizes the Revised

Standard Version of the scriptures, or the more recently
published (1976) Oxford Study Edition, utilizing the New
English Bible translation, there are included introductions
to each book of the Bible, annotations on each page regarding the meaning of obscure words or historical clari-
fications, as well as numerous other interpretive aids.
This is the type of endeavor to which the higher critic
directs his attention.

Applications of Biblical Criticism

Biblical criticism has numerous methodological applications. For the Hebrew scriptures we shall investigate
one broad application, an understanding of the Pentateuch,
and one more specific application, an interpretation of
the hail plague recorded in Exodus 9:13-35. Similarly,
for the New Testament we shall look in a broader perspective at the interrelationships of the four Gospels and
more specifically at the application of form criticism
to the Gospels.

All Old Testament scholars do not view the historical
development of the Pentateuch in precisely the same way.
Only the most conservative interpreters assign the first
five books to Mosaic authorship, however, and this position
is taken in defiance of Biblical criticism. In determining
how much should be ascribed to Mosaic derivation, however,
there is disagreement, as indeed there is not consensus
whether investigators should work with the Pentateuch or
the Hexateuch (including the book of Joshua). There is
also dispute as to when this material assumed written
formulation, Scandinavian scholars especially maintaining
a lengthy oral transmission period before the material was
placed in written form. In spite of the unanswered questions, most scholars accept as the Pentateuch's most probable reconstruction the documentary hypothesis.

The documentary hypothesis is hypothesis, meaning that new evidence could cause the discarding of this explanation in deference to a view better satisfying all available data. In brief, however, the documentary hypothesis builds upon the type thinking earlier associated with Jean Astruc, namely the recognition of diverse sources or strata in the Pentateuch. The documentary hypothesis is associated with two German scholars, Karl H. Graf and Julius Wellhausen. Graf's principal study was in the legal portions of the Pentateuch, publishing his findings in 1865. Wellhausen complemented Graf's work, doing his primary work in the narrative portions of the Pentateuch, publishing his conclusions in a series of monographs between 1876 and 1885, with perhaps his most important publication appearing in 1883, published in English as the <u>Prolegomena</u> <u>to</u> <u>the</u> <u>History</u> <u>of</u> <u>Israel</u>. Because of the efforts of these two men one often sees the documentary hypothesis referred to as the Graf-Wellhausen theory.

The documentary hypothesis recognizes four primary sources gradually compiled over the centuries to form the Pentateuch. These four sources are given the alphabetic designations J, E, D, and P, with the diagram on the following page indicating their derivation and compilation.

The J source derives from the Kingdom of Judah (the South), taking its alphabetic designation from the first letter in the name most used for deity in this source, Jahveh or Yahweh. In the Hebrew language words were earliest written consonantally without the inclusion of vowels, with the vowels being inserted during the sixth and seventh centuries A.D. The consonants of the sacred name are JHVH or YHWH, frequently designated the sacred

<u>Pentateuch</u>=<u>Torah</u>=<u>Five</u> <u>Books</u> <u>of</u> <u>Moses</u>

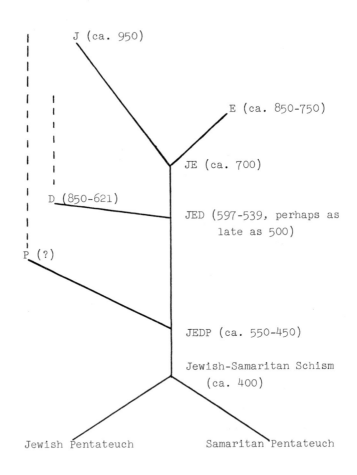

tetragrammaton. This is translated as "Lord," and when one finds the word capitalized (LORD), as in the Revised Standard Version or the New English Bible, this indicates the translation of the sacred name.[2] While the word is cryptic as regards its meaning, it probably was intended as the causative form of the Hebrew verb "to be," thus conveying the sense of the deity as the "one who causes to be."

The J source was written during Solomon's reign, apparently before the Kingdom began to wane during his latter years. The material is highly nationalistic, emphasizing particularly southern sites such as Beer-Sheba. A date of 950 B.C. is often attached to this source, remembering that Solomon ruled from 961 to 922 B.C.

Of the various sources, J manifests the best literary style, being artistic in weaving a story. For example, Genesis 2:4b-3:24 is associated with J[3] and records the simple but moving paradisiac story. Genesis 24 recounts the way divine providence directs as a wife suitable for Isaac is sought. In like fashion, the Yahwist artfully brings Yahweh's promise to Abraham (Genesis 12:1-3) to fulfillment. The promise's realization was continually threatened as hopes were repeatedly brought to the abyss of extinction, with Sarah's sterility, Jacob's inadequacy, the Hebrews' servitude in Egypt, and numerous other examples. In each case, however, Yahweh acts at the last possible moment to redeem an apparently impossible situation.

In the J source, especially the earlier materials, the thought pattern derived from a wilderness sociological base. For example, at the story's beginning no vegetation exists because "the LORD God had not caused it to rain upon the earth" (Genesis 2:5). One can envision the rocky, barren wilderness of Judah in this comment. Likewise, when man was brought into being, Yahweh scooped up "dust from the ground (adhamah)" (Genesis 2:7) and formed man (adham). Interestingly, this wilderness-oriented narrative never mentions fish! The sociological set seems apparent.

Finally, deity's portrayal in the J source is the most anthropomorphic (assigning human characteristics to deity) of the various sources, as would be expected in this earliest stratum. Yahweh walks in the Garden of Eden and calls out to Adam (Genesis 3:8-9), Yahweh closes the door of Noah's ark once all the people and animals were inside (Genesis 7:16), and Yahweh in the guise of a stranger eats with Abraham (Genesis 18:1-5). This anthropomorphism does not demean the majesty of deity. In the portrayal's naiveté there is expressed an exalted faith commitment.

The second strand of tradition is designated E. In this source the deity name utilized until the divine name's revelation at the burning bush (Exodus 3:13-15) is Elohim. This form, the Hebrew "plural of majesty" usually translated in the English text as "God," was used in the Hebrew when the singular insufficiently expressed the majesty and grandeur of deity.

E was written in the North, where the primary tribe was Ephraim, with date assignment varying between 850 and 750 B.C. As the J source focuses on primary sites in the South, the E source concentrates on northern locations, such as Bethel. Most scholars agree that the E source begins in Genesis 15 with the Abrahamic convenant's recording.

The E material, written approximately one to two centuries after J, contains a more exalted concept of God. While anthropomorphisms are still present, more often deity

is more distant from man. Given a more acute sense of
holiness, God reveals himself to man through dreams rather
than personal encounter.

Ethical concerns have also become more pronounced in
E, as evident in Genesis 20. In the doublets of this
chapter (Genesis 12 and 26), no attention is given to the
propriety of Abraham's actions while in the land of
Abimelech. In 20:12 there is explicit concern to demonstrate that the Patriarch had not lied when asserting
that Sarah was his sister!

In 722/721 B.C., Israel fell victim to the mighty
Assyrian Empire. Shortly thereafter, approximately
700 B.C., the southern and northern traditions, the J
and E sources, were combined. Many of the traditions in
the two sources paralleled, and in such cases the materials were simply superimposed on each other. Sometimes
variant traditions existed, and frequently these dispirate
traditions were both included, creating difficult interpretive entanglements for later readers. Regardless,
referring to our earlier chart, we have seen now the
emergence of the first two sources and their eventual
fusion.

The next stratum to be incorporated was D or the
Deuteronomic source, which material is dated from 850
to 622 B.C.[4] Probably a portion of Deuteronomy formed
the basis for Josiah's Reformation in 622 B.C., although
it would be debated how much of the material was known
at that time--chapters 12-26? Chapter 5? Regardless
this puts a terminal date on one end of the spectrum
and accounts for our 622 B.C. date earlier mentioned.
Few individuals today seriously debate Mosaic authorship
of Deuteronomy, but many follow the lead of Gerhard von

Rad in placing the emergence of the material during the period of Elijah.

Elijah adamantly resisted Baalism during the reign of King Ahab and Queen Jezebel in the mid-ninth century. Anti-Baalism is a central thrust of Deuteronomy and is most logically viewed against this emerging prophetic attitude in Israel. This position is strengthened by a prescribed antiphonal service (Deuteronomy 11:26-32) having been set in the area of Shechem, with the blessing proclaimed from Mount Gerizim and the curse from Mount Ebal. These Israelite mountains give the material additional northern rather than southern flavor.

The material perhaps emerged in the North during the time of Elijah, about 850 B.C., with its centralization concern focused on Shechem. After Israel's fall to Assyria in 722/721 B.C., however, the material migrated into Judah, becoming the basis for Hezekiah's (715-687 B.C.) reform. That reform was short-lived, however, for Manasseh (687-642 B.C.), who followed Hezekiah to Judah's throne, was a committed assimilator. During his reign numerous pagan practices were either re-instituted or introduced, while fervent Yahwism was discouraged. Probably during Manasseh's reign the Deuteronomy manuscript was edited by fervent devotees of Yahweh and ultimately preserved by being concealed in a niche in the Jerusalem Temple. It was here that Josiah's workmen found the scroll as the Temple was being refurbished. This material became the literary basis for Josiah's Reformation and later for the editing of the so-called Deuteronomic historical materials--Joshua, Judges, Samuel, and Kings. Finally, during the Babylonian Exile, the D material was added, or attached, to the JE corpus. One could say attached, since the D material is found at the conclusion of the Pentateuch. Thus between 597 and 539 B.C. the D material was edited into JE, although this process may have continued as late as ca. 500 B.C. after the exiles returned to Jerusalem.

The final pentateuchal source is P, or the Priestly material. Unlike the other sources, this corpus derives its designation directly from the responsible individuals, the priests of Yahweh. No one can say how early P originated. Some would argue that P's roots must be as early as J, although certain aspects depict a more developed thought pattern. For example, deity designation shows a clear evolution in P. From Adam to Abraham the name Elohim is primarily used, whereas from Abraham to Moses El Shaddai is more often used. Finally, with Moses, the sacred name, Yahweh, was revealed and used henceforth in the Priestly material.

The Priestly material exemplifies the southern mentality of Jerusalem priests and demonstrates characteristic priestly concerns, such as the holiness of Yahweh God, the determination of tribal boundary lines, the proper procedures for offering various sacrifices, and the enumeration of various laws and covenants governing Israel's life together. Conversely, many of these concerns make P the least interesting of the four sources. One would not deny, however, the beauty of some Priestly passages. For example, Genesis 1:1-2:4a, the Priestly creation account, is one of the more sublime Biblical texts.

The Priestly source was edited into JED both during the Babylonian Exile and probably during the early post-exilic years when zealous Yahwistic worship was being re-instituted in Jerusalem. It was the Priestly editors, therefore, who were the final redactors of the Pentateuch, giving the materials essentially the form known today.

The documentary hypothesis of the Pentateuch's origin and transmission is one view of the Pentateuch, albeit
the view most often accepted by scholars. Our primary
point, however, is that the documentary hypothesis demonstrates the kind of literary critical analysis demanded
by the Biblical critical methodology.

Having looked broadly at the source analysis of the
Pentateuch, this same type of analysis may be applied
more narrowly to Exodus 9:13-35, the hail plague. The
sources might be separated as follows:

J: 13, 17-18, 23b-24, 26-30, 33-34
E: 22-23a, 25
P: 35
Redactor: 14-16, 19-21, 31-32[5]

In the J material a coherent account of the hail
plague is recorded. With the editing of the E material,
however, problems appeared. For example, in the E material Moses' role is heightened considerably. More importantly, according to E "the hail struck down every
plant of the field, and shattered every tree of the
field" (9:25b). If this be true, a problem existed regarding the next plague, the locusts. What would they
devour? The redactor, sensing this problem, added 9:31-
32, which resolved the issue by limiting the hail's
devastation. Finally, in 9:35, the typical Priestly note
is sounded--ostensibly the plague did not achieve its
goal, the release of the Hebrews, but Yahweh God is in
control of the entire sequence of events and his purpose
is being accomplished!

Several examples of the Biblical critical method as

applied to the New Testament will now be pursued. Attention will be directed initially to the relationship and interrelationships of the four canonical Gospels, focusing on the relationship of the three Synoptic Gospels (Matthew, Mark, and Luke) to the Fourth Gospel, John.[6]

The Synoptic Gospels and the Fourth Gospel differ considerably; and, while estimates vary, it is usually suggested that approximately ninety per cent of the Fourth Gospel is unique. This difference is more than wording; rather, the Fourth Gospel's distinctiveness lay in a totally different outline and in events not mentioned in the Synoptics. Some of the differences are as follows:

1. In the Synoptics Jesus apparently came to Jerusalem only once, at the time of the crucifixion. In John Jesus came to Jerusalem at least four times (John 2:13; 5:1; 7:10; 10:23).
2. In the Synoptics Jesus' ministry began with John the Baptizer's arrest, which could enlighten Jesus' self-understanding. In John, a parallel ministry for Jesus and John the Baptizer is depicted in the Jordan River valley prior to John's arrest.
3. John placed the cleansing of the Temple as one of Jesus' initial acts, whereas in the Synoptics this event occurred during the final week of his ministry.
4. In the Synoptics there are numerous exorcism accounts (casting out of demons), while this emphasis is missing from the Fourth Gospel.
5. In the Synoptics Jesus is portrayed as having been crucified on the initial day of Passover (Nisan 15), while the Fourth Gospel indicates that Passover began a day later and thus Jesus was crucified the day before Passover began. While we cannot discuss this fully, the Synoptics present problems in that it is

unlikely the Jews would clamor for crucifixion on this
holy day. On the other hand, John's portrayal is
problematic because it seems so infused with theological interpretation, namely Jesus is introduced as
the "Lamb of God" (1:36) and he dies as the Paschal
Lamb (19:36). The calendar distinction between the
two accounts might be depicted as follows:

	Thursday	Friday	Saturday
Synoptics	14*	15**	16
Fourth Gospel	13*	14**	15

  *Evening of final meal and arrest
**Crucifixion

6. In the Synoptics Jesus would have eaten a Passover
   meal with his disciples on Thursday evening (recall
   that the day begins and ends with sunset), while in
   the Fourth Gospel this would be a meal preparatory
   to Passover rather than the Passover meal.

7. In the Synoptics the mighty acts (or miracles) are
   commonplace, whereas in the Fourth Gospel signs re-
   place the mighty acts. In the Synoptics these mighty
   acts generally point toward the inbreaking of the
   Kingdom of God, but the signs are purposefully evi-
   dential in assisting the observer-reader to recognize
   Jesus (John 20:30-31).

8. In the Synoptics there are few long discourses. Even
   in the Sermon on the Mount (a construct of sayings
   found in Matthew 5-7), the brief, pithy sayings and
   the "sermonettes" are easily recognized. Characteristically in John, however, long discourses move continually away from the original question to the concerns of the church.

9. The most important difference lay in the portrait of

Jesus, for in the Synoptics Jesus comes to a gradual awareness of his role and destiny. To the contrary, in the Fourth Gospel Jesus from the very beginning fully understands his person and his mission, eliminating any need for growth in this area (thus one finds no temptation scene in the Fourth Gospel as in the Synoptics).

These differences should not be emphasized overly, for it is probably true that a stranger to the New Testament tradition could read the Synoptics and the Fourth Gospel and recognize the uniformity of the tradition. Nonetheless, the differences are real and should not be minimized. It is virtually impossible to harmonize the Fourth Gospel with the other three Gospels; but the latter are sufficiently similar in outline, incidents recorded, sayings ascribed to and conversations with Jesus, and wording that one can designate them Synoptic Gospels.

If it be true that there are three Gospel witnesses against one, why do the scholars pay any attention to the variants in the Fourth Gospel? To answer this, we turn to the theory best expressed by B. H. Streeter in 1924 regarding the "Synoptic Problem."[7] The Synoptic Problem refers to the extensive similarity in the Synoptics, not only the parallel outline but more so a verbatim record extending over rather long sections. The resolution to the problem must account for these similarities while yet allowing for the differences which are present. Looking ahead, we respond to the initial question by noting that it is really Mark versus John, for Matthew and Luke are heavily dependent upon Mark. This obviously makes more difficult resolving problems existent between the Synoptics and the Fourth Gospel.

According to Streeter's four-document resolution to the Synoptic Problem, the Gospel of Mark is the earliest canonical Gospel, written in Rome about A.D. 64-69. The author was apparently John Mark, but there is a second-century tradition which links John Mark as the recorder for Peter's remembrances.[8]

The Gospels of Matthew and Luke were both written between A.D. 80 and 85, with the former being written in Antioch and the latter in Achaia (Greece). The Gospel of Luke was authored by Luke, the traveling companion of Paul; but the authorship of Matthew's Gospel is more problematic. Generally speaking the Protestant tradition suggests the Gospel to be anonymous, while the Roman Catholic Church accepts the Apostle Matthew as author.

The fourth source is hypothetical and assigned the designation Quelle (or Q), the German word for "source." This is suggested to have been written between A.D. 50 and 60 in Antioch; and, while authorship is uncertain, Matthew is often suggested. This is a hypothetical source in that no copy of Q has ever been found; rather, it is reconstructed from the Gospels of Matthew and Luke (no evidence that Mark used Q) where verbatim sayings and/or conversations of Jesus exist.

According to this resolution of the Synoptic Problem, both Matthew and Luke used Mark extensively, not only the Marcan outline of the ministry but also the Marcan content (Matthew used 90% and Luke 60% of Mark). In addition Matthew and Luke share approximately 200 verses of parallel materials not found in Mark, usually suggested to be derived from Q. A good example of this parallel material is found in Matthew 3:7-10 and Luke 3:7-9, as illustrated on the following page. In this Q section each writer utilized the materials to correlate with his unique interests. For Matthew it is the narrower Jewish

Matthew 3:7-10

But when he saw many of the
Pharisees and Sadducees coming
for baptism, he said to them,
"You brood of vipers! Who
warned you to flee from the
wrath to come? Bear fruit that
befits repentance, and do not
presume to say to yourselves,
'We have Abraham as our
father'; for I tell you, God
is able from these stones to
raise up children to Abraham.
Even now the ax is laid to
the root of the trees;
every tree therefore that does
not bear good fruit is cut
down and thrown into the fire."

63

Luke 3:7-9

He said therefore to the
multitudes that came out to be
baptized by him,
"You brood of vipers! Who
warned you to flee from the
wrath to come? Bear fruits that
befit repentance, and do not
begin to say to yourselves,
'We have Abraham as our
father'; for I tell you, God
is able from these stones to
raise up children to Abraham.
Even now the ax is laid to
the root of the trees;
every tree therefore that does
not bear good fruit is cut
down and thrown into the fire."

perspective of Pharisees and Sadducees coming to John, while in Luke it is the broader, more universal "multitudes" who came. Beginning with "You brood of vipers" the material is verbatim parallel, with the exception of the underlined words, which differences are inconsequential. Such lengthy verbatim passages are not accidents. A source from which both Gospel writers drew must be postulated (since Matthew and Luke were written at approximately the same time and in widely separated geographic sites one could not have borrowed from the other), and Quelle seems the most logical suggestion to this point. Finally, there are unique sections in both Matthew and Luke explained by material exclusively used by each of these writers, approximately 300 verses in Matthew (Special Matthew) and 400 verses in Luke (Special Luke).

According to this Biblical critical analysis, therefore, an understanding of the Synoptic Gospels emerges which allows both for the commonality and uniqueness of the three Gospels. The view recognizes the Gospels to be portraits rather than photographs. As is true with any good portrait, each Gospel presents Jesus as the writer perceived or understood Jesus. In this way a Gospel conceptualization emerges with which one can work critically and intelligently.[9]

A Biblical critical tool which has had major impact on New Testament studies is form criticism. While form critics are numerous, probably Rudolf Bultmann should be credited with developing the methodology in such fashion as to make it available to the broad scholarly public.[10]

Form criticism was earliest applied to Old Testament studies, but between World War I and World War II this methodology became practically equated with New Testament studies. Form criticism as applied to the Gospels is the investigation of the Gospel literature in order to isolate the individual unit of tradition (pericope), to analyze each pericope as regards its use in the early church, and to enlighten the interpreter concerning the oral transmission era of the church through this process of investigation.

Form criticism is based upon four basic presuppositions. Initially, the form critic assumes that the earliest Gospel traditions were placed in written form about A.D. 50, resulting in an oral transmission period from A.D. 30 (crucifixion) to A.D. 50. During this oral transmission period stories about Jesus and his sayings circulated without any concern for geographic or chronologic detail. For example, the pericope in which Jesus asserts "Let the children come to me" (Mark 10:13-16; Matthew 19:13-15; Luke 18:15-17) might have come from any time in his ministry and from any location. There is nothing in the pericope to give it geographic or chronologic setting.

Second, each pericope isolated may be categorized according to a fixed number of literary types. The basic premise is that a people of limited literary ability and awareness would have transmitted these materials in a restricted number of literary types. Unfortunately, not all form critics agree as to the categories and the same categories are not always used with parallel meaning. Some of the types used are as follows:

1. Pronouncement Story: This is a story having a unity of time and place culminating with a saying by Jesus. One may be more certain of the saying than of the context in which it is set in this literary type, for the saying could be intelligible in any number of contexts. Mark 2:23-28 is a good example:

One sabbath day he was going through the grain-
fields; and as they made their way his disciples began to pluck ears of grain. And the Pharisees said
to him, "Look, why are they doing what is not lawful
on the sabbath?" And he said to them, "Have you
never read what David did, when he was in need and
was hungry, he and those who were with him: how he
entered the house of God, when Abiathar was high
priest, and ate the bread of the Presence, which it
is not lawful for any but the priests to eat, and
also gave it to those who were with him?" And he
said to them, "The sabbath was made for man, not man
for the sabbath; so the Son of man is lord even of
the sabbath."

This final pronouncement could easily be set in numerous other contexts.

2. Miracle Story: This is an account of a mighty act
taking such forms as exorcism, healing, and nature
miracle. A healing mighty act is represented in
Mark 3:1-5:

Again he entered the synagogue, and a man was
there who had a withered hand. And they watched him,
to see whether he would heal him on the sabbath, so
that they might accuse him. And he said to the man
who had the withered hand, "Come here." And he said
to them, "Is it lawful on the sabbath to do good or
to do harm, to save life or to kill?" But they were
silent. And he looked around at them with anger,
grieved at their hardness of heart, and said to the
man, "Stretch out your hand." He stretched it out,
and his hand was restored.

66

3. Legend: This is a story recounting the activities
   of an individual who played a role in the Gospel
   account. In the trial before Pilate, the crowd was
   asked if they would prefer the release of Jesus or
   Barabbas. At this point Pilate's wife enters the
   scene:

   Besides, while he was sitting on the judgment seat,
   his wife sent word to him, "Have nothing to do with
   that righteous man, for I have suffered much over
   him today in a dream" (Matthew 27:19).

4. Myth: This is a story in which supranormal characters
   and events play a major role. The temptation scene
   in Mark 1:12-13 exemplifies this:

   The Spirit immediately drove him out into the
   wilderness. And he was in the wilderness forty days,
   tempted by Satan; and he was with the wild beasts;
   and the angels ministered to him.[11]

5. Controversy: This is a story portraying the conflict between Jesus and his enemies, particularly
   the Pharisees. In reading these narratives the
   controversy between the church and the synagogue
   which emerged post-Jesus is transparent. Mark 2:15-17
   is a good example:

   And as he sat at table in his house, many tax
   collectors and sinners were sitting with Jesus and
   his disciples; for there were many who followed him.
   And the scribes of the Pharisees, when they saw that
   he was eating with sinners and tax collectors, said
   to his disciples, "Why does he eat with tax

collectors and sinners?" And when Jesus heard it,
he said to them, "Those who are well have no need of
a physician, but those who are sick; I came not to
call the righteous, but sinners."[12]

6. Parable: This is a story told to make a singular
    point about the Kingdom of God. Numerous examples
    of parables are found in the Synoptics, but Mark
    4:30-32 is a brief but adequate example:

    And he said, "With what can we compare the
    kingdom of God, or what parable shall we use for it?
    It is like a grain of mustard seed, which, when sown
    upon the ground, is the smallest of all the seeds on
    earth; yet when it is sown it grows up and becomes
    the greatest of all shrubs, and puts forth large
    branches, so that the birds of the air can make nests
    in its shade."

    There are other examples of literary types, but the
    foregoing are sufficient to indicate the form critic's
    concerns.
    Third, after the pericope has been isolated and
categorized, it is then assumed that one can make determinations regarding the pericope's age by the amount of
ecclesiastical influence exerted upon the material. It
is asserted that a later derived pericope will show the
greater influence of the church's development and is
designated an impure or mixed type. To the contrary, a
pericope circulated from early on will demonstrate little
of the church's influence and is labeled a pure or un-
mixed type.
    The form critic's final assumption is the most im-
portant and the one to which the other three logically

lead. Once the pericope has been isolated, categorized, and dated, the pericope may then be evaluated in terms of its setting in the life (Sitz im Leben) of the early church. The strictest form critics conclude that this setting in the early church is the earliest traceable context. They argue that, since everything in the Gospels derives out of the church's life, it is virtually impossible to trace the pericope through the church into the ministry of Jesus. For many form critics, therefore, one can never know the Jesus of history. One must be satisfied, they would contend, with an awareness of the Christ of faith who confronted the early church.

The form critical methodology, while skeptical, has proven to be of immeasurable value in enlightening the oral transmission era of the church. This Biblical critical tool serves to open that hidden part of the church just as depth psychiatry reveals the hidden recesses of the mind.

Conclusion

The possibilities for clarifying the meaning and implications of the Biblical text through the use of Biblical criticism have been the focus of this portion of our study. We have barely touched on the myriad of possibilities open to our investigation, but the material discussed makes sufficiently clear that Biblical criticism is a necessary rather than an optional tool for the individual who would understand the Biblical tradition. We conclude, therefore, with some suggestions as to why the methodology of Biblical criticism is helpful.

Biblical critical tools permit the Bible to speak out of its own context. This assists the interpreter to understand the origin and intention of Biblical passages. To grasp content one must understand the context.

Biblical criticism discourages the individual's reading his preferred interpretation into a passage. This interpretive process facilitates reading the meaning out of the passage (exegesis).

Biblical criticism prevents bibliolatry. The worship of the book, the Bible, is ill advised both academically and ecclesiastically. It should be clear why this is true academically, but ecclesiastically this sets as ultimate the vehicle rather than that which the vehicle seeks to convey. Bibliolatry is a form of idolatry.

Biblical criticism helps place in proper perspective the significant role played by man in the emergence and transmission of the scriptures. One must forego the concept of scripture's divine dictation if the materials are to be accorded the serious concern they deserve and if literary-critical tools are to be applied to the Biblical text.

Biblical criticism enables man to recognize historical errors as man's errors. For example, the apparent confusion of Ai and probably Bethel in Joshua 7-8 is understood as an error which has found its way into the text during the process of transmission. In like fashion, limited scientific awareness may be recognized as man's finiteness. One thinks, for example, of the three-tiered cosmos presented in the early chapters of Genesis. One can deal with this as the accepted cosmological view of ancient man. One can also recognize the prejudice found in scripture as being the inevitable result of the human condition. For example, in the Hebrew scriptures there are many instances of the Hebrew antagonism against the Canaanites. In like fashion, in the Christian scriptures one finds numerous examples of hostility toward the Jews. In using Biblical criticism, one can accept such short-

comings as being resultant to man's part in the writing
of the scriptures. If instead one assumes the divine
dictation of scriptures, then one must either ignore
the problems or assume that insufficient evidence is at
hand to make intelligible what "appears" to be a problem.

Biblical criticism encourages the individual to utilize his full humanity, reason as well as emotion. This
recalls in Chapter I that any authentic understanding of
religion and religious experience must grapple with the
effect upon the individual's full humanity--belief,
emotion, and action.

These reasons give adequate support for the use of
Biblical criticism in interpreting the Biblical text.
The scriptures have the potential either of enslaving or
liberating the individual. The crucial issue revolves
around the presuppositional bases with which one approaches
scripture. Biblical criticism offers the opportunity for
scripture to fulfill its liberating possibilities.

IV

YAHWISM-JUDAISM: A FAITH WITHIN HISTORY

Yahwism-Judaism was unique among the religions of
the ancient Near East in the importance attached to history. Within history Yahweh revealed himself and man
found the meaning of existence. History was the only
medium through which the actions of God were understandable.

While the Biblical histories convey definite prejudices, no attempt was made to conceal these from the
reader. These writers had a perspective which precipitated their recording. Reading the material, therefore,
the message fairly leaps from the page. Resultingly,
the message frequently takes precedence over the historical account.

When attempting to interpret an historical passage,
one must seek first to understand the recorder and his
concerns. Each of the three histories found in the
Biblical text--the Priestly, Deuteronomic, and Chronicler's
histories--must be so investigated. What was the context
out of which the writer(s) recorded? What were they seeking to accomplish? How do the histories interrelate?
Before turning to these questions, however, some semantic
and geographic questions need resolution in order to
assist in reading the histories more intelligently. Only
as verbal designations are used properly and the locale
of Biblical faith's development understood will the

histories recording that faith's emergence and growth
have their proper impact.

Semantic and Geographic Clarifications

A problem in reading the Bible is the presence of
anachronisms. These occur especially with reference to
the geographic designation where the Hebrew faith developed, the identification of the people, and the name of
their cultus.

Geographically, the land where Judaism was born has
been designated by numerous names. When the Israelites
entered after the Egyptian sojourn, it was designated
Canaan.[1] While the derivation of Canaan is disputed, it
clearly was used before Palestine. The latter, the Roman
designation for the land being Palaestina, was derived
from the Philistines, who inhabited the coastal region
south of Mount Carmel approximately 1150 B.C. While different names were used to designate individual portions
of the land--as Canaan, Judah, Israel, Edom, and Moab--
the entire land was called Palestine, the term derived
from the name of the invaders.

The name Israel was not proper until the thirteenth-
century invaders gradually settled into the land by conquest, intermarriage, and treaty, making the land their
own. The earliest possible use of Israel would be the
Davidic era, when this warrior-statesman established the
monarchy and lifted the Israelites into the international
monarchical competition. Even Israel is problematic,
however, for following the death of Solomon in 922 B.C.
the Kingdom inherited from his father David returned to
its earlier bipartite existence. During this dual monarchy era, the northern Kingdom was designated as Israel
while the southern Kingdom was Judah. Israel persisted

as a Kingdom from 922 until 722/721 B.C., when it was conquered by Assyria. Judah continued until 597/87 B.C., when Babylonia on two occasions attacked Jerusalem, the capital of Judah, and deported some of Judah's inhabitants into exile in Babylon.[2]

Following the Babylonian Exile both Israel and Judah were used to refer to the totality of the land, although Israel was the primary term used. When the State was reconstituted on May 14, 1948, it was determined that Israel should be its designation.

Both in the Biblical text and interpretive materials, earlier designations continue to be used after a new term has evolved. Canaan persisted after Palestine came into use, just as Israel and Judah were used alongside Canaan and Palestine. Careful attention must be given to these designations, both to assure accuracy and to avoid anachronistic use. Isaiah was a prophet in Judah, not Israel, while Hosea was a prophet in Israel, not Judah. Also, it would be inaccurate to say that the Israelites came into Israel beginning about 1250 B.C. Keeping these geographic terms clear is important for understanding Biblical history.

The designation of the people with whom we deal is also important. Hebrew indicates a broad grouping of ancient Near Eastern peoples, some of whom migrated into Egypt, perhaps in the eighteenth century B.C. There they remained until the thirteenth century, when the exodus led by Moses occurred. Upon leaving Egypt, however, it is still Hebrew that is proper.

Israel and Israelite are covenant terms, referring either to the people or to the individual knit in covenant relationship with Yahweh. These words, therefore, should not be used until after the Sinai covenant has been ratified (Exodus 24). Biblically speaking, the Hebrews arrived at Mount Sinai, while the Israelites departed Sinai (it would be helpful to compare John Bright, A History of Israel, 2nd ed., and Martin Noth, The History of Israel, rev. ed., regarding the Sinai period). A problem in using these designations accurately is that Biblical writers frequently use the terms anachronistically, so that it is not unusual to read that Israel was in Egypt. These people, however, were not historical analysts. They tended to view the current situation as being indicative of the way life had always been. Ancient peoples characteristically did this, but with our modern historical tools we should read the material with greater enlightenment.

Through the divided monarchy one was either a citizen of Israel or Judah, and his national designation took its clue therefrom. Post-exilically, however, it is Israelite that prevails. In the current situation, the citizen of Israel is an Israeli rather than an Israelite. Israeli is specifically a national designation and has no reference to religious affiliation, so that there are both Jewish and non-Jewish Israelis.

The final semantic clarification is the name for the religious faith espoused by these Biblical peoples. There are two distinct designations, with the Babylonian Exile (597/87-539/38 B.C.) being the separator in their use. Prior to the Exile Yahwism was the proper term, used for a worship structure where Yahweh was worshipped in monolatrous fashion,[3] where a King ruled over the people, where the prophets communicated Yahweh's message, and where God's revelation was understood in a dynamic and multi-faceted fashion. Judaism and Jew are post-exilic designations developing as a result of the exilic and early post-exilic thought patterns. Monotheistic worship of Yahweh became normative; kingship even if politically feasible was rejected in the conviction that their exilic plight was dependent on their rejection of Yahweh as King (theocracy); prophets ceased to be viable spokesmen early in the post-exilic period and were replaced by scribes (lawyers of the Torah); and, as indicated in Chapter III, the Torah reached its final stages of formulation during the Exile and the early post-exilic era. The evolvement of the Torah is crucial, for this made Judaism a reality as the people of the Torah and consequently rendered the prophets unnecessary. The prophets were dynamic spokesmen for Yahweh who spoke to emerging situations, but with the Torah and its attendant authority there was no need for this type of dynamic voice. One looked to the Torah for the response of God to the specific problem or situation, and the priests and scribes came to play uncommonly important roles in Judaism.

Historically it is inaccurate to refer to Moses as a Jew; and in like fashion it would be anachronistic to refer to any of the pre-exilic figures as Jews--Josiah, Amos, Hosea, Isaiah, Jeremiah, as well as others. Judaism is a term specifically reserved for the post-exilic religious phenomenon, and the worship structure of the contemporary Jew obviously still goes by the same designation. While contemporary Judaism is built upon the Torah and Talmud (Babylonian Talmud codified A.D. 499), differing interpretations through the centuries have resulted in various "denominations" within Judaism, ranging from the Orthodox, who are most bound to the ancient traditions, through the Conservative to the Reform, who judge themselves the least restricted in terms of literal adherence to the ancient traditions.

Attention will now be directed to the geographic context in which Yahwism-Judaism emerged. Some understanding of geography is important for at least three reasons: to give awareness of the diverse areas which constitute Palestine as well as the areas surrounding the country; to clarify why the faith of Yahwism-Judaism is a melding of differing if refined perspectives; and to indicate why Palestine was and continues to be important far out of proportion to its size.

Palestine is made up of two distinct areas, Cisjordan and Transjordan. Since all directions are given as if one were standing in Jerusalem, Transjordan refers to the area east of the Jordan River, roughly four thousand square miles. Cisjordan refers to the area between the Jordan River and the Mediterranean Sea, approximately six thousand square miles. Biblically, the northern and southern boundaries were characteristically set at Dan and Beer-Sheba, approximately one hundred fifty miles. West to east the country is even smaller. The widest portion of Cisjordan runs from the Mediterranean Sea to the Dead Sea, a distance of fifty-four miles, while in the north it is only twenty-nine miles from the Mediterranean to the Sea of Galilee. Incorporating both Cisjordan and Transjordan, there is a land space of about ten thousand square miles, an area approximately equal to the state of Vermont. Palestine was never a large land area.

Individuals acquainted with the climate of southern California have a good key for understanding much of Palestine's climate. A rainy season extends from October through April. During this period there will usually be some precipitation each day, but from May through September rain is rare. The saving factor for the land during the long dry period is a heavy dew which blankets the ground during the night. Even during the rainy season, however, there is never sufficient rainfall. In recent years, for example, Jericho along the Jordan River has averaged five and one-half inches per year, Jerusalem twenty-six inches, Tel-Aviv twenty-one inches, and forty-seven inches near Safad.[4] In order for this amount of waterfall to be minimally satisfactory, precaution must be taken to preserve the water through the building of dams and cisterns; and, where they exist, springs must be used effectively.

Palestinian topography is amazingly diverse for a country so small.[5] The most distinctive feature of the topography is the geologic fault creating the Jordan River Valley, an area sometimes designated as the Arabah (suggesting aridity and sterility) or the Ghor (meaning depression).[6] This depression cuts the country from north to south, a depression originating in the Mesopotamian Valley and terminating in the North African continent. Within Palestine, the Jordan River Valley began in antiquity with Lake Huleh in the north, a lake situated approximately 229 feet above sea level. Practically this entire area has now been drained and reclaimed for agriculture. Only a few miles south of Lake Huleh is the Sea of Galilee, but in this short distance the fault has dropped significantly so that the Sea of Galilee is roughly 696 feet below sea level. The Sea of Galilee is approximately six miles wide and twelve miles long and has always been more important for fishing than for agriculture, since there is a relatively narrow rim of arable land around the Sea. In this area today, however, a number of Kibbutzim are located, as Ein Gev on the eastern shore; and the ancient city of Tiberias is located on the western shore.

Emptying out of the Sea of Galilee, the Jordan River—
78

fed by two primary rivers on the east, the Yarmuk and the Jabbok, and the River Jalud from the west, as well as numerous wadis from both the east and the west--makes its serpentine way to the Dead Sea. The River is not wide, but because of its rapid descent it is often rather swift. As a result, the Jordan did present some barrier to communication between eastern and western sectors of the land.

The Jordan River empties into the Dead Sea just south of Jericho. The water level of the Dead Sea is approximately 1,290 feet below sea level, and the floor level is roughly 1,300 feet further below sea level, making the Dead Sea the lowest inland body of water on earth. The Sea has no outlets, so all water emptying into the Sea must evaporate out. This results in numerous chemicals being found in the water, one element giving the water a tarry quality, clarifying Josephus' designation of the Sea as Lake Asphaltitis. The Sea has also been called the Salt Sea, and estimates vary between twenty-five and thirty-three per cent as regards the salinity of the water. While swimmers use the Dead Sea primarily because of its uniqueness, it is not a pleasant place for swimming. The Dead Sea is larger than most people realize, measuring as much as ten miles wide and approximately fifty miles long. After the 1967 War, the Israelis paved a road along the Dead Sea to the town of Eilat at the northern tip of the Gulf of Eilat. The considerable size of the Sea is recognized as one rides for mile after mile along the water, with steep rock cliffs and hills rapidly ascending on both sides of the Sea.

In terms of the topography-geography of Palestine, we have touched on this one aspect which lends the most unique flavor to the land. Palestine incorporates four, or for clarity one could say five, major land divisions.

Beginning at the Mediterranean coast and moving eastward, the initial land division is the Coastal Plain, or the Maritime Plain. This incorporates some of Palestine's most fertile area, particularly was this true of the land occupied by the Philistines, the so-called Philistine Plain to the south, where Palestine's largest block of level land is found. Generally this area had sufficient rainfall, although there were some springs located here to assist in irrigation when and where needed. As one moves further to the south the area becomes increasingly arid, as is particularly witnessed between Gaza and Beer-Sheba.

Located north of the Philistine Plain was the Plain of Sharon. While this area had its fertile locations, much of it was marshy; and the coastal region was characterized by sand dunes. It is in this sand dune area that the modern city of Tel-Aviv was constructed, beginning in 1909. Today, through careful use of water, much of this area blossoms with fertility; and many of the approximately two million trees which have been planted since the State of Israel was constituted in 1948 are found in this area, a fact vividly attested as one approaches landing at the David Ben-Gurion Airport at Tel-Aviv.

The northern terminus of the Plain of Sharon is Mount Carmel, a mountain which rises 1,736 feet.[7] This mountain, a spur off of the central mountain highlands, literally juts out a distance only a few feet short of the Mediterranean Sea. Modern Haifa, Israel's principal seaport, nestles at the base of Mount Carmel and presents a majestic sight from atop Mount Carmel.

The area north of Mount Carmel never had definitive designation. As one looks at a map, however, it is that portion of the Maritime Plain which was ultimately a part of the northern portion of the country known as Galilee.

The second land division was the foothills, or what was designated the Shephelah. This was the gentle rising hills before one actually reached the more abruptly rising mountain area. This might be seen as Palestine's Piedmont region, a region that was particularly suited for the grazing of flocks and herds. Remembering that the Israelites, when they were early occupants of the land, were more associated with the flocks and herds than with agriculture, we recognize that we now move to the area where the greater early Israelite occupation was found. The Shephelah, however, is more often considered a part of the next major land division, the central mountain ridge.

The central mountain range divides Palestine from north to south. Arising out of the mountains to the north of Palestine, the central mountain ridge runs with only one significant break from upper Galilee to lower Judah, this break being the Pass of Jezreel (or Esdraelon), which separates Galilee from Samaria. This Pass cut the hill country in the vicinity of Mount Carmel, providing Palestine's best access between east and west. Because the Pass was so important to communication and transportation, control was vital. At Megiddo, the primary city at the western entrance to the Pass, King Josiah was killed in 609 B.C. fighting against Pharaoh Neco of Egypt (2 Kings 23). Numerous significant battles were fought in this area. Drawing on this fact, the Book of Revelation portrays the symbolic final battle to be fought between the forces of evil and righteousness as the battle of Armageddon (Revelation 16:16), meaning "Hill of Megiddo" (see Judges 5:19; 2 Kings 9:27; and 2 Chronicles 35:22). Besides being a strategic military location, the Pass of Jezreel was also important economically, both because of trade routes and because exceptionally fertile land was found therein.

The central portion of the mountain country is designated Samaria, the area where many early Israelites settled. This is rugged mountainous region, broken by numerous valleys, one of the most important being that between Mount Ebal (3,085 feet) and Mount Gerizim (2,890 feet) where the ancient city of Shechem was located. Besides Shechem, other significant cities such as Samaria, Bethel, and Shiloh were located in this central hill country. Many of the valleys were fertile, possessing sufficient rainfall for agriculture.

The southern portion of the central mountain range was Judah, which received less rainfall than Samaria, was more rugged in its terrain, and was less productive agriculturally. Because of climatic and topographical conditions, Judah was the least attractive and most easily defended of the hill country regions. The principal city was Jerusalem, which sits atop the mountain range at ca. 2,600 feet above sea level. The eastern and southern regions of Judah become increasingly barren and arid, although among the significant Biblical cities located in Judah were Lachish, Debir, Hebron, and, lying along the southern extremities, Beer-Sheba.

Moving eastward, the next land division would be the Jordan River Valley, which has already been discussed. To the east of the Jordan Valley is the final land division, the Transjordan. The Transjordan region is, generally speaking, of higher altitude than its Cisjoran counterpart and has suffered even more from ravaging erosion through the centuries. In Biblical times we recall such names as Bashan, Gilead, Ammon, Moab, and Edom (north to south) occupying the Transjordan; but currently we find Lebanon to the north of Israel, Syria to the northeast, Jordan to the east, and Saudi Arabia to the southeast.

To the south of Palestine was the region known as the Negeb, a Hebrew word meaning "south country." Most properly this referred to the vicinity of Beer-Sheba. This was basically a barren region, with only a few springs giving evidence of fertility.

Moving further southward one enters the Sinai peninsula, bordered on the west by Egypt and the Gulf of Suez and on the east by the Gulf of Aqabah. The traditional location of Kadesh-Barnea (focal point of Israel's wilderness wandering) is located in the northern, and the most accepted site of Mount Sinai in the southern portion of this region. Saint Catherine's monastery, first constructed in the fourth century, sits at the base of Mount Sinai. This is a forbidding region of Nubian sandstone and granite. Whereas the sands usually associated with desert regions exist in the northern area, most of the Sinai peninsula is made up of craggy mountain ranges, so rugged and barren as to make any kind of sustenance difficult. Occasional oases are found, and the Bedouin peoples cluster around these life-giving sources of water. Traditionally the peninsula has not been a part of Palestine; but during the 1967 War Israel gained control of the Sinai peninsula, although ownership/possession continues to be debated.

The remarkable diversity that has characterized Palestine is evident, but why has this land always been so important? First, a primary reason has been location. To the east of the Transjordan was the Arabian Desert, an expanse so wide that today it is usually traversed only by night automotive trip. In ancient times, the physical impracticality of crossing this vast expanse meant that movements of peoples occasioned by designs of conquest, threats of famine, or mass migratory cycles had to avoid the Arabian Desert. Since Egypt and the Mesopotamian

Valley were primary power and population centers in the ancient Near East, one to the southwest of Canaan and the other to the east-northeast, all peoples had to navigate the narrow Syria-Canaan land bridge. Control of Canaan was necessary to control the east-west trade routes. It is no wonder that this little land always had an importance which was far out of proportion to its land size, population, or resources. Canaan was inexorably drawn into the arena of international affairs, this being truer for Israel than for the more remote Judah.

Second, religiously Palestine was the birthplace of both Judaism and Christianity; and Jerusalem and the Dome of the Rock (Islamic mosque) located there are highly revered by the Muslims. Multiple claims upon the land make impossible easy solutions to interrelationship problems.

Third, economically the oil problem is a major concern. While the Negeb does not possess the quantity of oil resources found in Saudi Arabia, nonetheless a major portion of the world's oil resources are located in this general area. Every nation located in proximity to the oil reserves, regardless of the resources in the particular country, assumes a note of international significance by virtue of its location.

Geographically, religiously, and economically Palestine has been a principal participant in world affairs. This has not always been a self-appointed role, however, but it has been an inescapable destiny.

Judaism's Three Histories

Judaism's canonical scriptures contain three Histories, each unique. These are the Priestly, Deuteronomic, and Chronicler's Histories.

In Chapter III the documentary hypothesis of the

Pentateuch was discussed. The Pentateuch and the Priestly History refer to the same books of the Hebrew scriptures--Genesis, Exodus, Leviticus, Numbers, and Deuteronomy. Pentateuch means "five scrolls." It is of Greek derivation and conveys similar connotation as the "Five Books of Moses," also referring to these five books. Another Jewish designation for the five books is "Torah," meaning guidance, law, or instruction. Thus, all of these designations--Priestly History, Pentateuch, Five Books of Moses, and Torah--refer to the same corpus of material. The designation used is determined by the intent of the user.

The Priestly History covers the period from creation to Israel's preparation for entrance into the land of Canaan. As noted earlier, this material was placed in its present form during and immediately following the Babylonian Exile. A dating between 550 and 450 B.C. suffices; and editorial changes of significance had been completed by 400 B.C., when the schism between Jews and Samaritans occurred. When these two communities separated, each retained the Pentateuch. Comparing the Samaritan and Jewish Pentateuchs, little significant dissimilarity is found.

The Deuteronomic History incorporates the books of Joshua, Judges, Samuel, and Kings and covers the period sequential to the Priestly History. It begins with the entrance into Canaan under Joshua's direction and concludes with the fall of both Kingdoms, the North to Assyria in 722/721 B.C. and the South to Babylonia in 597/587 B.C.

The Deuteronomic History does not include the book of Deuteronomy, which is incorporated into the Pentateuch. The designation, the Deuteronomic History, is derived from Deuteronomy, however, for the editing of these "history books"[8] was based on the religious perspectives of Deuteronomy. This viewpoint was one of divine retribution based on human conduct--do good and be rewarded, do evil and be punished. While not a part of the Deuteronomic History, therefore, Deuteronomy was a primary factor influencing the final formulation of the Deuteronomic History.

As will be discussed, King Josiah of Judah was instrumental in initiating a sweeping political-religious reform beginning at least by 622 B.C. Prior to his untimely death in 609 B.C., it is conjectured that the initial editing of the Deuteronomic History took place, probably about 610 B.C. With the Exile beginning in 597 B.C., however, fresh impetus was given to editors operating under this divine reward-judgment perspective. During the Exile, therefore, the Deuteronomic History was placed in its present form. These editors interpreted the life of their people according to actions precipitating divine favor and conversely, given their circumstances at the time of the final editing, actions incurring divine wrath.

The final canonical History was the Chronicler's History, formulated about 300 B.C. during the post-exilic period. Materials included were the books of Chronicles, Ezra, and Nehemiah. These writers sought to be more inclusive chronologically, beginning with a type of primeval history, attempting to place Abraham and his descendents among all the peoples of the earth, and concluding with a perusal of the post-exilic era in which the Chronicler(s)[9] actually stood.

Before turning to an investigation of these Histories with emphasis both to the events recorded and to the principles governing the record, the following chart indicates the way these three Histories relate to and complement each other:

PRIESTLY HISTORY	DEUTERONOMIC HISTORY
Creation-----Readiness for entrance into Canaan	Entrance-----Fall of Israel and Judah

CHRONICLER'S HISTORY

Abrahamic placement-------------------Post-exilic era
among the nations

Thus the Priestly and Deuteronomic Histories are sequential
to each other. In the latter portion of the Priestly History, the early chapters of Deuteronomy summarize what
Yahweh God has done in the life of this people, bringing
them to birth and making them a viable nation, even though
at this point they are landless (Deuteronomy 1:1-4:43).
This is internal duplication within the Priestly History,
however, for once the Deuteronomic History begins the focus
is on the actual entrance into Canaan. With the Chronicler's History, however, what has been recounted in both
the Priestly and Deuteronomic Histories is also the Chronicler's concern; but he takes his account further by cover-
ing the early post-exilic period. To relay the material
even as thoroughly as the Priestly and Deuteronomic Histories, the Chronicler's History would have to be as
lengthy as both of these plus some additional materials.
A comparison of pagination in any edition of the Hebrew
scriptures conveys that this is not the case, for the
Chronicler has been very selective in his coverage. We
will wish to investigate this more fully later as we discuss the Chronicler.

The <u>Priestly History</u> reaches into Israel's early stages of development. As earlier indicated, traditions were gradually brought together to create the Priestly History. We have discussed four of these generally accepted sources--J, E, D, and P--but various scholars make effective cases for additional traditions.[10] For our present concern, however, interest focuses not on the individual components but upon the character of the narrative as placed in its final form.

The Priestly editors were preoccupied with cultic matters. Their interests, however, focused more on the mechanics of the ritual acts than on the intended meanings associated with the acts.[11] It may be that the significance of the rituals were inherent and were conveyed by the officiating priests in the cultic act. If this be the case, then the meanings did not need to be conveyed so much as did the proper procedure for the ritual. The inherited nature of the priestly office tends to support this assumption.

This should not indicate a lack of priestly interest in the more sublime, however, as evidenced particularly by the emphases on ritual purity (as in Leviticus 21:1-24) and the exalted holiness of God. Ritual purity was associated not only with the sacrifice but also with the acceptability of the worshipper.

The priests performed a four-fold service in the Yahwistic cultus--keepers of the sanctuaries, responsibility for the deliverance of oracles, transmitters of the sacral tradition, and officiation in the making of sacrifice. These services gave priests watchcare over the entire cultus; and, while these duties potentially emphasized methodology over motivation, this was not the intent. When a segment of the society understands itself on the basis of ancient tradition, frequently an obsession

for maintaining the status quo develops. Certain abuses
may attend their zeal, particularly the misuse of power.

Basic to priestly thought was the concept of the
holiness of God. While creation theology apparently did
not develop within Israelite thought until the seventh
and sixth centuries, Genesis 1:1-2:4a (P) is a good example of the Priestly History's focus on the holiness of
God. The creation story is presented as myth, namely
that God brought into being not only man but also the
entire cosmos. Creation was seen as prologue to the
Israelite drama, as Bernard W. Anderson has properly
stated:

In Israel's understanding, then, creation and history are
inseparably related. Creation is the foundation of the
covenant; it provides the setting within which Yahweh's
saving work takes place.[12]

This dramatic prologue sets the stage for the view of
God which prevails throughout the Priestly History. God
was affirmed as the highly exalted other who demanded
emulation of his holiness, as set forth in the Holiness
Code of Leviticus 17-26. This emphasis had inherent dangers, however, as expressed by Walther Eichrodt:

We cannot . . . ignore that this Priestly language
about God promoted the development of conceptual theological thought and laid the foundations for a monotheism
defined in abstract terms. Such a development involves
the danger of losing that sense of the nearness of God
which is part of the endowment of faith, and of sinking
into the nothingness of despair in the face of an inaccessible Deity.[13]

89

As Eichrodt discusses further, this emphasis on the re-
moteness and otherness of God aroused abuses within developing Israelite thought;[14] but this fact should not
obscure the exalted concept of God maintained by the
priests.

As succinctly as possible, let us turn our attention
to the narrative concerns of the Priestly History. There
is a distinction between simply recounting the narrative
and discussing critically Israel's emergence. The pivotal event in all Biblical history was the exodus and the
events associated therewith, whereby disparate peoples
were united in covenant relationship with Yahweh at Mount
Sinai.[15] Historically, any account of Israel's existence
prior to this birth point must be recognized as faith's
"history," recorders looking through and influenced by
the exodus record their understanding of the events preparatory to the nation's emergence. With this acknowledgment, let us note the succession of events as found
in the Priestly History.

The History begins with the Primeval History recorded
in Genesis 1-11. Differing creation accounts are given
in Genesis 1:1-2:4a (P) and Genesis 2:4b-3:24 (J), the
former cosmogonic by thrust and the latter anthropogonic.
Both accounts set the stage for the emergence of man and
for the delineation of man's history prior to the initial
Hebrew's emergence, Abraham. The story of man begins with
primeval man and woman and their offspring (all male!) and
the emergence of traumatic interpersonal problems. Cain
murdered his brother Abel, and then with Cain we see the
flowering of urban-life wickedness. Chapter 5 moves the
reader from this point to a considerably later era when
men are abundant, the time of Noah. Yahweh's judgment
upon man's sinfulness results in the flood, but Noah and

his family are preserved in order that God might continue
the human experiment. Unfortunately, the experiment continues to go poorly; and after chapter 10, where again
the reader is transported by a genealogical table to yet
a later period, mankind's corruption is demonstrated in
the aborted attempt to build a tower from which finite
man might control God. Following the flood, however, God
had given his covenant oath that he would not deal so
harshly with man again; and thus a new experiment is initiated. Again Yahweh God chose one man, Abraham, through
whom His blessings should be manifest to all mankind.

This divine decision takes us into the remainder of
the book of Genesis where the Patriarchal story is recorded. Genesis 12-25 concentrates on Abraham, while
chapters 26-36 focus on his son and successor, Isaac.
Jacob, one of Isaac's sons, received his primary blessing;
and thus Israel's descent is traced through him. Genesis
37-50 depict this part of the cycle, although the bulk
of this narrative focuses on one of Jacob's sons, Joseph.
It is emphasized that Jacob had twelve sons; but it was
by virtue of Joseph's ascending to power by divine providence that ultimately all of the sons made their way
into Egypt. This set the stage for the Egyptian sojourn
and for the contest between Yahweh and the gods of Egypt,
resulting in the Hebrew's deliverance from Egypt.

This is the story of the book of Exodus. Moses is
depicted as Yahweh's instrument in the exodus. The exodus
is couched in the midst of numerous mighty acts, the
plagues, with the result being the Hebrews' release from
oppression. After their encounter with the Sea of Reeds,
the Hebrews finally arrived at their destination, Mount
Sinai. According to Biblical depiction, they arrived
Sinai at Exodus 19:1 and did not depart until Numbers
10:11, eleven months later. All of the intervening

material, including the Ten Commandments in Exodus 20 and
the covenant ratification ceremony in Exodus 24, purport
to come from Sinai. Much of the material is of later
derivation, but our concern is to chronicle the drama as
told in the Priestly History.

Following the departure from Sinai, the Israelites[16]
made their way northward with the intent to enter Canaan
from the south. When a scouting party brought back a
majority report which was negative concerning the people's
possibilities for success in taking the land, they wavered
in their intention. This was judged a rejection of Yahweh's
leadership, resulting in Yahweh's declaring that the people who departed Egypt would not enter Canaan, save for
the two spies who brought back a positive report. One of
these spies was Joshua.

Following a period of wilderness wandering, during
which a generation died, under Moses' direction the people traveled along the southern tip of the Dead Sea,
northward by its eastern side, to a spot just north of
the Dead Sea and opposite Jericho.

According to present placement and intent of the
book of Deuteronomy, Moses delivered here three final
addresses to the convened people. He recapitulated for
them what God had done (Deuteronomy 1:1-4:43), he sought
to clarify for them what God required (Deuteronomy 4:44-
28:68), and he briefly asserted what God proposed for
them (Deuteronomy 29-30). The remaining chapters (31-34)
of Deuteronomy chronicle the transition of leadership
from Moses to Joshua, and then Moses ascended a lofty
mountain from which he could overlook Canaan. Moses was
never seen alive again. The leadership transition was
complete.

This is the point to which the Priestly History takes
the narrative. While much of the history lacks excitement

and vivid color, particularly the book of Leviticus, it
is an important record and essential for understanding
Israel's comprehension of herself.

The Deuteronomic History is totally different from
the Priestly History, its governing principles and the
period of history recorded. The relationship of this
material to the Priestly History is disputed, especially
the possible continuation of the pentateuchal sources in
the Deuteronomic History.[17] In like fashion, the date of
the final editing and the number of editions upon which
the deuteronomistic editors worked is debated. Regardless, most would agree with Otto Eissfeldt that, at least
in the book of Kings, the nature of the editing process
was different. He states: "for the period after David
there was available, particularly for the Jerusalem kings,
a great deal of material in narratives and reports, and
the compilers could therefore choose as they wished."[18]
Again, however, for our summary we wish to capture the
essence of the principles governing these deuteronomistic
editors.

Whether it be one or several editings through which
this material evolved, the influence of the thought pattern expressed in the book of Deuteronomy cannot be gain-
said. Pivotal for Deuteronomy were the affirmations that
Yahweh was to be worshipped sacrificially only in the
Jerusalem Temple; that Yahweh alone was to be worshipped;
that Yahweh enacted his purposes in history; and that
divine retribution, whether for blessing or bane, results
from the actions of men individually and peoples corporately.

The conviction that Yahweh is to be worshipped only
in the Jerusalem Temple could become a major concern only
with Solomon and the construction of the Temple. This

evaluative principle used in the book of Kings constitutes one of the decisive differences in the deuteronomistic editing of the book, for every ruler was judged on his contribution to the centralization of worship in Jerusalem. As a result every king of Israel was judged negatively, for none of the northern kings encouraged their subjects to worship in Jerusalem. Even in Judah only Josiah, the king responsible for the Deuteronomic Reformation beginning in 622 B.C., was given unqualified approval. Hezekiah, also a reforming king, was given a more qualified approval; and the remainder of the southern kings received only limited acclaim (as Asa, Jehoshaphat, Jehoash, Uzziah, and Jotham) or fell victim to the deuteronomistic evaluation.

The deuteronomistic editors concentrated their attention on the South, for this was where Yahweh had caused his name to dwell. They were primarily interested in cultic matters as they affected the life of the people. Consequently, greater attention was focused on the prophets, for example, than on important kings who affected the international political arena but had little or no import religiously. A good example of the latter would be King Omri, who established Samaria as Israel's capital and controlled certain portions of the Transjordan area. In spite of this, Omri is summarily presented and dismissed with a mere six verses (1 Kings 16:23-28). The deuteronomistic editors made no attempt to conceal their biases!

Yahweh was to be worshipped exclusively by the people. Whether this be monotheism or monolatry is debatable, but nonetheless the conviction is clear. In the Deuteronomic History, turning aside to other gods, described in formula fashion as "serving the Baals and the Asheroth" (Judges 3:7), is depicted as the people's basic problem.

This same evaluation was used with the kings, for to walk "in the way of his father" conveys not only that centralization was not encouraged but also that the worship of Yahweh was compromised.

The deuteronomistic editors were convinced that history reveals the purposes of God. This also helps to explain their interest in the prophets, for they held equally to this dictum. For these editors, therefore, not only Israel and Judah, the international situation was important. The movements of kings and nations who knew not Yahweh were interpreted in terms of Yahweh's governance of history, usually as messengers of divine judgment. All persons, events, and nature itself were potentially the means for manifesting Yahweh's divine purpose.

Finally, one of the clearest principles of the deuteronomistic editing is that of divine retribution. They never doubted that righteousness was rewarded and evil actions punished. This conviction is exemplified in the formula used in the book of Judges, with Judges 3:7-12 being the best example. Also indicative of the retribution principle is 1 Kings 11, where it is indicated that the division of the Kingdom following Solomon's death resulted from Solomon's being too tolerant of the religious predilections of his foreign wives. Of all the deuteronomistic principles, probably this evaluative concern has had the most negative impact on Israelite religion. Such an evaluation is intensely subjective and open to radical abuse, as evidenced in contemporary Judaism and Christianity.

A summary of the Deuteronomic History covers a major period of Israelite history, approximately six centuries filled with significant events and persons. Any summation does violence to the materials, but we seek primarily the continuity of events.

The book of Joshua divides into three basic parts.
Chapters 1-12 record the conquest-settlement of the land
under Joshua's leadership, following the military strategy
of "divide and conquer." Attacking first at mid-country,
Jericho is depicted as succumbing to the invading Israelites; and the southern and northern portions of the
country fell in turn to them. While the general picture
is one of absolute domination, obviously this is exagger-
ation. After the death of Joshua, the question of the
people was: "Who shall go up first for us against the
Canaanites, to fight against them?" (Judges 1:1). Not
until David did the Israelites thoroughly dominate the
land. Joshua 13-23 records the division of land among
the Israelite tribes, while chapter 24 depicts a covenant
renewal ceremony at Shechem, perhaps the initial association of persons with Israel's covenant relationship when
they were not direct descendents of the exodus participants. The governance system characteristic of this
period is a type of tribal confederacy, designated by
some as an amphictyony, a grouping of autonymous tribes
knit together around a central religious shrine, namely
the Ark of the Covenant.

The book of Judges portrays the situation during
the tribal confederacy period with judges, or deliverers,
ruling over individual tribes. These men, and one
woman (Deborah), were primarily military deliverers who
emerged during a period of crisis and continued to exercise authority over the tribe for a brief period. During
this era there was one aborted attempt to establish a
monarchy by Abimelech (chapter 9), an indicator of what
was to develop among the Israelites. This book is important because it gives us some glimpse, however faint, of
the people during this period, their life and their

problems. It also demonstrates the moral-religious lesson which the deuteronomistic editors sought to impress by literary formula, namely that only absolute loyalty to Yahweh was acceptable.

Unfortunately the tribal confederacy proved to be unsatisfactory for meeting external military threats, for building economic security, or for providing an internal structure capable of engendering growth and development. Thus, with the book of Samuel,[19] the monarchical relationship developed. Samuel is the first major character on the stage, depicted as the final judge-deliverer and Yahweh's choice for ruler over his people. The Israelites clamor for a king like the other nations, however, and ultimately Saul was crowned by Samuel.[20] Saul was more attuned to the tribal confederacy than to the monarchy. The nation had its first authentic king with David, ruling first over Judah but ultimately over all Judah and Israel (2 Samuel 5:5). David's reign was marked by progress in every aspect of national life: economics, politics, international relations, and religion. With the rise of the monarchy, the prophetic movement emerged as Yahweh's dynamic spokesmen. Indicative of the prophet's role was Nathan's relationship to David, particularly as recorded in his parable of the lamb (2 Samuel 12:1-25). To their credit, the deuteronomistic editors included an account which many scholars judge a record from the time of David himself, 2 Samuel 9-20 and 1 Kings 1-2. This should be read with care, for it probably gives our most authentic portrait of David: a failure as a father and a national leader losing the following of his people. At his death (1 Kings 2) he is depicted as a tragic, sad figure.

The monarchy was to survive, however, and David was succeeded by Solomon, his son. Solomon was an extensive builder, among his credits being the Jerusalem Temple. He was an extravagant and self-indulgent figure, however, who lost the support of his people, particularly among the northern tribes. Thus, when Solomon died in 922 B.C., the Kingdom which had been ruled by David and Solomon divided, returning to an earlier bipartite existence. Throughout the pre-exilic period, however, this division persisted.

The deuteronomistic editors did not give equal coverage to the various kings, their chief criterion for evaluation being religious. Some of the more significant kings should be noted, first for Israel, then for Judah.[21]

Jeroboam I (922-901 B.C.) was Israel's first ruler, a clever labor leader. He was not of Davidic descent, a characteristic true of all the northern kings.

Shortly after Jeroboam I, Omri (876-869 B.C.) ascended the throne. As noted earlier, he is discussed only briefly but was a significant figure. He established Samaria as his capital, attempting to place Israel in the international scene, for this situated the capital along major trade routes.

When Ahab (869-850 B.C.), son of Omri, ruled, the Tyrian princess, Jezebel, exercised considerable influence as one of Ahab's queens. Jezebel sought to establish Baalism, the worship of the Canaanite god of the storm and agriculture, as Israel's state religion. This attempt brought the prophet Elijah into direct confrontation with the royal household.

The anti-Baalism struggle initiated by Elijah was concluded by a coup directed by Jehu (842-815 B.C.). This coup also terminated the Omrid Dynasty (876-842 B.C.) and assured the preservation of Yahwism in the north, although the overthrow was characterized by extensive bloodshed.

With Jeroboam II (786-746 B.C.) Israel was lifted
out of the doldrums of her national existence and reached
a peak of power and prestige. Along with this national
revival, however, Israel was religiously corrupt, bring-
two major prophetic figures on the scene, Amos with his
message of social justice and Hosea with his demand for
loyalty to Yahweh.

Following Jeroboam II the nation went into rapid
political decline, with the final king being Hoshea (732-
721 B.C.). During his reign Israel refused to pay the
required tribute tax to Assyria, with the result that a
siege was laid against Samaria by Shalmaneser V, which
siege was completed by Sargon II with Samaria's fall in
722/721 B.C. Thus it was that Israel was brought to a
conclusion, with a number of the inhabitants, particularly
in the environs of Samaria, being deported.

In Judah, Rehoboam (922-915 B.C.), son of Solomon,
was the first ruler. While Rehoboam was responsible for
the ultimate breach between Israel and Judah, Jehoshaphat
(873-849 B.C.) was a southern ruler who encouraged the
strengthening of ties with Israel. A political marriage
between the northern and southern houses during his reign
while Ahab ruled in the North served ultimately to bring
a female, Athaliah (842-837 B.C.), to the throne in the
South. Athaliah was a fervent Baalist who tried to turn
Judah from Yahweh to Baal. This encroachment upon Yahwism was short-lived, as demonstrated by the later rule
of Uzziah (783-742 B.C.), a stalwart Yahwist. At the
death of Uzziah the ministry of Isaiah was initiated,
this zealous prophet who proclaimed that his people must
put absolute trust in Yahweh.

Isaiah's ministry continued through the rule of
Uzziah's son, Ahaz (735-715 B.C.), who faced the threat
of Assyrian domination of Judah. It was during this

crisis that Israel fell to Assyria in 722/721 B.C. Even
as Isaiah spoke more to the powerful, Micah spoke of the
nation's ills and of Yahweh's inevitable judgment upon
Judah.

Hezekiah (715-687 B.C.), son of Ahaz, was a reforming
king. The Assyrian threat continued throughout his reign,
and the next ruler responded to this threat by capitulating.
Manasseh (687-642 B.C.) was pro-Assyrian, and significantly
there are are no name prophets speaking during his reign.
He instituted a campaign designed to suppress over-zealous
Yahwism!

Shortly after Manasseh, however, Josiah (640-609 B.C.)
came to the throne. This was the reformer par excellence
for the deuteronomistic editors. At least by 622 B.C.,
he initiated a Reform which was supported by a recently
discovered scroll (generally thought to be a portion of
the book of Deuteronomy) and by the prophet Jeremiah, at
least during the early stages of the prophet's ministry.
Josiah was killed, however, in 609 B.C. in a struggle with
the troops of Pharaoh Neco of Egypt. Thus, this Reform,
which had the political ambition of unifying the North
and South, as well as the religious aspiration of purifying
Yahwism, lost its major advocate.

Judah's time was now short-lived. Babylonia was
rapidly rising as a major power, and the kings of Judah
misjudged her vitality. When tribute was withheld, King
Nebuchadrezzar of Babylon appeared in 597 B.C. and Jerusalem was felled. Zedekiah was installed as a puppet
ruler for Babylonia, while King Jehoiachin was exiled.
Unfortunately, Zedekiah joined a revolt against Babylonia
which brought Nebuchadrezzar to Jerusalem again in 587 B.C.
This time the city was dealt with more harshly, as the
Temple constructed by Solomon was destroyed, portions of
the city walls were torn down, and a second deportation

occurred (a third grouping was taken in 582 B.C., a total of 4,600 persons--perhaps men?--according to Jeremiah 52: 28-30).

At this point the Deuteronomic History concludes, with Jehoiachin in Exile but being treated favorably by the Babylonian ruler. The editors were not devoid of hope, the Davidic dynasty was still alive!

Israel's third history is the Chronicler's History, dated approximately 300 B.C. As indicated earlier, the Chronicler recorded the time span covered in the Priestly History and the Deuteronomic History; yet he obviously did not incorporate everything in these two sources. The Chronicler portrayed Israel-Judah in their ideal contexts, thus he excised materials which reflected unfavorably on David or Solomon as well as large blocks of northern traditions. In the Deuteronomic History, for example, David's illicit affair with Bathsheba, which resulted in the murder of Bathsheba's husband, was viewed by the deuteronomistic editors as the crucial event for understanding David's decline. To the contrary, because of the negative reflections on David, the Chronicler did not even record this narrative.

The Chronicler also had other objectives in this History. In 333 B.C. Alexander the Great conquered Palestine as he moved toward Egypt, and the Hellenization process in Palestine was evident. This writer retold Israel-Judah's story to focus on the purity of worship in the second Temple. Hellenization posed a real threat to that purity, but he hoped to encourage steadfastness in the people's resistance to Hellenization. The Chronicler is not as reliable in his pre-exilic record, for he often read the post-exilic ritual with which he was associated into the pre-exilic era. Obviously, in reading the Chronicler's history, the portion recounting the post-exilic period should be read with the greatest seriousness.

One of the Chronicler's primary purposes was to prove the supremacy of the Jerusalem tradition over the Samaritan cultus practiced at Gerizim. Quite obviously the dispute continued regarding the authentic spot to worship Yahweh; and the Chronicler--with his emphasis on David, Solomon, and the kings of Judah--affirmed the absolute supremacy of the Jerusalem Temple and its traditions. As Otto Eissfeldt expressed this: "The aim of the whole work is . . . to prove that in contrast with the godless Northern Kingdom, it is only the Southern Kingdom of Judah, with its Davidic dynasty and its Jerusalem Temple, which is the true Israel, the legitimate bearer of the divine rule which is actualised in the Kingdom of David, and that it is only the community of Jews who returned from the Exile, and not the religious community of the Samaritans, which was in the process of coming into being at the time of the Chronicler, which faithfully maintains and continues this tradition."[22]

The Chronicler extended his coverage into the post-exilic era to assert the legitimacy of the reconstituted Jerusalem cultus under the leadership of Ezra and Nehemiah. This places the latest focus of the History approximately 398 B.C., the most probable date for Ezra's coming to Jerusalem.

In addition to the aforementioned characteristics of the Chronicler's History, Eissfeldt notes the following characteristic features:

(1) the arrangement and correction of the events according to the religious pragmatism of retributive doctrine, (2) a religious conception of history which reckons with direct divine intervention in events and limits human action to

prayer and song, and (3) the marked predilection for Temple and cultus, for Levites and cultic music.[23]

We need not give a summary of the Chronicler's History. It is worthwhile to affirm the obvious, however, that the Chronicler's alterations to the Priestly and Deuteronomic Histories do not significantly alter the interpreter's approach to the earlier record. One uses the Chronicler primarily for the post-exilic era where the Chronicler stands. The Chronicler is indeed helpful as one attempts to understand the problems confronted by the post-exilic community as it sought to reconstitute itself. An understanding of this period is greatly enriched by reading the Chronicler; and other writings from the period are helpful as well, including Isaiah 56-66, Obadiah, Malachi, Haggai, and Zechariah.

Conclusion

A summary of issues so broad as those presented in the present Chapter would not be helpful. It should be clear, however, that it is absolutely essential to understand the historical context of the Biblical record if content is to be interpreted properly. The Hebrew tradition encompasses an historical faith which affirms that the actions of God and his relationship to man may be understood only by the viewing of history.

As one seeks to understand this history and the developing religious perspectives of Yahwism-Judaism, there is no substitute for the actual reading of the three Histories here briefly discussed. Comments about the Biblical text never substitute for reading the text.

A survey of the type here undertaken cannot do justice to Yahwism-Judaism's penchant for action and reaction. The Hebrew mind borrowed freely from surrounding peoples, sometimes purposefully, sometimes unconsciously. In reading the materials, however, the dynamics of the situation should be evident, recognizing that an end product in religious thought is marked by lengthy development.

The developmental nature of Yahwism-Judaism makes it impossible to set down a basic theology of "Yahwism" or "Judaism." The faith was dynamic and resisted crystallization, although in post-exilic Judaism the normative sense attached to the Torah encouraged rigidity. The existence of diverse thought patterns today in Judaism--Orthodox, Conservative, and Reform--indicate on the one hand that vitality is still present while on the other that any effort to reduce Judaism to a monolithic structure drains the faith of its vibrancy.

A survey of Israel's Histories does not take one sufficiently into the rich experiences of the prophetic nor at all into the wisdom literature.[24] Because of the dating of the Chronicler, the significant developments associated with the Maccabean period also fall beyond our focus. A thorough involvement in the development of Israel's faith must necessarily be considerably more expansive than the Histories. Nonetheless, the Histories both open for us the Hebrew thought pattern and direct us into some of the primary elements of the Biblical tradition.

Finally, we should recognize that Israel's faith defies schematization. It is history, and thus Gerhard von Rad's concern that one does theology through reciting the history demands careful thought (see his Old Testament Theology, I-II, trans. D. M. G. Stalker [London: Oliver and Boyd, 1962 and 1965]). The student of religion in western culture must have an awareness of Israel's historical perspectives and development.

V

RELIGIOUS AND INTELLECTUAL CURRENTS
IN EARLY CHRISTIANITY

It was emphasized in Chapter IV that Israel's faith
was historically conscious in that Yahweh's revelation
was experienced in the historical process. Christianity,
emerging from first-century Judaism, conveyed similar
emphasis. As Christianity's early record is studied,
however, we recognize both similarities and dissimilar-
ities to Judaism. In part the rationale for these apparent inconsistencies is Judaism's diversity. It is this
diversity and some of the ties to Christianity upon which
we first focus attention. It is important to recognize
that early Christianity's environment was not exclusively
Jewish, however, so we shall also indicate some of the
Gentile religious situation. We shall then discuss some
characteristics of the early Jerusalem church as recorded in the Acts of the Apostles. These characteristics
derived from a developing Christological understanding,
however, which raised many problems within the life of
the church as accommodation was sought between the reality of the Jesus of history physically encountered and
the Christ of faith consistently affirmed. What did this
mean to early Christianity, and what does it mean today?

Christianity's Early Environment: Jewish and Gentile
First-century Judaism was characterized by numerous

sects, such as Pharisees, Sadducees, and Essenes. We cannot focus intensively on each group, but we should indicate Christianity's relationship/indebtedness to each.

The Pharisees probably exerted more influence upon early Christian thought than any other sect. Even in the Gospels, Jesus is depicted in relationship to the Pharisees more often than any other group, a fact which may be explained in at least two ways. On the one hand, according to Synoptic presentation, Jesus spent only his final week in Jerusalem, the city where he would have encountered the Sadducees. The Pharisees, however, were associated with the synagogues scattered throughout Palestinian and Diaspora Judaism; thus Jesus in Galilee would have had more contact with the Pharisees simply because of the geographic factor. On the other hand, Jesus' contact with the Pharisees may stem from his thought affinity with the Pharisees. It is natural to have the greatest contact and discussion with those whose thoughts you most nearly share.

The Pharisees were resistant to influences upon Judaism from external sources. They were separatists in this sense, but they nonetheless lived in the midst of the society. Living amidst so much defilement, however, the Pharisees were exceedingly zealous in maintaining the traditions of the Fathers. This could on occasion lead to hyper-legalism; but it is a Christian perversion, especially as recorded in the Gospels, which equates all Pharisees with such superficiality. The Pharisees were dedicated to the preservation of the best of Judaism. A balanced view of the Pharisees must derive from inspection of both Jewish and Christian sources.

The Pharisaical view of scripture exerted considerable influence upon Christians. The Pharisees accepted as authoritative the Law (Torah), Prophets, and, to the degree possible to use the division at this early time, the Writings.

This view of scripture had particular repercussion on the resurrection belief. There are only two generally accepted references to resurrection in the Hebrew scriptures, Isaiah 26:19 and Daniel 12:2, the former in the Prophets and the latter in the Writings. To the contrary, the Sadducees did not affirm resurrection, a disagreement upon which Paul purposefully played (see Acts 23). Paul was obviously a Pharisee (Acts 23:6; Philippians 3:5); and, given both his influence upon early Christian development and the importance of the resurrection for the church, Christianity is most logically seen as developing out of Pharisaical Judaism.

The Sadducees differed markedly from the Pharisees. Whereas the Pharisees were more of a popular, layman's party, the Sadducees were constituted of the priestly, aristocratic, and wealthy individuals and were primarily restricted to Jerusalem. Even after the church's emergence, the Sadducees did not associate with the church to any significant degree.

The Sadducean view of scripture made participation in the church difficult. Only the Law was accepted as binding scripture, and thus the tenet of resurrection was not accepted. Obviously a Sadducee would have to reverse radically his thought to become a follower of Jesus as the Christ.

At one point, however, possibly early Christians were influenced by Sadducean thought pattern. The Sadducees accepted more openly non-Jewish relationships. In one sense their social-religious positions dictated this stance, for the Sadducees stood to lose more than any other group if the status quo were seriously shaken. Regardless of motive, they were much more able to work constructively with their Roman overlords. This type of openness characterized at least a portion of the early church.

Earlier the Essenes were also mentioned. This group is not mentioned in the New Testament, but some information is given by both Philo and Josephus. Most scholars are convinced also that the Qumran community at the Dead Sea was populated by Essenes. Many have suggested a communal influence upon the early Jerusalem church by the Essenes. Some have also suggested a possible relationship of Jesus with the Essenes. Judgments on the former are still indeterminate, while few take seriously the latter suggestion.

This discussion of Pharisees, Sadducees, and Essenes indicates too briefly the diversity of influences potentially acting upon early Christianity from within Judaism.[1] As indicated, these are not all of the sects. For example, is it possible that any of Jesus' followers were Zealots, individuals so obsessed with Judaism's preservation that they would take up arms rather than submit to assimilation? Few first-century Jews would have affirmed a direct relationship to any one of these sects. Maybe no more than five per cent would have been so associated, but this was a vocally expressive and activist minority who shaped the directions of Judaism. Finally, in such sectarian expression it would have been easy for Jesus' followers to become another sect within Judaism. Might we conjecture that apart from Paul and unknown others who reacted in similar reactionary fashion this would have been the result?

Within Palestine an inevitably close relationship
existed between Judaism and Christianity. Whereas
Christianity rapidly became predominantly Gentile when
it moved outside of Palestine, Judaism nonetheless contributed significantly to Christianity even in the
Diaspora (Judaism beyond the borders of Palestine). During the first century there were actually more Jews in
the Diaspora than in Palestine, with approximately
2,500,000 Jews in Palestine and about 3,200,000 in the
Diaspora--about one million Jews in each of Mesopotamia,
Egypt (primarily Alexandria), and Asia Minor.[2] Reginald
Fuller notes that the Jews in the first-century Roman
Empire constituted perhaps seven per cent of the population.[3] This is not an insignificant figure, for individuals like Paul found a Jewish foundation upon which
to build, a broadly spread awareness of Jewish history
and thought pattern. It was not necessary to begin the
Christian proclamation with the story of Abraham or Moses.
Such could either be assumed or built upon, as Paul often
did.

One of Judaism's problems which most influenced the
church was the believer's relationship to the non-believer.
From Israel's first entrance into Canaan, she presented
postures both of acceptance and rejection of the Canaanite
peoples and their culture. Uncertainty persisted regarding Israel-Judah's reaction until the Babylonian Exile,
but during the Exile Deutero-Isaiah sounded a clarion
call for inclusivism. He suggested that Israel's role
was to be "a light to the nations" (Isaiah 42:6), Yahweh's
instrument of revelation to all men. While this reiterated Israel's early commission to be "a kingdom of
priests and a holy nation" (Exodus 19:6), post-exilic
life indicates that the issue remained unsettled. Among
post-exilic writings conveying the continuing controversy

are Jonah, encouraging an inclusive stand, and Esther, supportive of radical exclusivism.

The book of Jonah was an Oriental humor story with didactic intent (another good example being the story of Balaam and Balak in Numbers 22-23). The writer of Jonah would doubtlessly have been amused had he realized that people of later generations would attempt to interpret as historically literal his purposefully humorous, non-historical narrative.

During the post-exilic period there was a radically conservative swing spearheaded by men like Ezra. This movement even demanded the dissolution of marriages between Jews and non-Jews (Ezra 10:11). Judaism was becoming exceedingly introverted, with the result that Jewish responsibility to the non-Jew was being either ignored or denied. To assert that Yahweh is concerned for all men, this writer purposefully chose the eighth century pre-exilic Assyrian context for his story, the people remembered as among the most bitter and cruel of Israel's enemies.

The central character of the story is Jonah, a prophet scarcely mentioned in 2 Kings 14:25. Jonah was commissioned by Yahweh to preach to the people of Nineveh, the infamous capital of Assyria. Jonah wanted no part of this, so he chose the one possible escape from Yahweh, the sea. Recalling that the Israelites were landsmen having little contact with the sea, we recognize Jonah's logic. Thus Jonah boarded a ship destined for Tarshish.

From the outset of this aborted attempt to escape Yahweh's commission, the writer's humor is evident. We can imagine this poor, weary, frustrated figure who boards the ship and immediately goes to the hold of the ship and falls into deep sleep. So soundly does he sleep that not

even a terrific storm which frightens the sailors stirs
him from his slumber. As the sailors cried to their gods
and heaved the cargo overboard to lighten the ship, they
searched diligently to find the party responsible for
this disaster. All through this ordeal exhausted Jonah
slept! But eventually lots were cast and it was determined that Jonah was the culprit. Not being one to evade
responsibility (!), Jonah readily admitted: "I am a
Hebrew; and I fear the LORD, the God of heaven, who made
the sea and the dry land" (Jonah 1:9). Eventually, with
Jonah's consent, it was determined that their only hope
was to cast Jonah overboard!

Upon hitting the water, Jonah was immediately consumed by a great fish prepared by Yahweh. After three
days in this situation, however, Jonah decided that there
may be things worse than preaching to the people of
Nineveh! Thus he struck a bargain with Yahweh--release
me from this confinement and I will fulfill the commission. Jonah was then emitted from the great fish and
the commission given anew: "Arise, go to Nineveh, that
great city, and proclaim to it the message that I tell
you" (Jonah 3:2).

Eventually, therefore, Jonah would preach to Nineveh. The story records how he went to Nineveh, going a
full day's journey into the city which is described as
being "three days' journey in breadth" (Jonah 3:3). This
clearly indicates that we are dealing with a non-historical story, for archaeologists who have excavated Nineveh
have demonstrated the city to have been roughly three
miles in length and one and one-half miles wide. By the
time this story was written, however, Nineveh had been
in ruins for centuries; and in tradition this evil city
loomed considerably larger than it had in fact!

Jonah finally issued his proclamation, a typical

prophetic message of doom: "Yet forty days, and Nineveh shall be overthrown!" (Jonah 3:4). Much to his chagrin, however, the king of Nineveh responded by proclaiming a city-wide repentance! And "God repented of the evil which he had said he would do to them; and he did not do it" (Jonah 3:10)!

Jonah was distraught and angry and wasted no words telling Yahweh. Eventually he took a seat on a hillside overlooking Nineveh to see what would happen to the city. Yahweh appointed a plant which grew up over Jonah to shade and comfort him, which action pleased Jonah. But then Yahweh designed a worm which attacked the plant so that it withered and died, and Jonah was exceedingly angry. He asserted that "It is better for me to die than to live" (Jonah 4:8). Yahweh used the plant to drive home the lesson, however. Jonah, you have compassion for the plant, even though you did nothing to bring it to birth or nourish it--"should not I pity Nineveh, that great city . . . ?" (Jonah 4:11).

Jonah had succeeded in spite of himself. Yahweh's compassion had been showered upon this people despised by Jonah. And the post-exilic writer had quite by design also succeeded. Anyone who read or heard this story must grasp its point for a community becoming increasingly nationalistic and exclusive. If Yahweh has concern for all men, so too should we!

The story of Esther just as emphatically argues the opposite position, Israel's right to a narrow, exclusive orientation. Like Jonah, Esther is a post-exilic writing formulated for didactic purposes. Like Jonah, the story of Esther is not an historical account. Unlike Jonah, this anonymous post-exilic author set his story in the post-exilic Persian context. This legendary

112

account apparently was written to support the post-exilic festival of Purim. Were it not for this festival association, it is unlikely that the book would have been incorporated into the Hebrew canon. Its failure to include references to the historical events so important to Judaism plus the absence of any mention of God (unless Esther 4:14 be so interpreted) caused the rabbis to discuss at length its inclusion into the canon. Eventually additional material was written to make it more acceptable. This material, "The Additions to the Book of Esther," is found in six additions, a total of one hundred seven verses. These additions were simply worked into the translated Hebrew in the Septuagint, although they are placed in the Apocrypha in present English translations.

The story is set in the reign of Xerxes I (486-465 B.C.), called Ahasuerus in the story; and it should be noted that it is not absolutely clear from the story which Xerxes was intended. King Ahasuerus gave a great banquet in his capital of Susa, which festivity lasted for seven days. On the seventh day, the King commanded that Queen Vashti should come before his entourage in royal attire. Queen Vashti refused, however, greatly angering the King. After consultation with his wise men, it was determined that she should be deposed from her position because of her disobedience. Interestingly, the rationale for her judgment plus a royal decree sent throughout the empire as regards her action and resultant judgment was the fear of an uprising of wives against their husbands on a broad scale should Vashti's action go unpunished!

With Vashti deposed, a type of "beauty contest" was held to pick a new Queen for Ahasuerus. Esther, a woman of enhancing beauty, was chosen. At the direction of

Mordecai, her cousin who had raised her and who was himself some type of minor official, Esther did not reveal
her Jewish background. Significant for the story, since
it will be Esther and Mordecai who assure Judaism's preservation, is this intentional silence and the fact that
both seemingly bear names derived from foreign deities.
The chief god of the city of Babylon was Marduk, while
Ishtar was his consort. The name Mordecai was apparently
derived from Marduk and Esther from Ishtar.

Eventually Mordecai learned of a plot against the
life of the King. Relaying this to Esther, she informed
the King. When the plot was investigated and proved
true, the two would-be assassins were put to death. As
a result of these actions, Haman was advanced to the
position of grand vizier.

Haman was unfortunately an exceedingly haughty man
who demanded everyone meeting him to give obeisance.
Mordecai refused because this was offensive to a Jew and
because as a Benjaminite (like Saul, Esther 2:5), he
resisted such action toward Haman, who was an Amalekite
of the Agag family (see Esther 3:1; see also 1 Samuel
15:7-9 for the early enmity). This so angered Haman that
he dedicated himself to the death of Mordecai; but he
determined to accomplish this by the annihilation of
Mordecai's people, the Jews. Lots (Purim) were cast to
decide the proper time to approach the King. Eventually,
Haman presented his plan to the King and gained his approval. It was decided that on Adar 13 all the Jews
would be killed and their goods plundered.

News of the impending pogrom came to Mordecai, who
went into mourning. Indirectly word filtered to Esther
through Mordecai of the danger for the Jews. Esther,
realizing that she could be put to death if she appeared
unsummoned before the King, was convinced that she should

do so by a two-fold message from Mordecai: (1) do not think that you will escape Haman's wrath, and (2) consider the possibility that providence has placed you here for just such a time as this (Esther 4:13-14).

Thus Esther appeared unsummoned before Ahasuerus, where, not only was she received with favor by the King, but also Ahasuerus and Haman agreed to appear for a meal prepared by the Queen. Even before the meal, however, the King was reminded of how Mordecai had saved his life and that nothing had been done to repay Mordecai. Thus Mordecai was exalted in finery by royal decree, much to Haman's dismay. When the meal was held, Esther appealed for the King's preservation of her people.

Esther's appeal was obviously effective. Haman immediately fell in disfavor and was hanged from a gallows which he had prepared for Mordecai's hanging. Not only was the massacre of the Jews called off, Adar 13 and 14 were set aside for the Jews to put to death all of their enemies, both in Susa and throughout the empire! Thus the enemies of the Jews were eliminated by the tens of thousands, including Haman's ten sons, and Mordecai was elevated to a rank second only to the King.

The intense nationalism and pride in the Esther story are evident. The writing was obviously intended to exalt the Jews with very little concern for others. The book, still read during the festival of Purim, portrays a Jewish attitude the polar opposite from the book of Jonah. But this distinctive perspective is important for indicating the continuance of the inclusive-exclusive controversy well into the post-exilic period.

There is a clear continuation of this controversy in the early Christian church. The picture derived from the Acts of the Apostles and the letters of Paul indicates that there was a strong resistance, apparently primarily focused in the Jerusalem church, to accepting Gentiles as Gentiles into the church. In essence, the argument suggested that Jesus was the Jewish messiah and that one who claimed him as messiah must do so by becoming Jewish. There was another opinion, the view that ultimately dominated, that Jesus was the Christ for all men. Paul, in particular, argued that it was unnecessary for the Gentile to assume the ritual encumbrances of the Jewish law to become a Christian (see the letter to the Galatians). This dichotomy within the church created one of the earliest and most disruptive conflicts within the early church. It is important to recognize, however, that this was not a problem unique to the church. It was because of the church's Jewish background that this conflict emerged so quickly and in such disruptive fashion.

The Jewish environment, both Palestinian and Diaspora, constituted only one of the factors influencing the development of early Christianity, however. As just indicated, the inclusive-exclusive question resulted in a rapid inclusion of Gentiles in the church. The church resultingly became rather quickly primarily Gentile rather than Jewish. This meant not only that a body existed whose roots were not Jewish but whose scriptures were the traditional Jewish scriptures but also that the various competing thought patterns in the Gentile world were brought quickly into encounter with the church. We cannot investigate all of these influences, but something of the diversity should be indicated.

The Emperor Cult at its inception was apparently only a pledge of allegiance to the Emperor demanded annually of each citizen. Each citizen was required to sprinkle a few grains of incense or a few drops of wine

on an altar-like structure before an image of the Caesar.
In some of the outlying areas of the Empire, the subjects
viewed this act as worship. Unfortunately, some of the
later Emperors, such as Caligula (37-41) and Domitian
(81-96), accepted such deification. This created a two-
fold problem for many Christians. First, the persistence
of Jewish thought patterns regarding idolatry made this
an inconceivable act. Second, as Judaism and Christianity
increasingly separated the exemption to this act granted
the Jews was not given to Christians. Inevitably, therefore, Christian resistance to the Emperor Cult resulted
in persecution of Christians. Thus, the first Empire-
wide persecution of Christians as Christians occurred
during the reign of Domitian. The apocalyptic book of
Revelation reflects this persecution.

There was a broadly grouped religious phenomenon known
as Mystery Religions which had significant impact on the
Gentile world. As we shall see, one could also argue that
it influenced the Christian thought pattern.
The Mystery Religions were primarily of eastern derivation and exhibit Oriental mysticism. Participation was
restricted to individuals properly initiated into the cult,
but the cults were non-restrictive in that a person could
belong to as many as desired. They are "mysteries" both
in that the associated rites were known only to the ini-
tiates and also in that a participatory relationship gave
the individual the secrets and assurance of life after
death. The cults, therefore, appealed to the common man--
.assuring life after death, providing an intimate relationship with deity, meeting a sensual need since most of the
cults practiced imitation acts of the lord of the cult and
his consort, and giving persons often displaced a sense of
belonging. In the Mysteries various rites were observed,

but characteristically each cult observed both a baptismal rite and a sacred meal.

It is understandable that the early Christian movement could have been judged another Mystery. There was a dying-rising Lord of the cult, a baptismal ritual enjoined, and a sacred meal regularly observed by the devotees. Given the Gentile movement into the church, doubtlessly a constant vigil had to be maintained to' prevent corruption of the church's life, as indicated in Paul's Corinthian correspondence. In addition, the church found it necessary to clarify constantly the symbolic and nonsensual nature of their acts, their allegiance to one deity, and their emphasis upon obedience to rather than union with deity. This religious phenomenon, while its actual influence upon the church will continue to be debated, obviously could not be ignored by the early church.

In like fashion, the church had to reckon with Gnosticism, a designation derived from the Greek gnosis, "knowledge." A Gnostic was an individual possessing a particular type of knowledge whereby full knowledge of self and assurance of life after death was achieved. In a sense, therefore, the Gnostic sects were really more man- than deity-centered. In the first-century world, there were Jewish Gnostics, Christian Gnostics,[4] and Gnostics associated with neither.

Given the diversity of Gnostic sects, we cannot examine them individually. We shall focus our attention, therefore, on some characteristics shared by most of the sects.

A dichotomy between matters material and spiritual was a basic tenet. The Gnostics were convinced that anything material, whether the tangible cosmos or the physical body, was inherently evil. God was pure spirit, and the physical was the antithesis to God.

This material-spiritual dichotomy dictated deity's relationship to the physical world. Quite obviously the pure god could not be defiled by the world of matter, nor could god have been directly responsible for the world's creation. Most Gnostic sects, therefore, explained creation as a series of emanations. God in his absolute goodness "spills over" to a next lower level. As creative goodness "spills over" from this level a degree of the positive goodness is diminished. This process continues as spirit is continually decreased and matter gradually increased. Ultimately, the world is created. For Christian Gnostic sects, Jesus was understood as the final emanation in this de-spiritualizing process.

The spirit-matter duality also influenced the view of man. Basically all men were divided into one of three categories. The most exalted group, necessarily small by number, were those having achieved gnosis to such a degree that not even the physical limitations of the body could prevent the freedom of their spirit. At the opposite extreme, and again relatively few by number, were those so beset by the physical that spiritual release was impossible. The vast majority of individuals, however, were those in whom the conflict between matter and spirit was yet active and indeterminate as regards the final outcome. These individuals, if they achieve gnosis, could achieve liberation of the spirit. It is evident that such classifications inevitably bred arrogance among those in possession of gnosis.

Christian Gnostics were faced with a difficult problem as regards Jesus. How could one so obviously beset by humanity be God's Messiah? This apparent inconsistency was met by one of two responses, both of which were declared heretical. On the one hand, there was docetism,

119

derived from the Greek word meaning "to seem" or "to appear." In other words, Jesus only seemed to have a body, to be physical. On the other hand, adoptionism was also used to escape the problem. This view suggested that at the baptism the spirit of God filled the body of Jesus of Nazareth. The spirit departed Jesus' body, however, while he was on the cross. While preserving Jesus' humanity, therefore, this precluded the need that he be subject to those purely human attributes of being born and dying while acting as God's peculiar agent.

Within Christendom Gnosticism presented several threats to the life of the church. If it be true that matter is evil and the spirit good, then there were two polar reactions possible for the individual. On the one hand, there was the danger of sexual license (see Paul's Corinthian correspondence). If the body and the spirit are totally separated, and if one has nothing to do with the other, why not permit the flesh its indulgence? But the argument could also be reversed. By bringing the body under subjection through a life of asceticism, the spirit could be subjected. Both of these reactions were rejected by the church.

A thought pattern such as that associated with Gnosticism could not have threatened the church had the church not weakened its Hebraic roots and accepted Hellenization. Hebrew thought affirmed the unity of the individual, a psychosomatic wholeness. Man did not have a separable or distinguishable spirit or soul; man was a unity who was a living being. Such dissection of man as seen in the Mysteries or in Gnosticism could only occur in a strongly Hellenized church.

There were those in the first-century world who found unappealing the sensual aspects associated with the religious options, who judged the inherent polytheism unsatisfactory, and who failed to find any intellectual challenge and stimulation in the various religious structures. For many such individuals, Epicureanism and Stoicism, two current philosophical formulations, offered at least a quasi-religious alternative.

Epicureanism was based on the teaching of Epicurus (342-270 B.C.). As a teacher, he was partially reacting to the excessively anthropomorphic deities associated with the Mysteries. He taught instead that the universe was constituted of vast, empty space and of material bodies divided into atoms. He suggested that the gods inhabit this empty space far removed from the world. Furthermore, these gods are without interest or power either to help or to hurt man. Thus, the gods simply have nothing to do with man. Nonetheless, man should worship the gods. Why? The gods live ideal lives of perfect happiness totally removed from either pain or pleasure. It is this condition that is worthy of man's worship, which worship takes the form of imitation. The highest good for man, therefore, is pleasure; but this could never be life dedicated to sensual pleasure. A life of pleasure is one lived in freedom from anything which would cause pain or disturbance of any type either to body or mind.

Stoicism was based on the teachings of Zeno (336-263 B.C.), and derived its name from the "painted porches" (stoa) in Athens where Zeno taught. For the Stoic, ultimate reality was rational pneuma (breath or spirit); and the world was understood to be constantly in flux between two basic entities. On the one hand, there is God, also designated as Pure Reason, the Divine Fire, the one Logos. On the other hand, there is the world into which a portion of the Divine Fire or one Logos is distributed, whether understood as Divine Sparks, or as seminal rational forms. The basic good for man, therefore, is to recognize that spark-rational form within him and to seek to live by reason, absolutely freed from all externals or emotions which would prevent man's accomplishing his full potential.

While Stoicism has perhaps contributed positively to Christian thought (does the Logos Prologue to the Fourth Gospel have any relationship?),[5] it also had negative impact in encouraging a "sparkology" view of man, the view that a spark of the divine rests in every person. The New Testament is clear in its re-affirmation of Hebrew thought, however, that man is absolutely finite, that nothing he can accomplish alters this basic fact. According to Judeo-Christian thought, man does not have a spark of the divine within.

Stoicism did make some significant contributions to the first-century world, however. First, Stoicism's "spark" within the individual ignited a sense of self-sufficiency for each person. Second, in such an unsettled environment Stoicism provided a rationale for brotherhood wherever circumstances dictated the individual's settlement.[6]

There are numerous other influences, both Jewish and Gentile, which acted upon the church as it was being formulated. One should recognize, however, that Christianity did not emerge in a religious vacuum. The possibilities, quantitatively and qualitatively, open to first-century man were endless. Christianity's success can hardly be attributed to religion's scarcity! Furthermore, emerging in such a context it was inevitable that Christianity should absorb certain attributes and characteristics of what it encountered, whether in friendly fashion or in direct conflict.

Characteristics of the Early Jerusalem Church

No records of the earliest church's development exist whose writing actually corresponds to the historical period. Our first New Testament records derive from Paul, whose earliest letter cannot be dated very much prior to A.D. 50. Not only is this source roughly twenty years post the church's initial development, but also Paul's correspondence deals with concerns focused outside Palestine, only touching tangentially the Jerusalem church where this influenced directly his own work.

Our sole record of the Jerusalem church's early development is the Acts of the Apostles, written about A.D. 85-90 by Luke, the traveling companion of Paul. Although many influences have acted upon the material prior to its written formulation, because it is our only record of the church's genesis period it is obviously important and instructive.

The earliest followers of Jesus were designated "followers of the Way" (Acts 9:2). For the eastern mind, "way" conveyed what the westerner would express by "relationship." Thus the "followers of the Way" were those affirming themselves in proper relationship with God. This designation depicts the Hebraic orientation of the early church, conveying basically that these people had acknowledged Yahweh's Messiah, Jesus of Nazareth, when he was among them.

The name "Christian" was used first at Antioch of Syria (Acts 11:26). It is probable that this was initially a term of derision, applied by others to the followers and only later accepted by them as their designation.

Regardless of nomenclature, certain characteristics were associated with the early followers. Since these characteristics are derived from the Acts of the Apostles, they apply specifically to the Jerusalem church. While most of these characteristics would be common to the expanding church, it is the Jerusalem setting to which Acts refers.

The earliest followers in Jerusalem were Jews. It is true that in Acts 1-12 there are references to Jews and Hellenists, but logically the Hellenists may be viewed as Jews. Perhaps they were Diaspora Jews migrated to Jerusalem but still influenced by the Hellenistic culture, or possibly they were Palestinian Jews who responded positively to certain Hellenistic influences. Regardless, there was sufficient division of opinion among the Jews and Hellenists to create relationship problems, exemplified particularly in chapters 6-7 where questions were raised regarding the attention being given to Hellenists' widows and orphans within the church. This was an attitudinal problem, however, rather than a basic presuppositional difference such as existed between Jews and Gentiles. The followers of Jesus in Jerusalem continued to function as Jews, maintaining their relationship to and veneration for the Jerusalem Temple and its associated ritual. There is no evidence, for example, that sabbath observance was rejected. In addition to sabbath observance, however, they met together to commemorate what they affirmed to have happened on the first day of the week, their kairos event (significant point of time), the resurrection of Jesus of Nazareth.

They affired the resurrection of Jesus as sine qua non for their existence. This affirmation will be discussed more in the next section on Christology, but suffice for now to understand that this affirmation stands

124

in parallel relationship for the early Christian community as the exodus event for Israel's existence. Apart from this affirmation, however understood by contemporary investigation, the community of faith would not have been born.

The Jerusalem community practiced a communal existence, a characteristic witnessed only in Jerusalem in the New Testament. This was a type of classical communism in that it was "from each according to his ability, to each according to his need." Some have suggested an influence from Essene lifestyle on the church at this point. The pooling of resources in the Jerusalem church, however, was a voluntary rather than an enforced sharing. The Greek word koinonia, "fellowship" or "togetherness," is frequently used to describe this relationship. It was this communal existence which precipitated the earliest recorded problems within the church. Because of the honor bestowed upon Barnabas who shared fully with the church, a man and his wife, Ananias and Sapphira (Acts 5), sold some property and pretended to share the full proceeds with the church. Their deaths emphasized that the community could not survive external pressures if beset by internal deceit, not that everyone had to emulate Barnabas. In like fashion, Acts 6 depicts the dissatisfaction of the Hellenists with the way their widows and orphans were being treated. This controversy led to an extension of the ministry within the church as seven individuals were chosen "to serve tables" (Acts 6:2), the two most notable of these being Stephen, the first recorded Christian martyr, and Philip.

The early followers practiced the rite of baptism. Beyond the Passion Narrative, there are few incidents

recorded in some fashion by all four Gospels; but Jesus'
baptism is one such event. While there is no indication
of Jesus' having baptized anyone, the church obviously
saw this as an important practice. Derivation of the
church's practice is uncertain, but several possibilities
exist. First, some link the practice to an early Jewish
proselyte baptism. While it is known that this ritual
was followed in the second century, it is not so clear
for the first century. Second, some relate the baptism
within the church to the rituals of the various Mysteries.
As earlier indicated, however, a prime intent of the
Mysteries' ritual was union with the deity, whereas in
some fashion the church saw itself in obedience to Jesus'
command (most explicitly stated in Matthew 28:19-20).
Third, the Christian ritual has been associated with the
Essene ritual washing. This seems unlikely since the
Essene rite was a constantly recurring purificatory act,
whereas the Christian action was done only once. Fourth,
and apparently the most probable option, the Christian
baptismal act is linked to the baptism of John the Baptizer. As earlier indicated, preserving John's baptism
of Jesus was obviously important to the church, in spite
of the fact that it was problematic that Jesus should
submit to baptism by John (most clearly spoken to in
John 1:29-34, where John witnessed to the superiority of
Jesus). Jesus had participated in this ritual, however,
and the church sensed a need to incorporate similar action.
It was similar rather than identical, however. John's
ritual was a baptism of repentance for sins in anticipation of God's coming Messiah. For the church baptism
was also an act in repentance for sins, but it was done
in recognition of the Messiah's having already come. The
distinctive difference between John and the church, therefore, may be seen in the contrast between anticipation

and actualization.

The early Christian community shared a strong didactic concern--"they devoted themselves to the apostles' teaching . . ." (Acts 2:42). As Jews the scriptures of the early community were the Hebrew scriptures. The study of this material could not be done in unbiased fashion, however, for these were people convinced that Jesus was the Messiah, the fulfillment of promises made to the Jews. With this conviction they studied the scriptures to discern supportive passages relative to the Messiah whom they affirmed. They were not seeking to be convinced; rather, they were verifying their faith affirmation. Approaching the Gospels in this fashion, it was unavoidable that some passages would be misinterpreted, forced to apply to Jesus as Messiah while they actually had a clear reference otherwise. For these early interpreters, therefore, whether the interpretation be accurate or not is ultimately unimportant. If they understood a passage to refer to the Messiah, and Jesus be the Messiah, then Jesus must have fulfilled the passage's intent. For example, in the Gospel of Matthew, the writer used Isaiah 7:14, which passage had a clear historical context, to support the idea of Jesus' virgin birth.[7] In like fashion, Hosea 11:1 was used to give the basis for Jesus' having been taken into Egypt by Joseph. It is not as though fraudulent use of the material was consciously chosen over proper historical application. Conviction simply loomed more importantly for these pre-scientific expositors.

The community was also motivated by the Holy Spirit. According to Acts 1:4-5, Jesus told his followers to wait in Jerusalem until the Holy Spirit should come upon them. According to the Lucan account, the Spirit's bestowal occurred during the festival of Pentecost, seven weeks following Passover.[8] It is this event, encumbered with its symbolism, which marks the birth date for the church. The community was convinced that the Spirit energized and brought it into being, aided them in their interpretation of the scriptures, gave protection to believers when confronted by persecution, and commissioned the faithful on a mission to spread the "good news" (gospel) of Jesus the Christ. Thus the Holy Spirit was affirmed as an indispensable factor for the church's existence.

Regarding the emphasis on mission within the early church, there was considerable disagreement concerning the church's relationship to Gentiles. The general picture of the Jerusalem church in Acts 1-12 portrays a body resistant to inclusion of the Gentiles apart from their conversion to Judaism. The one significant exception, perhaps historically accurate although likely formulated by Luke to point ahead to the second half of his book where Paul's journeys are recorded, is found in the record of Peter's activity (Acts 9:32-11:18). Peter is depicted as the first of the Twelve to engage in mission activity among the Gentiles, although his work was restricted to Palestine. One of his most important contacts, with the Roman Centurion Cornelius, is recorded in Acts 10. Since it was ritually defiling for a Jew to cross the threshhold of a Gentile, obviously Peter's activity was a major step for the community. Significantly, however, upon Peter's return to Jerusalem he was called upon to explain his activities before a type of church council. The clear impression is the church's displeasure with his activity; but nonetheless when Peter had recounted his deeds the judgment was rendered: "Then to the Gentiles also God has granted repentance unto life" (Acts 11:18). If this reaction accurately reflects the church's conviction,

the inclusive-exclusive problem should have been resolved.
Unfortunately, it probably does not give majority opinion
since the Jerusalem church never actively pursued the
Gentiles. This role was left to Paul, who fancied himself apostle to the Gentiles. It was the church at Antioch,
Syria, apparently a church of mixed Jewish-Gentile constituency, which was the base for Paul's three missionary
journeys.

Throughout Paul's first journey (A.D. 47-49), problems persisted as regards the Gentile question, resulting
in a Conference convened at Jerusalem in A.D. 50. This
Conference's decisions are recorded in Acts 15. While
many questions are unanswered, such as whether Galatians 2
records a doublet of this Conference from Paul's perspective or a different Conference, one thing is clear--neither
in Acts 15 nor in Galatians 2 is circumcision enjoined of
the Gentile. There seems to have been a conscious movement of the church away from its ritualistic Jewish heritage, a decision that inevitably led to the division of
Judaism and Christianity as differing faith structures.[9]
While this had the positive effect of opening the church
into the mainstream of the Greco-Roman world and increas-
ing its potential for becoming a universal faith structure,
it also had the negative effect of severing the newly-born
faith from its historical roots. This severance made it
increasingly difficult for Jews to associate with the
church, opened endless possibilities for the Hellenization
of the church, and initiated the beginning of a long and
difficult history between the church and the synagogue.
It may be that Christianity is only now beginning to recognize anew the importance of its roots and is seeking
through various means to associate itself meaningfully
with the faith structure which gave it birth.[10]

Grappling with Christology

For contemporary Christians, one of faith's most difficult problems is understanding precisely who Jesus was and the importance which should be attached to him. Many Christians sense a tinge of guilt as such questions arise, for ecclesiastical tradition has seemed to encourage affirmation rather than question. Surely this is an area to which the believer must give his attention, however, for this is the basic question within Christendom. As clarification is sought, we find that the question of Christology, the understanding of the person and nature of Jesus as the Christ, is not unique to our time in history. The church has historically grappled with this problem, most notably through the numerous Councils convened from the third through the sixth centuries. Contemporary believers recognize, however, that a faith position accepted without question is generally shallow and does not do justice to the richness of the tradition. The believer has become increasingly convinced that a faith that cannot withstand his scrutinizing investigation does not deserve his acceptance. In this light one continues to grapple with Christology, not seeking those points to be denied but searching for those basics which constituted the earliest affirmation. It is in this recovery that Christology will be meaningful to modern man.

The earliest portion of the Gospel literary tradition to be recorded was the Passion Narrative. This affirmation expressed the basis for the early church's conviction about Jesus, and central to the Passion Narrative is resurrection.

This affirmation was a negative turned positive in that the church could not stop with the belief "He is not dead!" This conviction continued, "Because he is not dead, he will come again!" Resurrection affirmation, therefore, encouraged eschatological belief. It was this anticipation that precipitated the early community's lifestyle. Its centrality is hardly to be questioned.

Our earliest record of the resurrection derives from Paul's Corinthian correspondence, 1 Corinthians 15, dated about A.D. 55 or 56. This account does not mention the empty tomb tradition at all. While each of the Gospels at a slightly later date included the empty tomb in their accounts, we must conclude either that Paul was unfamiliar with the tradition or that he did not judge it important to his presentation. Regardless, the empty tomb is obviously the weakest argument to use in support of the resurrection. Even in the Gospels, there is indication that this problem was recognized, as the reader is told that precautions were taken so that the disciples could not have stolen the body (see Matthew 27:62-66). Whatever be said regarding the resurrection, therefore, must be asserted apart from the empty tomb tradition.

When one seeks to understand historically the resurrection affirmation, the real problem is confronted, for it becomes obvious that the precise event cannot be recovered. When attempting to understand history, an event may be grasped and interpreted if there be in the interpreter's awareness an event historically analogous to the one being interpreted. For example, acts motivated by love, hatred, jealousy, greed, anger, or numerous other emotions may be understood because of direct human experience. Suffering may likewise be comprehended; and death, even though indirectly confronted, may be interpreted through general human experience. The problem with resurrection is apparent, however, for there is no historically analogous event upon which the interpreter may draw for

understanding and interpreting resurrection. And since
the New Testament does not hesitate to affirm the uniqueness of Jesus' resurrection, we are drawn to a singular
conclusion--for the modern man, just as for the ancient,
whatever one says about resurrection must be understood
as faith's affirmation.

Regardless, individuals have constantly sought to
explain what happened in the resurrection event. For
example, it has been suggested that Jesus was psychologically resurrected in the minds of his followers; but
the problem with this theory is that the Gospels do not
portray the disciples as having such anticipation, a
necessary prerequisite for the view. It has also been
suggested that the followers went to the wrong tomb, discovered it empty, and thus was begun the tradition. It
seems unlikely, however, that no one could have known
the tomb's location, surely the only requirement for
refuting such a misconception. Furthermore, the disciples
have not escaped accusation, questioning whether they
might have stolen the body. At this point, the veracity
of the followers and their willingness to give themselves
to such a purposeful hoax must be evaluated.

Another possibility might be built upon the Pauline
statement found in 1 Corinthians 15. Paul referred to
the sarx (flesh) and the soma (body), but only the soma
was resurrected (1 Corinthians 15:35-38). The Jew was
aware of the dissolution to which the body was subjected
at death; but the resurrection of the soma affirms a continuing being, not physical continuance.[11] Whether Paul
understood the resurrection of the soma individualisti-
cally or corporately, most assuredly the resurrection of
Jesus was individually portrayed. This leads to the
conclusion that if the empty tomb were not a consideration, it would be possible to affirm Jesus' resurrection

as a continuing soma even if the sarx still be in the
tomb. The only prerequisite would be the affirming
community's conviction that their relationship with Jesus
had not been broken by the shackles of death. This perspective, while impossible to maintain with the Gospel
tradition, is acceptable within the framework of 1 Corinthians 15. Such a view would give a possible alternative
for those who experience irreconcilable difficulties with
the traditional resurrection affirmation.

Martin Buber suggested that the earliest Christian
affirmation was ascension rather than resurrection.[12]
He noted that in Jewish background figures such as Enoch,
Moses, and Elijah provided for an ascension foundation.
He suggested further that it was only under the influence
of Paul and Hellenistic Christianity that this essentially
alien and Greek idea of individual resurrection became
associated with Jesus. This is an interesting suggestion,
for if the primary intent of the resurrection is to affirm
God's action, would not ascension convey the same thought?

The resurrection narratives were preserved for didactic purposes. Clearly the early believer had equally
as much difficulty as modern man trying to understand
the risen Lord whom he encountered. Two examples help
to clarify.

In Luke 24 the story is told of two men walking from
Jerusalem to Emmaus in the period following the crucifixion-
resurrection event. Being joined by a stranger, they did
not become aware of his identity until he broke bread with
them, a clear Eucharistic reference. Physically and chronologically separated from Jesus, this story enabled the
early community to understand how the meaning of the
resurrection could become assured for them. Yet the figure encountered, akin to the Jesus of history, is radically unlike the Jesus earlier known, both appearing and

133

disappearing mysteriously.

Similar didactic interest is expressed in John 20,
where the "Doubting Thomas" story is recorded. During
Thomas' absence, the risen Lord appeared to the disciples
on the first day of the week. When Thomas was told of
the encounter, he refused to believe unless he could see
for himself. Eight days later, with Thomas present, the
risen Lord appeared again and invited Thomas to verify
his presence. Thomas, however, acknowledged by affirming,
"My Lord and my God!" To this affirmation Jesus responded:
"Have you believed because you have seen me? Blessed are
those who have not seen and yet believe" (John 20:29).
Typical of Johannine style, Jesus' remark was not really
directed to Thomas but to the church whose response to
Jesus was necessarily dependent upon the continuing apostolic witness. The Lord who appears and disappears
mysteriously in a room with shut doors and who invites
the doubter to verify his authenticity by observing his
crucifixion wounds is no longer available. The faith
expression of the individual or of the church is now dependent upon the apostolic witness.

The church could not explain this phenomenon. They
were neither philosophers nor abstract thinkers; and
thus they expressed themselves in the only language style
available to them--concrete perspectives. They referred
to the risen Lord, therefore, as though to the Jesus of
history, the fully recognizable one. Nonetheless, he
was not recognizable by the two travelers on the road to
Emmaus. He is akin to what he was, yet his mysterious
appearances and disappearances verify that he is unlike
what he was. Clearly the early church was not affirming
a simple bodily resuscitation, which incidentally would
place the individual subject anew to all the problems
of finite flesh. The believers sought to affirm that

the relationship experienced with Jesus of Nazareth, the Jesus of history, had not been terminated by his death. That relationship continued through God's act of resurrection, so that now the Christ of faith continues to be with them, to teach them, to compel their continuing to work for the establishment of God's Kingdom even as he had worked.

At this point the ascension motif becomes important to the church. Both in the Lucan (Acts 1:4-5) and the Johannine (John 16:7) views, Jesus' departure was the prerequisite to the Spirit's bestowal. Thus resurrection, while vitally important as the affirmation of continuing relationship, was not sufficient. Ascension was necessary if the geographically-localized Jesus, now the resurrected Lord, were to have a domocratized and universalized relationship. By the ascension, therefore, all believers profited. With the ascension, however, the church linked resurrection; and the latter assuredly became the dominant motif. As expressed by Paul: "the gospel concerning his Son, who was descended from David according to the flesh and designated Son of God in power according to the Spirit of holiness by his resurrection from the dead . . ." (Romans 1:3-4). Thus while resurrection and ascension are integrally related faith affirmations, resurrection was the key event within the church. In the New Testament, furthermore, resurrection is characteristically affirmed to be God's act--God raised him, not Jesus raised himself. This deity-centered focus was necessary if the affirmation were to project its intended Hebraic rootage.

Because of the resurrection-ascension affirmation, birth narratives developed and became important within the church. One does not begin postulating a great person at the time of birth; rather, because an individual has become esteemed, interest is focused upon birth. Because

Jesus had been recognized as a principal focus of the power and love of God, the authors of the Gospels of Matthew and Luke, each in their unique manner, affirmed how that power and love found embodiment within the human situation, not how God became man, an unthinkable concept for the Hebrew.

At this point an interesting parallel exists in the development of Hebrew and Christian thought. Both communities began as the result of a crucial event, the exodus event for Israel and the cross-resurrection-ascension event for the church. In both bodies life progressed as the faith communities came to a sense of historical consciousness, self-awareness, and purpose. This maturation process precipitated an interest in the circumstances existent prior to their communal birth experience. Neither community could understand its "pre-history," however, except through the eyes of faith developed during their natal events. For Israel, the first step in this backward projection of faith was the patriarchal narratives, faith's history in the ideal as events were moving toward the Hebrews' sojourn in Egypt, the necessary preparation for the exodus event. For the church, the Gospels of Matthew and Luke depict a similar first step by relating their nativity narrative (the Gospel of Mark begins with Jesus' baptism by John). In both communities, however, there was a desire to project faith yet another step backward. For Israel this portion of faith's projection is found in the Primeval History of Genesis 1-11. It is affirmed that God was responsible not only for bringing Israel to birth but also for creating the cosmos upon which the historical drama would be enacted and for directing the events leading up to the selection of Abraham. The Fourth Gospel fulfilled this role within the church's life as the Prologue (John 1:1-18)

relates how the Word (logos) was with God in the beginning, was the agent of creation, and was the very source
of true light and life. Eventually, however, the Word
assumed flesh and dwelled among men--Jesus of Nazareth.
John does not give a birth narrative, but obviously this
Word portrayal is more exalted and theologically astute
than a birth narrative could ever be! Diagrammatically
this theologizing process might be depicted as follows:

```
Primeval◄------Patriarchs◄---------Exodus---->Israel
History                            Event
   D              C                  A           B
John-Logos◄----Birth Narrative◄----Cross/----->Church
                                   Resurrection/
                                   Ascension
```

Recognizing the growth process of these crucial events
as understood within the faith traditions helps the interpreter to place them in proper perspective. In the
strictest sense, what preceded either the exodus event
or the cross-resurrection-ascension event is not historical record; but this recognition does not lessen the
theological impact of the narrative nor their importance
for understanding the respective faith communities.

This awareness of a parallel type development in
Hebrew and Christian thought is further manifest in messianic expression. In the New Testament Jesus is depicted
in multiple fashion as the Messiah. All of these messianic roles have their roots in Hebrew thought.

Both the Hebrew "Messiah" (mashiah) and the Greek
"Christ" (christos) mean "the anointed one." Thus, when
the church affirmed Jesus Christ, this was a pivotal
faith affirmation, Jesus is the Christ, or Jesus is the

Messiah.

In Hebrew thought, messiah designated anyone endowed with divine mission.[13] The designation might be used of prophet, priest, or king, and early conveyed an actual sense of anointment. Later, the word was used more broadly of anyone fulfilling divine mission, whether Israelite or not, as Deutero-Isaiah refers to Cyrus, the king of Persia, as the LORD's "anointed" (Isaiah 45:1). As messianic thought developed, it took many forms. We turn our attention now to some of these, stating briefly the Hebrew thought but also emphasizing the manner in which the concept was affirmed by the New Testament writers.

First, there was the anticipation of the New Moses (Deuteronomy 18:18). Moses holds an exalted place in Hebrew tradition as the recipient of the Torah. The people had failed to abide consistently by the Torah's demands, however, a theme constantly reiterated by the prophets. Perhaps one like Moses would come who could interpret anew the fullest intention of the Torah and enable the people to enjoy the relationship with Yahweh which their election intended. The author-editor of Matthew's Gospel has portrayed Jesus in precisely this role. Through the editorial framework of the Sermon on the Mount, Jesus is depicted as the one who ascends the mountain in order to teach the people. In Matthew 5:21-48, Jesus in formula fashion reinterprets the Mosaic law: "you have heard that it was said . . . but I say to you . . . ." Significantly, however, this section was preceded by a statement which should have assured Jesus' orthodoxy for the Jew: "Think not that I have come to abolish the law and the prophets; I have come not to abolish them but to fulfil them" (Matthew 5:17).

138

Second, Israel anticipated the coming of a messianic King, a thought built upon Davidic foundations. Not only had David amassed Israel-Judah's first and greatest kingdom, but also it was understood that God had covenanted with David to promise the throne to his house forever (2 Samuel 7:14-16). If circumstances made impossible the role of David's house, this temporarily negated the divine promise but could not permanently nullify it. The New Testament writers incorporated this theme, portraying Jesus as fulfilling this role by various means. Both Matthew and Luke use their nativity narratives to trace Jesus' genealogy through David and carefully place Jesus' birth in Bethlehem, the city of David, even though the genealogies agree on little else. Beyond this, the temptation narrative depicts Satan's offer for Jesus to rule over vast kingdoms (Matthew 4:8-10; Luke 4:5-8); and John's Gospel portrays the people's desire to acclaim Jesus King following one of the mighty acts (John 6:15). Both Jesus' teachings and his mighty acts focus on the imminence of the Kingdom of God, a concept which may be interpreted as either presently or eschatologically oriented. As much as he apparently eschewed personal acclaim, messianic kingship consistently confronted him.

Third, post-exilically the age of the spirit became an important messianic age concept. It was understood that God's spirit would be poured out upon mankind, effecting radical changes in both history and nature. Apocalyptically, this was the basis for Joel's vision of the future (Joel 2:28-32), which was quoted in the sermon of Peter at Pentecost (Acts 2:17-21). This relates messianically to Jesus in that the cross-resurrection-ascension-bestowal of the Holy Spirit at Pentecost was interpreted as fulfillment of this apocalyptic expectation. The church

understood itself to be living in the messianic age of
the spirit.

Fourth, the age of the servant is derived from the
servant poems of Deutero-Isaiah (42:1-4; 49:1-6; 50:4-11;
and 52:13-53:12). This prophet of the Exile asserted
that Israel would fulfill her responsibility as "a light
to the nations" (Isaiah 42:6; 49:6) by being Yahweh's
revelatory, suffering servant. This was an ego-renuncia-
tion role which demanded Israel's servanthood even if
fulfillment of the task compelled Israel's own demise.
Scholars will continue to debate the extent to which
Jesus interpreted himself in the light of the servant
poems. What does seem clear is that the church concluded
that the role of the servant had been lived out in the
life and ministry of Jesus.

Fifth, the son of man became an important messianic
figure. In the Hebrew scriptures, son of man has a varied
background. In the book of Ezekiel (2:1), son of man is
used as a form of address. In Psalm 8:4, it is only a
surrogate for man:

what is man that thou art mindful of him,
    and the son of man that thou dost care for him?

In this poetic parallelism "man" and "son of man" correspond. In Daniel 7:13, however, the apocalyptic vision
of "one like a son of man" appears. This is a divinely
ordained messenger, like man, but obviously more than man.
He will be the apocalyptic figure to marshall the forces
of good against the forces of evil. In the intertesta-
mental book of Enoch, the messianic associations with
son of man are completed. Seeking to interpret Jesus,

this summary also signals our problem, for during the
first Christian century son of man was used both as surrogate for man and apocalyptically. In the Gospels son
of man is used only as a self-designation by Jesus, not
as a form of address. The questions then are whether
Jesus used the phrase, and if he did how he understood
it? Personal conjecture would acknowledge that Jesus
likely used the phrase but that it is impossible now to
recover how he applied the phrase to himself. If the
church came to the conviction that Jesus was the son of
man, and if it came to that awareness through the spirit's
instruction, without any apprehension it would have substituted "son of man" for "I" or "he" in the Gospel
records. For example, the following doublet passage is
set in Caesarea Philippi:

Matthew 16:21
From that time Jesus began to
show his disciples that he
must go to Jerusalem and
suffer many things . . . .

Mark 8:31
And he began to
teach them that the Son
of man must
suffer many things . . . .

It is impossible to recover with certainty the authentic
Gospel record, but the church's identification of Jesus
with the apocalyptic son of man seems clear.

These are just some of the Old Testament messianic
motifs, but this is sufficient both to show their diversity and the church's identity of Jesus with numerous
messianic interpretations. Thus, when the church affirmed
Jesus to be the Christ, they were associating him with a
long-standing if multi-faceted Hebrew tradition. As one
uses the New Testament record today, therefore, it should
be recognized that a simple identification of Jesus with

141

the Messiah is insufficient. The specific messianic concept(s) being used as the interpretive focus for Jesus should be clarified.

The contemporary interpreter must search for mechanisms to make meaningful Israel's messianic perspectives for modern man. One possibility is messianic consciousness. During a Jewish-Christian dialogue, involving Congregation Beth Ahabah and St. Paul's Episcopal Church, both of Richmond, Virginia, it was suggested that the fulness of the Christ was not restricted to Jesus: "Whenever love is experienced, humanity is achieved, barriers are overcome, and community is created: there Christpower is experienced, messiah is revealed."[14] Messianic consciousness better preserves the Hebrew nuance of this thought both linguistically and in terms of the awareness of God's historical action over the span of linear time. This possibility of continuing historical activity offers exciting possibilities for an interpretation of Jesus. Obviously the church desires to make exclusive and unique claims for Jesus. To see Jesus as a manifestation of God's love and power within Hebraic messianic consciousness, indeed traditionally Christianity has affirmed the clearest focus which man has witnessed, is no minor claim. With this affirmation, however, the church would not be guilty of its traditional chauvinism; for this claim both accepts God's messianic manifestation of his love and power earlier and recognizes the continuing manifestations of same.

This thought pattern relates well to Martin Buber's "I-Thou" view in his classic book I and Thou.[15] Buber suggested that true life was realizable only in the relational present, particularly as two individuals (although not necessarily so restricted) meet in a dialogic relationship where each individual is affirmed and confirmed. For

142

messianic consciousness, wherever love is experienced so that personhood is affirmed and human potential confirmed, wherever power is experienced that brings one to a realization of humanity vis-a-vis my fellow, there messianic consciousness has been manifest. Not only is Jesus a messianic exemplification, therefore, so too may others act as messiah for their neighbors, acting in the love and power of God in an affirming, confirming relationship.

For the early Christians, Jesus was acknowledged as manifestation of this divine love and power. As such he acted to reveal God, although from a normative Hebraic view this would not have led to any metaphysical claim for Jesus. Certainly Buber is correct in his Two Types of Faith that such thought transition could only have occurred under Hellenistic influences. As Jesus and his message were proclaimed, however, there was an inevitable repulsive effect on most men. His summons was to "come, follow me" (Mark 10:21), a call for each individual to assume the same type of role as he. His ministry was one of self-renunciation, however, a task to which man qua man does not easily give himself. Thus Jesus was both revelatory and repulsive, true for his own day, characteristic in continuing fashion whenever the church truly seeks to manifest agape (self-giving love).

Thus, the church will continue to grapple with Christology. New ideas will continue to take form alongside the traditional affirmations of the ages. That questions can and will continue to be raised is perhaps the best attestation to the vitality of the church. That a simple resolution to the Christological problem continues to evade those who would formulate easy answers is perhaps the best witness both to the significance of the ministry associated with Jesus of Nazareth and to the richness of the Judeo-Christian tradition.[16]

143

Conclusion

The early Christian community emerged initially in a Jewish atmosphere, and those who were "followers of the Way" still associated themselves with Judaism. But the Greco-Roman world of the first century was an open and diverse environment, and once the Palestinian boundaries were crossed it was inevitable that numerous influences should act upon this young movement. Our brief survey has indicated only a few of the possible structures which Christianity encountered, but anyone desiring understanding of early Christianity must be cognizant that Judaism and Christianity did not exist in a religious vacuum.[17]

The church established in Jerusalem was tied to Judaism for its belief structure. A study of the Acts of the Apostles is instructive as regards this earliest situation, but it also raises some interesting questions which the actualities of history forbid our being able to answer. Had Jerusalem not fallen to the Romans in A.D. 70, would the church have remained a Jerusalem-based institution? If James, the brother of Jesus, had not been martyred in A.D. 62, would the leadership of the church have followed some type of kinship line to Jesus? Had circumstances been different, would the Pauline thought pattern have found so firm an establishment in the church? If the Palestinian church had survived in stronger fashion, would Hellenistic thought patterns have become so embedded in Christian thought? Would the church have developed into a sect within Judaism such as the Pharisees? Attempting to second-guess history is an impossible task, but these are interesting questions to pursue when asking "What if . . .?"

Some suggestions have been made regarding Christology, both in the text and for suggested reading. Vitally important, however, is the recognition that questions have been raised concerning the person and nature of Jesus as the Christ from the church's beginnings. Our humanity demands that we be involved in decision making, so that it is a basic denial of our human condition to accept without question traditional affirmation. One may discover that traditional affirmation is the most acceptable posture, a perfectly understandable position if personally derived. On the other hand, one's investigations may lead to radically new ways of perception.[18]

Surely within Christendom there is sufficient room for honest diversity. Messianic consciousness is sufficiently encompassing to permit divergent affirmations, for whenever Jesus is said to be Messiah it is affirmation rather than proof scientifically derived. Such expansiveness exists within Judeo-Christian messianic consciousness, however, only if each individual gives to his fellow the freedom of personal affirmation. There can be no enforced conformity, regardless of the individual or institution setting the standard.

The church's history is rich in its positive accomplishments--education, care for orphans, concern for the elderly, medical care, ethical inculcation, just to mention a few. But the church's history is also marked by numerous examples of cruel and inhumane treatment as conformity was enforced--the scriptures in the languages of the people, the Crusades, the Spanish Inquisition, and general anti-Semitism. It is to this anti-Semitic concern that we turn in Chapter VI as we leave now the formative period of the church and view the interaction of Judaism and Christianity since the latter's emergence.

VI

JEWS AND CHRISTIANS IN HISTORICAL PERSPECTIVE[1]

The study of western history usually means the investigation of white Christianity's contribution to the
development of western culture. In recent years, this
recognition has encouraged a justified resentment among
United States Blacks and has precipitated the emergence
of numerous "Black Studies" curricula in educational
institutions.

As noted, however, traditional studies of western
history focus upon "white Christianity's contribution to
the development of western culture." This means that not
only the role of the Black but also that of the Jew has
been largely ignored, leading to a parallel development
in Judaic studies.

In the limited space allotted this Chapter, this
historical deficiency might be addressed in either of two
ways. The subject might be developed biographically,
focusing on some significant Jewish figures who influenced markedly western culture: Francis Salvador (1747-
1776), English-born Jew who came to South Carolina and
was the first Jew in the colonies to hold elective office
(South Carolina's Provincial Congresses in 1775 and 1776),
perhaps the first Jew to hold elective office in the
modern world; Meyer Amschel Rothschild (1743-1812), German Jew who founded the banking house of Rothschild;
Alfred Dreyfus (1859-1935), French army officer falsely

accused of treason and later exonerated; Theodor Herzl (1860-1904), Austrian-born Jewish journalist whose disillusionment resulting especially from the Dreyfus trial led to his founding the modern Zionist movement; Louis Dembitz Brandeis (1856-1941), American-born jurist appointed to be an Associate Justice of the United States Supreme Court (1916-1939); David Ben-Gurion (1886-1973), Polish-born Jew who became the first Prime Minister of the State of Israel, serving two terms (1948-1953, 1955-1963); and Golda Mier (1898-   ), until 1974 Prime Minister of the State of Israel. This list obviously is not exhaustive; rather, these names serve only as a sampling of the individuals whom we might choose were we to take a biographical approach.

Another corrective to the historical deficiency would be to interweave some highlights of Jewish history with the data more traditionally studied. It is this approach chosen here. If the material seems to portray in biased fashion the plight of the Jews, explanation is sought in the fact that traditional historical recounting is readily available and in the assurance that the predominantly Christian society will benefit from an awareness of the historical interplay of Jews and Christians, a record more sordid than one would wish. Such an awareness enables the Christian to understand why the Jew often finds overtures to religious dialogue from the Christian community obscured by suspicion and doubt. The hard data of history left an indelible impression upon the Jewish people.[2]

The Formative Period, A.D. 30-500

Earlier it was indicated that the church became increasingly Hellenized as it spread beyond the borders of Palestine.[3] Such Hellenization caused the church to develop some thought patterns radically different from those which would have been espoused by Jesus of Nazareth.[4] One grants that it is virtually impossible to recapture the Jesus of history standing behind the Christ of the Gospels.[5] It is unlikely, however, that the Jewish Jesus, who probably never traveled beyond the borders of his native Palestine, could have worshipped in churches located at Ephesus, Thessalonica, Corinth, or Rome. The cultural gap would have been too great, the affirmation of Hellenism too pronounced for one immersed in traditional Jewish culture. Differences separating the Christian of the Empire and the Palestinian Jew would manifest themselves in numerous ways--attitudes toward the body, Jewish ritual traditions, etc. Jesus would not have been comfortable with this predominately Gentile body who ultimately took their name, Christian, from what they affirmed to be true about him--he was the Christ. Since such problems might safely be conjectured for Jesus, it should not be hard to understand why the first-century Jew generally had difficulty relating to ones "belonging to the Way" (Acts 9:2), or "Christians" (Acts 11:26). When the breach between Judaism and Christianity was finalized is debatable, but during the reign of the Roman Emperor Domitian (A.D. 81-96) Christians were persecuted because of their refusal to participate in the Emperor Cult while Jews were exempted from this practice.

In the Gospels, Jesus is portrayed as a practicing Jew. He participated in synagogue life (Mark 1:21ff.); and all of the Gospels attest to his going to Jerusalem, presumably to observe the Passover, a custom for devout Jews (see Mark 10ff. and parallels). According to the Acts of the Apostles, his followers in Jerusalem continued going to the Temple (3:1ff.); and there is no indication that the disciples' gathering on the first day of the week to commemorate the Easter event precluded their observance of the sabbath. Paul was a Jew, and in his missionary journeys he followed consistently the policy of taking his message about Jesus initially to the Jews and then to the Gentiles only after his proclamation was rejected by the Jews. Paul's arrest in Jerusalem occurred in the Temple (Acts 21:27ff.). He characterized himself as a "Hebrew born of Hebrews; as to the law a Pharisee" (Philippians 3:5).

Paul's self-image notwithstanding, his thought pattern lay behind much of the problem which has been experienced between Jews and Christians. As a Diaspora Jew, Paul did not hold Jewish ritual practices to be inviolate, as did the Palestinian Jew. Particularly, circumcision and dietary restrictions Paul determined to be unnecessary for the Gentile who accepted Jesus as Messiah (see the Galatian correspondence). This created insurmountable problems for the Jew who accepted the obligations of the Torah as absolutely binding. Not only must these commandments be obeyed personally, the Jew was also convinced that social contact with persons not adhering to these strictures ritually defiled him.

When one couples the ritual problems with the disciples' insistence that Jesus was the promised messiah, it becomes apparent why the Jew and the Christian had difficulty relating. The Jewish revolts against Rome in A.D. 66 and A.D. 132 sealed the separation of the two groups. The Zealots, a party particularly resistent to Roman control of Palestine, were especially influential in bringing about the revolt of A.D. 66. Prior to the revolt, however, they encouraged negative reaction to the Christians, culminating with the death of James, brother of Jesus and apparently leader of the Jerusalem Christians, in A.D. 62.[6] Fear of greater persecution caused Christians

to leave Jerusalem, and thus they were not available to
assist in the defense of Jerusalem when the revolt erupted.
The same result, with different preconditions, occurred
in the A.D. 132 situation. A revolt against Rome was
directed by Bar Kokhba, with this leader being judged
messiah by no less an authority than Rabbi Aqiba. It
was impossible for the Christians to aid in the struggle,
however, since they accepted Jesus rather than Bar Kokhba
as messiah. It has been suggested that the Christian inability to participate in this struggle occasioned the
identification of "Christian" with "traitor."[7] The line
of division was firmly marked; and, once clearly delineated, Jews and Christians have never recovered a sense
of unity.

Jews and Christians had become a problem for each
other. Already the nature of the Jewish concern with
Christians has been indicated, but the Christian problem
was no less real. Early Christians were Jewish Christians.
They were Jews who differed from their fellow Jews only,
but significantly, in their affirmation that messiah had
come. In their zeal, they were compelled to proclaim this
conviction to fellow Jews. Furthermore, they were convicted that once the Jew heard this message he would
respond affirmatively to the Gospel. When the Jew rejected the Christian message, the church had to deal with
this. One example of this is seen in Paul's Letter to
the Romans (chapters 9-11), where the Jewish resistance
is judged to accord with God's plan. Paul asserted that
it was God's intention for the Jews to resist the Gospel
that the message might be taken to the Gentiles. Once
the Gentiles had heard, however, he was convinced that
the Jews would respond.

Unfortunately, this thought pattern deprecated the
integrity of the Jewish faith, affirming Judaism to be

only a forerunner, a type of custodian or a teacher, leading men to the Christ (Galatians 3:23ff.). It was inevitable, particularly as the church became predominantly
Gentile, that Jewish ritual was adamantly rejected. During the second century, in the judgment of some of the
Church Fathers, it was anathema (a thing accursed) for
the follower of Jesus to observe Jewish rituals, such as
sabbath observance.

The eventual resolution to the problem was politically enacted in a manner which foretold severe problems
for Judaism. Constantine, born A.D. 280 (?), rules as
the Emperor of Rome A.D. 306-337. His embracing Christianity in A.D. 312 signaled the eventual adoption of
Christianity as the official religion of the Empire.[8]
In A.D. 313 Constantine issued the Edict of Milan, assur-
ing toleration for Christians throughout the Empire. This
should have assured also religious freedom for the Jew.
The proclamation of Christian toleration, however, indicates the tenuous nature of Jewish freedom. This is veri-
fied by a decree issued in A.D. 329 forbidding the Jew to
hold a Christian slave or to convert the pagan, with the
latter being punishable by death.

Also, during the fourth century, the Arian controversy
arose. As the Empire increasingly "Christianized," the
Jew looked to Egypt where Arius and his followers were
not so hostile to Jewish thought. Arius (A.D. 256?-336)
affirmed that Jesus was not of the same substance as God.
To the contrary, he asserted that Jesus was an agent created by God and was God's instrument in the creation of
the world. Thus, while God has neither beginning nor end,
Jesus had a beginning. Therefore, one must acknowledge
that the Son was not a part of God.

Arius' view, while understandably more acceptable
to the Jew, differed with developing Christian theology.

151

This threat to orthodoxy led to the Council of Nicaea in
A.D. 325 and ultimately to the development of the following creedal statement:

I believe in one God the Father Almighty, Maker of
heaven and earth, and of all things visible and invisible:
And in one Lord Jesus Christ, the only-begotten Son
of God; Begotten of his Father before all worlds, God of
God, Light of Light, Very God of very God; Begotten, not
made; Being of one substance with the Father; By whom all
things were made: Who for us men and for our salvation
came down from heaven, and was incarnate by the Holy Ghost
of the Virgin Mary, and was made man: And was crucified
also for us under Pontius Pilate; He suffered and was
buried:
And the third day he rose again according to the
Scripture: And ascended into heaven, and sitteth on the
right hand of the Father: And he shall come again, with
glory, to judge both the quick and the dead; Whose kingdom shall have no end.
And I believe in the Holy Ghost, the Lord, and Giver
of Life, Who proceedeth from the Father and the Son; Who
with the Father and the Son together is worshipped and
glorified; Who spoke by the Prophets: And I believe one
Catholic and Apostolic Church: I acknowledge one Baptism
for the remission of sins: And I look for the Resurrection
of the dead: And the Life of the world to come. Amen.[9]

The Arian position was rejected, declaring by majority
vote the heresy of the minority. Arius and his followers,
who refused to accept the Council's judgment, were exiled
from the Empire. For Christianity, the Council and its
repercussions had the effect of precluding an alternative
Christological point of view. In the name of that "sacred"

aspiration, orthodoxy, man's freedom to think, to judge, to affirm was curtailed. Unfortunate as this was for the Christian, the effect on the Jew was perhaps more dramatic, for now there was no place in the Empire to turn in the expectation that his faith affirmation would find reasonable reception.

The church's proclamation demonstrated the negative reaction to Judaism. Typical during the fourth century was Ambrose John Chrysostom, who was designated "the golden-mouthed" because of his oratorical ability. He was particularly adamant to bring all pagans into Christianity, and the Jews were a prime concern. One of his sermons began as follows:

. . . a great number of the faithful have for the Jews a certain respect and hold their ceremonies in reverence. This provokes one to eradicate completely such a disastrous opinion . . . Instead of greeting them and addressing them as much as a word, you should turn away from them as from the pest and a plague of the human race.[10]

As the Jew anticipated the future, what would later be designated the Middle Ages, he did so with fear and foreboding. His relationships with the Christians gave him no reason for hope.

The Medieval Period, A.D. 500-1500

The Medieval Period is one of Judaism's saddest periods, for persecution and death was the Jew's constant companion throughout this era. In like fashion, it is one of the most sordid eras in church history, for unfortunately the responsibility, and thus guilt, for this extensive persecution and death falls upon the church.

Typical of the church's reaction to the Jews during

153

the early Medieval Period, Pope Gregory the Great (590-604) issued an edict which forbade the forced conversion of Jews. Nonetheless, strictures were laid upon the Jews which clearly indicated their second-class citizenship. For example, it was stipulated that no new synagogues could be built, Jewish physicians could not be employed by Christians, and Jews could not hold Christian slaves. Even more devastating was the reaction to Jewish children.

It was determined that it was in the interest of the salvation of the Jewish child to baptize the child into the church. Only one step further was the conclusion to remove the child from the corrupting influence of the Jewish home. This thought pattern was sanctioned by the Fourth Council of Toledo (633), which encouraged the wresting of baptized Jewish children from their parents. The continued deterioration is evident in the Ninth Council of Toledo (655), which decreed that the baptized Jew must remain in the presence of a Christian clergyman during any Jewish or Christian holy season, to assure no relapse into Jewish customs during these periods.

During this era the feudal system and craft guilds were developing. With the former the Jew was excluded from land ownership, forcing the Jew into urban existence.[11] Once in the urban setting, however, the Jew discovered the craft guilds, just like the feudal system, to be dominated by Christians. Thus the Jew, in spite of his own desires, was forced into lending money as a vocational pursuit. Looking ahead, Cecil Roth stated: "By the thirteenth century the majority of Jews in those countries subject to the Catholic Church, with the partial exception of southern Italy and Spain, were dependent directly or indirectly, in spite of themselves, on this degraded and degrading occupation."[12]

During the seventh century, Islam burst upon the

world scene, a militant faith formulated on the teachings
of Mohammed (570-632). This faith rapidly spread westward
to Spain, completing the conquest of Spain by 715, and
eastward into the Mesopotamian Valley, resulting in the
decline of Mesopotamian Jewry by the beginning of the
eleventh century. The latter was a tragic loss, for Mesopotamian Jewry had for centuries been Judaism's chief
focus, producing the highly revered Babylonian Talmud.[13]

While the Jews did not always prosper under Muslim
rule, they often fared better under Muslim rather than
Christian domination. Christians found it difficult to
forget the charge of deicide against the Jews, often leading to persecution when Christians dominated politically.
In addition, Jews often made an uneasy alliance with Muslims as they established control over an area. This is
exemplified in the Muslim conquest of Spain, where, during the early years of Muslim control, Jews found warm
reception because of their linguistic and medical abilities, both valuable assets to the Muslims. Finally, Jew
and Muslim shared many traditions; and the Muslim faith
permitted acceptance of the Jewish scriptures. Thus,
the Jewish plight under the Muslims was not totally negative.

Charles the Great, Charlemagne, was crowned Emperor
of the Roman Empire on Christmas Day, 800. His reign
brought peace and stability to the Empire, and the Jews
thanked Yahweh for a ruler portending no harm to them.
His rule had lasting effect on the Jews, both in migra-
tions and in cultural development. Geographically the
Jews spread throughout Spain, into France, along the
Rhineland in Germany, and as far west as England with the
Norman conquest of England in 1066. Culturally, this period saw intensified Jewish participation in the professions
of law and medicine, an increase in the number of significant

Jewish poets, and perhaps most importantly the intellectu-
alization of Jewry through Talmudic studies, exemplified
in the esteemed Moses Maimonides (1135-1204).

This geographic spread, economic accumulation, and
cultural intensification unfortunately created animosity
toward the Jews in certain quarters. One result of increased hostility was excessive taxation, with the Jew
often being taxed beyond endurance. Seeking relief, the
Jews sought immediate relationship with the rulers where
they were settled. Consequently, by the ninth century,
the Jews were the direct property of the crown in their
various areas.[14] What they did not envision was the extent of taxation the rulers might impose and the deplor-
able uses to which the tax revenue might be directed.
The result, however, was now clear: "The commercial
supremacy of the Jew in Western Europe came to an end in
the tenth century . . . ."[15]

A classical example of the negative impact of this
relationship is seen in the Crusades. On November 26,
1095, Pope Urban II (1088-1099) delivered a sermon before
the Council of Clermont. The sermon was precipitated by
information filtered westward of Muslim maltreatment of
Christian shrines in Palestine, particularly in Jerusalem.
The sermon's emphasis was to encourage a militant Christendom to take the necessary steps to recover the Holy
Land from the infidel. Thus the trumpet sounded, resulting in eight crusades between 1096 and 1291. In financing
the Crusades, much of the revenue was drawn from the Jews.
This situation was particularly despicable, for while the
focus of the crusaders' wrath was ostensibly the Muslim,
many crusaders never reached Jerusalem. Nearer at hand
was a target, the Jew--judged responsible for the death
of Jesus, thereby guilty of deicide. The Jew was also
infidel. Consequently, untold Jews died during the Crusades,

with entire Jewish communities being destroyed.

During this period, Jewish options were greatly reduced. Earlier, when the situation became intolerable, he could move to a different area. During the Crusades such movement was practically precluded, for he knew that should he chance upon crusaders on the road he would be treated as the infidel enemy. Minimally he could expect radical persecution, maximally death. Thus the Jew had to make the best of his situation, regardless of how bad it might become.

Prejudice encouraged dehumanization of the Jew. Anyone familiar with Jewish tradition recognized that the Jew was forbidden by the Torah to eat meat improperly slaughtered, the prohibition against blood being linked to the Noachian covenant (Genesis 9:1-7). In spite of this, rumors circulated and were accepted as fact that Jews slaughtered Christian children, using their blood to make matzah. Regardless of the rumor's folly, this encouraged persecutions of the Jews as pogrom followed pogrom. The church affirmed as the Christ (Messiah) he who is recorded to have said: "This is my commandment, that you love one another as I have loved you" (John 15:12). Yet it was at Passiontide that the Jews experienced their greatest agonies. In the name of the one teaching love, Christians were "compelled" to correct the injustice of history, the death of Jesus at the hands of the Jews. Thus the Jews inevitably approached the Christian Easter season with great fear.

Church Councils continued to enact decrees negative to the Jew. In the Third Lateran Council of 1179, it was decreed that the Christian could not dwell among the infidel. While this decree was stated positively in that it was the Christian who was prohibited from living among the infidel, nonetheless the result was experienced primarily by the Jew. It was the Jew who was isolated so as not to contaminate the Christian.

On November 30, 1215, a Papal Bull was issued to implement the decision of the Fourth Lateran Council of 1215, namely that all Jews must wear a distinguishing badge.[16] While this dictum was not strictly enforced until the sixteenth century, the segregation of the Jew was gradually becoming fact and was being done with legal sanction.

Typical of the era was a Papal Bull issued June 17, 1242, whereby Pope Gregory IX ordered the gathering of all Hebrew manuscripts from the synagogues in Paris. The result was the burning in the streets of Paris of twenty-four cartloads of Hebrew manuscripts, copies of both the Torah and the Talmud. The sheer inhumanity, the injustice to Judaism, and the loss to critical scholarship are difficult to fathom.

Again, in 1278, Pope Nicholas III issued a decree giving Christians the freedom of Jewish pulpits. This decree permitted the Christian to enter a synagogue at any occasion of worship to preach for the conversion of the Jew. The Jew was required to remain seated, but obviously no one could legislate the Jew's listening!

Ultimately, the inevitable began to occur. The Jews, who by the eleventh century had spread as far westward as England, had become personae non grata in a Christian dominated environment. By economic and political sanctions, most Jews had been stripped of all material goods, nullifying their earlier value to the various rulers. Legal segregation and the badge of distinction could only partially convey Christian reaction; eventually it was determined that only expulsion would suffice!

On July 18, 1290, King Edward I of England issued a decree ordering all Jews to depart England within three months. In 1306 Philip the Fair of France had all Jews arrested simultaneously. They were informed that they must depart the country within one month and that all of their physical properties would become the property of the crown.

Given the tragedy which befell Jews in Germany during World War II, it is ironic that they were not forced to leave Germany. Nonetheless, German Jews endured radical persecution. Expulsions and persecutions continued; but it was in Spain that the final tragedy fell. In northern Spain[17] the Jews had reached the zenith of their cultural development. After exceedingly difficult times--including the unique phenomenon of unparalleled numbers of Jews "accepting" Christian baptism to avoid persecution (called Marranos, or "New Christians") and the Spanish Inquisition initiated on September 17, 1480--the Catholic rulers, King Ferdinand and Queen Isabella, issued a decree on March 30, 1492, compelling all Jews to depart Spain within four months.

Thus the westward movement of the Jews was brought to an abrupt halt. They were forced to begin anew an eastward trek searching for countries where they might find an acceptable reception.

The Post-Medieval Period, A.D. 1500-Present

As the Jews moved eastward, a continuous community was preserved in only two countries, Germany and Italy. In Germany considerable suffering was experienced, and the situation in Italy was not markedly better. Some Popes, such as Leo X (1513-1521) and Clement VII (1523-1533), gave positive encouragement to the Jews. Generally, however, the Jews were restricted to subservient positions, such as money lending.

During the sixteenth and seventeenth centuries, the

primary focus of Judaism was in the Turkish Empire, where Jews were welcomed for trading and marketing abilities, and in Poland, where religious freedom was practiced by royal decree. Poland became the seat of Jewish learning, a form of Talmudic interpretation developing here designated as pilpul (a "hairsplitting method of talmudic study"[18]).

Martin Luther nailed his ninety-five theses to the door of the castle church in Wittenberg on October 31, 1517. Apparently, Luther expected the Jews to respond to his proclamation; but the Jew found his interpretation of the New Testament totally unappealing. When the Jew responded negatively, Luther became exceedingly anti-Semitic. One of his sermons began: "What then shall we Christians do with this damned rejected race of Jews? . . . ."[19] Unfortunately, the Protestant Reformation did nothing to alleviate the plight of the Jews. Roland de Corneille states:

. . . while history will not permit us to lay the blame upon the doorstep of medievalism, it also refuses to permit us the scapegoat of the papacy or the Roman Catholic Church. The temptation to lay the responsibility there is made all the more attractive by the fact that the plight of the Jews was gradually ameliorated during the centuries which followed the Protestant Reformation. Therefore, it has occurred to some people that Protestantism provided a kind of driving force towards the establishment of tolerance and more humane attitudes towards Jews. As a matter of historical fact, however, Protestantism did nothing of the kind . . . nothing positive emerged from it to change the persistent negative stereotypes by which the Christian habitually judged them. Any opportunity which Protestantism had to rectify the past, or at

least to establish a segment of the Church on a new foot-
ing, was lost.[20]

The Jew was now caught in the middle--between the Protestant and the Roman Catholic Church, with both reacting
negatively to Judaism.

The situation was dismal, and recent developments in
Venice portended even greater ill for the future. In 1516,
Jews had been restricted to a quarter of the city designated Ghetto Nuovo, or "New Foundry." The Jewish plight
further deteriorated in the Autumn of 1553. On the Jewish
New Year (Yom Kippur), by Papal decree all available copies
of the Talmud were burned in Rome. Then in 1555, Cardinal
Caraffa, who was the master designer behind the Talmud
burning, ascended the Papal throne as Pope Paul IV (1555-
1559). He reinstituted the various anti-Semitic medieval
decrees. By Papal Bull in 1555 the medieval restrictions
upon Jews were implemented anew in Italy. The ghetto
spread throughout Italy and rapidly over Europe.

Ghetto life was a radical test for the Jew. In this
restricted area of the city property ownership was regu-
lated; building was restricted; the type of instruction
permitted was dictated; most vocational pursuits were
excluded; permission for marriage was legislated; and
exit from the walled ghetto was governed by Christian gate-
keepers. Living conditions were atrocious; food was inadequate; ceilings of rooms were low; doorways forced bend-
ing for human passage--culminating in a stooped bearing
and after an incarceration of approximately two centuries
a loss of several inches when compared with the Jew who
entered the ghetto.[21] The ghetto had far-reaching impact
beyond physical impairment. Emotionally an intense hatred
was engendered against all Gentiles, while an uncommon
allegiance to fellow Jews was encouraged. Religiously,

the traditional love of learning could not be exercised,
causing a deterioration in the level of Jewish scholarship. Socially, it was going to be difficult to enter
into interpersonal relationships with Gentiles apart from
a deep-seated suspicion of motivation.

The liberating forces for the Jews were not destined
to be religious:

So far as the relationship of the Church to the
Jewish people is concerned, there are few exceptions to
the rule that at no time did Christianity champion the
cause of the Jews. It was only when movements outside
the Church such as Humanism, Capitalism and Nationalism,
brought their influence to bear that the situation im-
proved at all.[22]

The clearest example was the French Revolution of 1789,
with its emphases on the dignity and equality of man embedded in the Declaration of the Rights of Man. No longer
could Jews be ostracized behind ghetto walls, and Napoleon's
troops literally crashed the gates of many ghettos. The
possibility for a normal life for the Jew now appeared a
reality, for throughout Europe the ghettos disappeared:
on January 28, 1790, Portuguese Jews were emancipated;
on September 2, 1796, Holland granted full citizenship to
the Jews; in Venice the ghetto gates were broken down on
July 10, 1797; in February, 1798, ghetto Jews were delivered in Rome; in 1811 restrictions were removed from Jews
in Frankfort, Germany; only in Russia were the restrictions upon the Jews not removed.

The westward movement of the Jews initiated anew
brought the first group to North America in 1654, with a
much larger wave primarily from Germany arriving in the
1840's. During the late nineteenth century, Russian Jews

experienced persecution, precipitating a migration of
approximately one-half million Jews to the United States
between 1880 and 1900. Evidence that the Jew continued
to experience hostility in the United States is indicated
by the establishment of the Anti-Defamation League of
B'nai B'rith (founded 1843) to battle anti-Semitic slurs
in the press.

The greatest physical tragedy to befall Judaism was
the rise of the Third Reich. Following World War I, Germany experienced an economic breakdown and the imposition
of heavy war reparations. When Adolf Hitler came to power
in 1933, the Jews gradually recognized that they would be
Germany's scapegoat for her misfortunes. Most German Jews
had rejected any Zionist inclinations. They had settled
in Germany, fully adopting Germany as their homeland.
This adjustment made more difficult the recognition of
Hitler's designs and hampered their ability to respond:

It was inconceivable to them that the constitution, the
basic law of the land, could be overthrown. They had become acculturated, hence could not fathom the possibility
of a whole nation turning against them at the behest of
a few maniacs. They abhorred violence, hence did not
take up arms (as their forebears had done in Germany
when Jews were attacked during the Crusades, and as the
heroes of the Warsaw Ghetto, after long hestitation when
their cup of misery was finally running over). Dwelling
in all sections of the German cities, they therefore had
no emotional preparation, physical training, or even
opportunity for united action.[23]

The Jewish plight in Germany rapidly deteriorated
once Hitler assumed governmental control. In 1935 racial
laws were enacted which forbade Jewish participation in

social, economic, and cultural aspects of the country's life. The Jews had truly become second-class citizens. In October 1938, a minor German official in Paris was killed by a young Jewish boy. The Germans used this as the rationale for carrying out their designs for the Jews in Germany. On November 9-10, 1938, a burst of destruction occurred in which practically every synagogue in Germany was burned; Torah scrolls were trampled in the streets; large numbers of Jews were either beaten, imprisoned, or killed; businesses were sacked; homes pillaged; and personal property wantonly destroyed.[24] Finally, in January, 1942,[25] the "final solution" to the "Jewish problem" was devised, namely extermination. Thus concentration-annihilation camps were set up with their disguised gas chambers and their ovens for the consumption of human flesh. The infamy of such places as Auschwitz, Dachau, Treblinka, Maidenek, Buchenwald, and Bergen-Belsen will resound in men's minds for as long as human civilization endures. It was in these places that six million Jews died during the Nazi regime in World War II, one-third of the world's Jewish population.

Jews ponder, indeed Christians wonder, where were the Christians of Germany throughout this degenerate period? But the blame should not be placed too squarely on the German Christian, where was Christendom in general? Hitler and his henchmen--Heinrich Himmler, Reinhardt Heydrich, and Adolf Eichmann--may have been the agents directly responsible for this black era in human history. The entire human family must bear the responsibility for this atrocity, however, for the history of the relationship of Jews and Christians--Talmud burnings, identification badges, ghettos, crusades, inquisitions, expulsions--made possible the inconceivable activities of the Third Reich! Some few churchmen spoke in behalf of the

Jews, but generally the voice of the church both in Germany and internationally was silent.

Out of the Holocaust of World War II, appealing to the 1917 Balfour Declaration indicating British support for the establishment of a "National home for the Jewish people," the State of Israel was constituted on May 14, 1948, when the British mandate in Palestine was terminated. Thus was begun a nation's rebirth which has been punctuated by Israeli-Arab conflict--the wars of 1948-1949; 1956; the six-day campaign of June 5-10, 1967; and the October-November 1973 war.

Conclusion

What does the future hold for Israel? Who wishes to act as seer? The dream of Theodor Herzl (1860-1904) that a homeland for the Jews be constituted was fulfilled forty-four years after his death. When Jews around the world commemorate Passover, they conclude the Seder meal with the words "Next year in Jerusalem!" with a more realistic intonation than was possible before 1948, and even more so once the Jews gained control of Jerusalem as a result of the 1967 conflict. The homeland is a reality which was absent almost two thousand years. International Jewry is determined that the homeland will continue for today's children, their grandchildren, and forever.

Perhaps equally important is the question, what will be the relationship of Christians and Jews as we face the future? For how long will traditional prejudices endure? How effective will be the numerous examples of Jewish-Christian dialogue that one sees taking place?[26] These questions as well as numerous similar questions cannot now be answered with assurance. It can only be hoped that the lessons of history are clear, that by learning

these lessons we will avoid the horrors of repeating our
own mistakes, that the affirmation of man's humanity is
more certain, and that Christendom will lead the way in
establishing new avenues of understanding and constructive
rapport between Judaism and Christianity.[27]

RELIGION IN CULTURAL EXPERIENCE

Religious expressions share certain basic characteristics, and a general phenomenological approach would
dictate seeking a compendium of common characteristics
for discussion. For example, Ninian Smart in The Religious Experience of Mankind[1] discusses six dimensions of
religious experience common to various religions: ritual,
mythological, doctrinal, ethical, social, and experiential.

This Chapter, however, does not focus on religious
experience so broadly. To the contrary, Judaism and
Christianity, the two religions primarily influencing
and shaping western traditions both in the past and in
the present, are emphasized. This is a limited phenomenological approach, therefore, as these two religious expressions are investigated regarding four shared characteristics: doctrinal, ritual, mythical, and social. The
presence of these characteristics in Judaism and Christianity shall be indicated, with the implications inherent
for each religious structure.

Sacred Versus Profane

It has often been asserted that ancient man experienced the holy much more vividly and extensively than
does his modern counterpart.[2] Modern man narrowly restricts
the arena in which deity may be discovered, a development
perhaps necessitated by the continual secularization of

modern man's existence. The ability to explain observed
phenomena has reduced considerably those areas assigned
to deity. Ancient man, however, recognized divine infusion in every aspect of life--nature and history--much
more than modern man. On the one hand, ancient man made
little distinction between matters sacred and profane,
while on the other he did recognize peculiarly holy ob-
jects and events. Thus, in spite of the greater availability of the sacred dimension for ancient man, one may
nonetheless speak meaningfully of the "holy" for ancient
man. Certainly Biblical man used this reference with
frequency and with meaningful content.

Mircea Eliade speaks pointedly to the understanding
of the sacred's manifestation among ancient peoples:

The modern Occidental experiences a certain uneasi-
ness before many manifestations of the sacred. He finds
it difficult to accept the fact that, for many human
beings, the sacred can be manifested in stones or trees,
for example. But . . . what is involved is not a veneration of the stone in itself, a cult of the tree in itself. The sacred tree, the sacred stone are not adored
as stone or tree; they are worshipped precisely because
they are hierophanies [act of manifestation of the sacred],
because they show something that is no longer stone or
tree but the sacred . . .

It is impossible to overemphasize the paradox represented by every hierophany, even the most elementary. By
manifesting the sacred, any object becomes something else,
yet it continues to remain itself, for it continues to
participate in its surrounding cosmic milieu. A sacred
stone remains a stone; apparently (or, more precisely,
from the profane point of view), nothing distinguishes
it from all other stones. But for those to whom a stone

reveals itself as sacred, its immediate reality is trans-
muted into a supernatural reality. In other words, for
those who have a religious experience all nature is capable of revealing itself as cosmic sacrality. The cosmos
in its entirety can become a hierophany.[3]

Recognizing ancient man's acceptance of hierophanic
experience within the commonplace, the double dimension
of encountered reality is clarified. The scientific revolution, however, made it difficult for man to accept such
hierophanic experience. Historically, therefore, the
movement to separate with absoluteness the sacred and the
profane is relatively recent in man's evolvement. Thus,
in "religious circles" which are characteristically marked
by a concern to preserve the past, it is perhaps inevitable
that difficulty should continue in clarifying the demarca-
tion between the sacred and the profane. Contemporary
man lives an existence governed by scientific principles,
and even when he does not fully understand all of these
principles he is a creature of modern culture and cannot
dissociate himself from these governing principles even
if he should desire to do so. At this point problems
arise, for if modern man attempts to transliterate ancient
concepts into modern modalities, and here we refer especially to the view of the sacred, a type of religious
schizophrenia results. Modern man can translate these
earlier conceptualizations for his use, but the thought
distinction between transliteration and translation is
important.

Again, Eliade makes the point vividly in discussing
the distinctive viewpoints for ancient and modern man in
the simplest physiological acts:

For modern consciousness, a physiological act--eating,

sex, and so on--is in sum only an organic phenomenon, however much it may still be encumbered by tabus (imposing, for example, particular rules for "eating properly" or forbidding some sexual behavior disapproved by social morality). But for the primitive, such an act is never simply physiological; it is, or can become, a sacrament, that is, a communion with the sacred.[4]

Ancient man reckoned all food as divine gift, but rarely would modern man make this same equation. In like fashion, contemporary slaughter-house methods for preparing meat stand in sharp contrast with ancient Hebraic conviction that every meat slaughter was a sacrifice to his God. While one cannot tranliterate every ancient concept, therefore, one may translate the thought pattern. By so doing, one recognizes, for example, in the kosher requirements of Judaism or the eucharistic meal of Christendom the basic thought pattern that attended ancient man's activities.

In summary, a meaningful distinction between ancient and modern man regarding perception of the sacred and the profane must be recognized. Nonetheless, just as the ancient Hebrew had that to which he attached the label "holy," so too does modern man have those areas of existence which continue to bear that label.

Manifestations of Religious Experience

The manifestation of religious experience perhaps most obvious for modern man is the doctrinal perspective. Essentially doctrines carry convictional intent for those within the community and a persuasive power for those outside the faith community. To fulfill this convictional and persuasive intent, the doctrine must be expressed as clearly as possible. Thus, one result of doctrinal expression is the systematization of the faith structure. Such systematization is an invaluable asset in enabling a faith community to achieve self-awareness and direction, whether the doctrine be in oral or written formulation. This is a difficult process, however, both because the language must convey in concrete form intangible and often inexpressible ideas and because language evolves so that words once used may over a lengthy time span develop totally different connotations. This difficulty of expressing the experienced but not enunciated in language is clear, but a second problem perhaps equally difficult is that of securing sufficient agreement within a faith community for an acceptable doctrinal expression to evolve.

Any transmitted doctrinal statement, therefore, inherently conveys problems. Among these are at least the expression of intolerance, the crystalization of thought characteristic of the community's struggle for survival, and the problem of language and ideas becoming outdated.

The formulation of a doctrinal statement often conveys a not too subtle intolerance since an enforced conformity process takes place when a faith community expresses a normative statement of belief. Once adopted the statement becomes the standard, and anyone not accepting such becomes thereby an unbeliever, an infidel. This occurred, for example, during the approximately six centuries following Jesus' death as conformity was sought in the Christological question. As creedal statements evolved, inevitably individuals fell in the wake of the church's advance as orthodoxy was enforced. Even in contemporary circles, let a clergyman affirm publicly that he does not believe the literal story of Jesus' virgin birth and note the effect that such a statement frequently will have on his career. Subtle, and sometimes not too subtle, measures are brought into play to enforce orthodoxy, namely conformity to the doctrinal statement. Moreover, these doctrines do not have to be written formulations. For example, the earlier mentioned virgin birth affirmation would not be a creedal formulation for the faithful in some Protestant denominations, at least the affirmation would not be expressed in written creedal statement. Nonetheless, deviation from that unwritten norm can draw various types of censure. In addition, traditional affirmations may have the same binding hold upon the devotee, as for example the understanding that Moses is the author of the Torah in Orthodox Judaism.

Especially a written doctrinal statement may evidence the crystalization of thought characteristic of a community's struggle for survival. This relates to the issue just discussed in that the community facing difficulty and/or extinction either by internal or external pressures may seek to fortify itself by drawing ever tighter its conformity requirements to meet the problem. The community will seek to clarify its assertions and will enforce rigidly these on all devotees. Basically a faith community recognizes that it cannot survive either if it be radically divided from within so that the very fabric of the structure is eaten away or if it be beset by external pressures when it lacks the strength resultant from internal agreement.

Most doctrinal formulations also tend to become woefully outdated in both language and ideas, especially written statements. This is almost inevitable when viewed not only in terms of short-range application but also in terms of a doctrinal statement's applicability perhaps centuries after its original formulation. Given the way language evolves and knowledge continually expands, it is practically inconceivable to envision a doctrinal statement's being formulated which could resist falling victim either to the language or knowledge pitfall.

Within Christendom a classic doctrinal statement, the Apostles Creed, illustrates the problems associated with doctrines:

I believe in God the Father Almighty, maker of heaven and earth, and in Jesus Christ his only Son our Lord, who was conceived by the Holy Ghost, born of the Virgin Mary, suffered under Pontius Pilate, was crucified, dead, and buried. He descended into hell; the third day he rose again from the dead; he ascended into heaven, and sitteth on the right hand of God the Father Almighty. From thence he shall come to judge the quick and the dead.

I believe in the Holy Ghost, the holy Catholic Church, the communion of saints, the forgiveness of sins, the resurrection of the body, and the life everlasting. Amen.

Kenneth Scott Latourette indicates that the present form of the Creed developed about the sixth century. He notes, however, that some portions of the Creed are quoted in second-century writings, concluding that the Creed authentically dates to the era of the Apostles. He conjectures that the Creed's origin lay in an early baptismal formula,[5] judging the Creed to be perhaps an expansion of the primitive baptismal formula found in Matthew 28:19-20. Nonetheless, there are few accidents of history; and Latourette is probably accurate in attributing the concern to expand the baptismal formula to the Roman Church's reaction to Marcion. As a second-century Christian, Marcion rejected

both the Hebrew scriptures and the God described therein.
Marcion conjectured that this world could not have been
created by a loving God, that instead the world had been
created by a Demiurge. He further asserted that Jesus
was a phantom and that the judgment would be by the
Demiurge. To this the Creed affirmed belief in "God the
Father Almighty," asserted the humanity of Jesus, and
affirmed that it would be Jesus who would act as judge.[6]

This brief background to the Apostles Creed has been
given both to affirm a specific context for the Creed and
to indicate that the context no longer has applicability
for contemporary man. Who is talking about a Demiurge
today? Does the same type of problem exist today as regards Jesus' humanity? Any doctrinal statement has a
context which gave it birth; and, while we cannot fully
recover that context for the Apostles Creed, we may be
assured that whether that context be affirmed as first,
second, or sixth century it is a radically different context from that confronted by modern man.

Beyond the specifics of the context and its early
anti-Marcionite use, however, we recognize numerous other
problems for the contemporary individual. For example,
no one today accepts the three-tiered universe with which
the Hebrews as well as other ancient peoples, including
the early Christians, worked. Yet this Creed clearly
operates under this mode of thinking--"He descended into
hell . . . he ascended into heaven"--and the modern Christian must be sufficiently knowledgeable and sophisticated
to translate that thought into its symbolic meaning. How
many Christians are capable of so doing? For how many
people does the Creed become a problem as regards the
enforcement of a literal interpretation of scripture?
How many Christians today would affirm belief in the virgin birth and the resurrection, particularly in the

concrete, fully human fashion expressed in the Creed?

In summary, the Apostles Creed manifests the three dangers inherent in the formulation of doctrines earlier discussed: a basic intolerance is expressed, the Creed emerged during the church's struggle for survival, and in many of its affirmations the statement is woefully outdated.

A second manifestation of religious experience is ritual, a form of visible behavior, either simple or elaborate, intended to convey an individual's inner expression. The action may be simple, as shutting the eyes in prayer, clasped hands in prayer, or the bowed head when praying. These are all personal rituals, which are not necessarily shared with a larger community. A ritual may be highly elaborate, however, as the Roman Catholic Mass or the Sedar Meal, the latter being associated with Passover in Judaism. Various types of music, dancing, art, and architecture may also be employed ritually.

Regardless of its manifestation, ritual must be subjective, even if corporately experienced, in order to express the individual's inner intention. This subjective aspect harbors a problem for ritual. The visible aspects of ritual may become the dominant element, the ritual's reason for being. During Jesus' ministry the Gospels portray a rather constant conflict between Jesus and the Pharisees, and ostensibly the problem was the latter's emphasis upon obeying the letter rather than the intent of the Torah. The problem focused on placing primary emphasis upon proper observance rather than viewing the Law in terms of its potential for establishing meaningful relationships betwen God and man as well as between men. The rituals associated with the various aspects of the Law--such as how far a person might walk on the sabbath, what type of burden might be carried on the sabbath, what should be done to assist a person in need on the sabbath-- had become ends in themselves rather than as means to an end. It has earlier been acknowledged that this portrayal may be a caricature of the Pharisees, but nonetheless the example makes a valid point. Christians are equally guilty of such facade, for frequently external observances of acts done (as church attendance or public prayer) or not done (as abstaining from alcoholic beverages or other social associations) loom larger in importance than the manifestations of love, compassion, and justice within society.

Ritual actions find diverse expressions. During the Medieval Age, for example, many European cathedrals were constructed, with the work usually instigated by a single individual or at least by a limited number of persons. Bishop Poore of Amesburg, England, petitioned the Pope to permit his building a new cathedral. When permission was granted, Bishop Poore selected the area of Salisbury and in the amazingly brief time from 1220 to 1280 the majestic Salisbury Cathedral was constructed. By the very nature of its construction--shaped in the form of a cross; flying buttresses which direct the eyes of the observer heavenward; and ultimately the spire (four hundred four feet, the highest in England), added during the fourteenth century, which further served to point the individual's attention toward God--inner intention was expressed through the cathedral. Obviously what was true for the Salisbury Cathedral was equally the case with the various medieval cathedrals. At the same time, as modern man views the cathedrals, he is not obsessed with the same type of cross-centered theology as the medieval individual, nor is his thought pattern governed by a three-tiered cosmological structure which would give parallel meaning to the flying buttresses or the towering spires.

Thus, a ritual, like a doctrine, which assumes too concretized a form, may become outmoded for later generations.
What was once a majestic expression of faith may become
for later generations essentially a museum!

Sharing material means may also be a ritual action
for modern man. For example, most denominations within
Christendom have been concerned with "foreign missions."
The fact that such giving may sooth a collective guilt
is evidenced by examples which could be enumerated. Money
so allocated supported diversified ministries among non-
Christian peoples, such as medical, educational, and
ecclesiastical concerns. On occasion, however, Black
Africans, themselves products of the mission fields, came
to the United States to prepare for the Christian ministry.
They were equipping themselves for service among their own
people. While in the United States some of these individuals tried temporarily to associate themselves with some
of the churches which had traditionally given the strong-
est support finanically to foreign missions. In some
instances these individuals were denied membership! One
acknowledges that diverse factors contributed to these
decisions during the racially troubled years of the sixties,
but nonetheless such actions indicate that ritual possesses
the potential of becoming an end in itself. It is acceptable so long as my money is sent to Africa, but when the
Black comes to my church I must grapple with the fact that
I have used this ritual act to mask my internal feelings.

Thus ritual is a meaningful expression of my inner-
most feelings, and as such it becomes a projection of my-
self. Nonetheless, the dangers associated with ritual
actions need also to be acknowledged.

A third aspect of religious experience is the mythical
perspective. Brevard S. Childs defined myth as follows:

Myth is a form by which the existing structure of reality is understood and maintained. It concerns itself with showing how an action of a deity, conceived of as occurring in the primeval age, determines a phase of contemporary world order. Existing world order is maintained through the actualization of the myth in the cult.[7]

This definition unites the concerns of deity orientation, past activity but present focus, and the importance of the cultus. In myths such as the Judeo-Christian myth of creation or the Christian myth of the resurrection, the tie to divine act in the past which is cultically related to the present is clear.

Myth is a controlling image whereby ancient man ordered his cosmos and modern man compartmentalizes and thereby comprehends his environment. The individual myths are conjoined to formulate a people's mythology, the entire structure of controlling images by which a people understand existence. Such myths must be descriptive of experience, in some sense explicative of function, and explanatory as regards what man cannot or wills not to explain in other terms.

Whenever one uses a myth, a faith affirmation has been made. In its classical view (not in the more inclusive way we frequently use the word today), myth refers to the action(s) of God or the gods. One cannot prove the existence of either God or the gods, but certain actions and/or activities may be ascribed to God or the gods as a faith affirmation. One could never "prove" to someone beginning from differing presuppositions, however, that God was active in the Hebrews' exodus from Egypt or in the resurrection of Jesus. Both of these events, pivotal in the faith communities of Judaism and Christianity respectively, are affirmed rather than proven events. No one today could take this case into a court of law and prove beyond reasonable doubt that either of these events historically occurred.

With reference to the classical view of myth, this should be contrasted with legend. As myth deals with deity, legend is concerned with the actions of a man. For example, in western tradition Paul Bunyon would be a legend, while any narrative involving suprahuman characters--as the transfiguration scene in Mark 9:2-8 (Matthew 17:1-8; Luke 9:28-36)--is a myth. One should be careful not to confuse these categories.

Yahwism (the pre-exilic Hebrew political-religious structure--see Chapter IV) and Judaism are recognized as historically oriented religions, meaning that history as the medium of God's revelation was accorded unique importance by Yahwism-Judaism. Christianity, as a development out of Judaism, has this same characteristic. This orientation caused Israel to translate myths encountered in surrounding cultures into historical associations. For example, characteristic of ancient Near Eastern peoples was the mythological view that the world had been brought into being resultant to the struggle between order (cosmos) and chaos, with order being ultimately victorious. This type of narrative is myth in that the characters, events, substance, in sum, everything is suprahuman. As a people who saw history as the arena of God's action, the Israelites could not accept such mythological statement. As a result, the Israelites tended to historicize such myths during the absorption process. One example of such historization was the equation of the forces encountered in their struggle to gain release from Egypt with the elements of chaos. In this fashion, the aura of myth is preserved, for it is Yahweh who is the ultimate victor, while the event is concretized by being related to

179

historical occurrence. Psalm 74:13-14 is typical:

Thou didst divide the sea by thy might;
   thou didst break the heads of the dragons on the
      waters.
Thou didst crush the heads of Leviathan,
   thou didst give him as food for the creatures of the
      wilderness.

The mythical sea monster representative of chaos (Dagon,
Leviathan) was defeated through Yahweh's providing the
Hebrews' escape from Egypt through the sea. Now it has
become a concrete, historical event which later generations might recall and celebrate, but as an historical
rather than as a mythical event!

   For Biblical man the controlling image was God; and
there is no evidence that the Israelite ever developed
a pantheon of deities, although there is indication that
Israelite worship was influenced by various deity patterns.[8]
Nonetheless, a pantheon never developed; although this
does not exclude mythological statement. For example, in
the Priestly creation account of Genesis 1:1-2:4a, one
encounters well-expressed myth. Indeed, the myth was precisely what the Israelite sought to convey--God is responsible for the creation process! Genesis 6:1-4 falls into
this same category, and this is perhaps the most authentic
mythological element found in Genesis 1-11:

When men began to multiply on the face of the ground, and
daughters were born to them, the sons of God saw that the
daughters of men were fair; and they took to wife such of
them as they chose. Then the LORD said, "My spirit shall
not abide in man for ever, for he is flesh, but his days
shall be a hundred and twenty years." The Nephilim were

180

on the earth in those days, and also afterward, when the sons of God came in to the daughters of men, and they bore children to them. These were the mighty men that were of old, the men of renown.

This is a typical mythological motif to explain persons of unusual stature and/or strength in ancient literature, as the Mesopotamian Epic of Gilgamesh describes Gilgamesh as being two-thirds god and one-third man. The only way pre-scientific man could understand extraordinary stature, strength, or wisdom was by divine infusion into the human situation. Myth of this more usual characterization is found occasionally but only rarely in Biblical literature.

In a myth no distinction is made between truth and falsehood. When one affirms what deity has done, the veracity of the statement is not questioned. There is, therefore, no value judgment involved. Thus, in the myth of God's deliverance of the Hebrews at the Reed Sea, there is no way to determine whether the account found in the book of Exodus accurately describes the historical details of what occurred. Again, in the myth of Jesus' resurrection (God raised him), there is no way to determine historical truth, namely the details of the event behind the myth. This inability to determine historical truth is fact even though these two myths constitute the primary affirmations for these faith communities. Any myth is accepted ultimately as a faith affirmation.

Another important related concept is symbol, an image that suggests, stands for, or points to something beyond itself. Such a symbol as used here would have basically a single referent rather than multiple referents.[9] The symbol has meaning, therefore, only as it points beyond itself to something else, as a street sign bearing the inscription "Campus Drive" is meaningful only when a street

named "Campus Drive" exists to which the sign refers.
Apart from such a referent the sign would be only non-
sensical juxtaposition of letters.

This referent association of symbols is true within
the religious community, and the sign's referent parallels
the view of myth in that there is no attempt to determine
historical veracity of the symbol. For example, the
Jewish festival of Purim is annually observed and has its
Biblical basis in the book of Esther. Whether the story
recorded in the book of Esther is verifiable history is
not asked as one observes Purim, at least not from faith's
perspective. One may question this academically, but this
is an entirely different question. As the story of Esther
is read, as the children respond to that reading, as
Hamantashen are consumed, these are symbols accepted within the community's practice without concern for or need
to demonstrate historicity. The same reaction is true
within the Christian community. In the observance of the
Eucharistic meal, the bread and the wine assume symbolic
connotations, regardless of how one understands the symbolism. As the sacramental meal is observed, however,
one does not question the reliability of the symbolism.

There is involved in symbolic association, thus, the
same faith affirmation apparent in so much religious experience. This is nowhere more apparent than in prayer,
perhaps most pointedly public prayer. As the community
gathers in prayer, the clergyman perhaps begins a prayer
with such words as "O God, Creator and Redeemer of mankind . . . ." When was the last time one of the faithful
rose to challenge the historicity of that affirmation?
Have all of the faithful been given irrefutable proof that
God is the "Creator and Redeemer of mankind"? Not at
all! The words "Creator" and "Redeemer" are symbolic
expressions utilized and accepted by the community of

faith as affirmation, not as proven academic assertion.

Two New Testament passages give examples of the intertwining of myth and symbol. The first of these is Luke 24:13-35, the Emmaus road experience. According to this narrative, which is set on the third day following the crucifixion, two men who had been in Jerusalem through the crucifixion event were returning to their home in Emmaus, a village about seven miles from Jerusalem. As they walked along they were joined by a stranger whom they did not recognize. Inquiring as to the nature of their discussion, the stranger learned of their dismay at the death of one Jesus of Nazareth, whom many had hoped might be the Messiah. At that point the stranger began explaining how this crucified one did indeed fulfill the expectations expressed in the Law and the Prophets. Coming to Emmaus, the two men invited the stranger to spend the night as their guest. At evening they gathered around the table and the stranger "took the bread and blessed, and broke it, and gave it to them. And their eyes were opened and they recognized him; and he vanished out of their sight" (Luke 24:30-31). Then the two men hastily returned to Jerusalem to relay to the disciples "what had happened on the road, and how he was known to them in the breaking of the bread" (Luke 24:35).

Recalling that the Gospel of Luke was not written until A.D. 80 to 85, we recognize several issues in this narrative. While the story asserts the community's assurance of the resurrection, namely that the relationship of the believers with the one whom they affirmed had not been broken by death, the story more pointedly relates to those second and third generation followers who never confronted Jesus. How were they to be assured of his continuing presence? Of the "reality" of the resurrection for them? The answer resounds clearly--through participation in the

Eucharistic meal the cross-resurrection event will be
opened to the believer, with the result that he who was
not a visual witness to the resurrection event may be
as equally assured of the "reality" of the event as he
who was. Mythological? Of course! Symbolic? Assuredly!
True? What does one mean by truth? Capable of being substantiated by historical, analytical research? Of course
not! Capable of affirmation as existentially true for
the individual or the community? Of course! But at this
point we recognize that we are using "truth" in distinctly
differing ways.

A second New Testament narrative demonstrating this
juxtaposition of myth and symbol is Acts 1:1-11. This
section recounts Jesus' association with his disciples in
Jerusalem immediately following the resurrection. Verses
6-11 state:

So when they had come together, they asked him, "Lord,
will you at this time restore the kingdom to Israel?"
He said to them, "It is not for you to know times or sea-
sons which the Father has fixed by his own authority.
But you shall receive power when the Holy Spirit has come
upon you; and you shall be my witnesses in Jerusalem and
in all Judea and Samaria and to the end of the earth."
And when he had said this, as they were looking on, he
was lifted up, and a cloud took him out of their sight.
And while they were gazing into heaven as he went, behold,
two men stood by them in white robes, and said, "Men of
Galilee, why do you stand looking into heaven? This Jesus,
who was taken up from you into heaven, will come in the
same way as you saw him go into heaven."

The mythical element is obvious with the resurrected Lord,
the ascension motif, and the mystical appearance of the

two figures in white robes. But symbolism leaps from the page as well--most especially the three-tiered universe and what the ascension motif thereby affirms about the resurrected Lord. The community was convinced of a special relationship existing between God and the resurrected one. This association they attempted to express through the Father-Son relationship and through the affirmation that the Jesus of history became for them the Christ of faith as a result of the cross-resurrection-ascension event.[10] In brief, the event as narrated in Acts points beyond itself to an understanding of the believer's relationship to God and to his ultimate future expectation, which is based on conviction relative to Jesus as the Christ and his unique relationship to God, and finally to a cosmological concept which is vitally important for the narrative as structured.

Nonetheless, this dependency on ancient cosmology raises barriers for modern man's understanding of the ascension event which makes it impossible for modern man to relate meaningfully to the resurrection-ascension affirmation unless it be demythologized and expressed anew in terms acceptable to modernity's comprehension. For example, if what is being affirmed is a unique relationship between Jesus and God which not even death could terminate, then this might be expressed in other terms. Using Tillichian terminology, we might speak of Jesus' unity with the ultimate "Ground of being," which statement avoids the problem of the impossible cosmological conceptualization of the figure rising to heaven. Such a restatement does not preclude the necessity of faith's affirmation quite obviously, for who can demonstrate conclusively that such a "Ground of being" exists? This, too, is a faith affirmation, just as was Luke's record; but at least it is not the type affirmation that causes modern man to violate known scientific views of our universe.

The mythological perspective is readily recognized as a vitally important element in both Judaism and Christianity. The understanding of God, man, the universe, indeed of practically all knowledge, however, has changed radically since Biblical times. One thing not significantly altered since Biblical times, however, is a recognition of man as egocentric being. Not only does the Biblical paradisiac narrative in Genesis 2:4b-3:24 portray such a view of man, so too does our modern study of history and psychology. In looking at the myth and symbol involved in the Biblical narrative, therefore, it is important not to reject a thought pattern simply because it does not accord with our contemporary conceptualization.

A fourth manifestation of religious experience shared by Judaism and Christianity is the social thrust of the faith.[11] Considerable attention is directed toward the doctrinal formulation of a faith structure and how that doctrinal understanding is expressed through ritual acts and myths, but the most authentic test of the faith structure is its influence upon lifestyle. Man conveniently makes his institutions correspond to his wishes, thus our institutions are often compromises between faith's demands and pragmatic desires. For example, both Jewish and Christian traditions teach the value of all men before God, a resultant social principle emanating from this being nondiscrimination. In practice, however, faith's practitioners affirm "Love your neighbor" in community worship and vote at their country clubs to exclude persons whose race or religion might not match the club's traditions (or prejudices?). One questions how Christian or Jew reconciles the affirmation that life is given and sustained by God with certain instances of warfare, public drunkenness whereby one makes himself a lethal weapon on the highway, or support of capital punishment. The affirmations of a religious community may have minimal effect on the lifestyle of the secular community individually and/or collectively.

It is frequently asserted that the United States is a Christian country, but this is an unfortunate misuse of "Christian." Life in the United States has assuredly been influenced significantly by Christian teachings and aspirations, in areas such as education; care of the sick, elderly, and orphaned; and certain societal associations such as the importance ascribed to Sundays. Surveying the history of the United States, however, it is difficult to view the nation which experienced such violent internal disruption during the Civil War, brought on in significant measure by the slavery question, as a Christian nation. Even if one wished to ascribe those circumstances to historical accidents, it is nonetheless fact that more than a century after that disruptive encounter emotions still flame around the issue and, more importantly, while the civil rights of the Blacks have now been assured by enacted law, those rights are not always so certain in daily practice. Is this what it means to be Christian?

There is an equally important reason for not calling the United States a Christian nation, namely the injustice to the approximately six million Jews in the United States. If one be tempted to respond that this is only approximately three per cent of the nation's population, recall that in most hard-core Communist countries it has been traditional that openly avowed Communists constitute roughly three per cent of the population! That percentage of the population is obviously not insignificant. Recall also that the six million Jews in the United States constitute the largest single block of Jewry found anywhere in the world, approximately twice as many Jews as settled in the State of Israel and about one-half of the entire global Jewish population. Obviously the Jewish population in the United States is a significant contributor to the cultural and intellectual development of the country, and it is incumbent upon the Christian majority to be constantly on guard lest the majority enact laws, such as the notoriously unjust "Blue Laws," which discriminate against the minority and seek to treat all peoples as being in one mold. This is not a Christian country and never has been.

Another aspect of religious social manifestation lay in the way religious affirmations guide ethical determinations. Protestant religious thought has been quite influential in the United States, one outgrowth of such being the so-called Protestant Ethic. According to the resultant work ethic, man's accountability to God was exaggerated, the rule of thumb being the axiom that hard work assures success. The end result was development of a lifestyle in which people became so work oriented that they could neither enjoy their labors nor life. Coupled with this viewpoint was the assumption that hard work assures success, the basic mentality underlying the axiom that any boy could become President. Thankfully, in the current day when as much emphasis is being given to a theology of play as to a theology of work, we are recognizing that many factors do influence one's standing and progress within the society. Fortunately, the current generation is questioning practically every truism which has governed societal actions to this point.

Finally, however one experiences religion in the Judeo-Christian framework, it is going to have a communal nature. Regardless, the authenticity of the experience ultimately depends existentially on the individual.

Religion does influence the society in which it finds itself, but basically it is the individual within society
who will affect society's direction. In other words,
individuals determine historical events rather than vice
versa.

It must also be recognized that the subjective nature
of religious experience carries with it inherent social
dangers against which the devotee must constantly guard.
First, religious experience may be only a self-gratifying
experience, an ego trip for the individual. While not
restricting this criticism to a single group, this is a
basic flaw inherent in much of the so-called Jesus Movement. These groups, generally characterized as radical
right-wing Christianity, would be judged by many, both
the traditionalist and the not so traditional, as pseudo-
religious, irreligious, or some other depreciatory designation. There are numerous such groups, particularly
strong on the west coast but well established across the
country, especially on college and university campuses.
Among these groups are the Children of God, the Christian
Foundation, the Christian World Liberation Front, the
Navigators, the Campus Crusade, the Intervarsity Christian
Fellowship, even a Jews for Jesus faction. These groups
are not identical, obviously, yet for all there are common
factors, namely a fanatical fundamentalism as regards the
Bible and a poorly developed Christology. Their Biblical
literalism incorporates such basic doctrines as the virgin birth of Jesus, Jesus' death on the cross as payment
for the sins of man, the physical resurrection of Jesus
coupled with the expectation of his imminent return to
establish his kingdom, with all of these affirmations
being based on the absolute inerrancy of the scriptures.
Numerous studies have been made of the Jesus Movement

phenomenon.[12] Generally the participants are authoritarian
by nature or are amenable to an authoritarian structure.
The typical participant has been unable to cope with life
as experienced and thus the seclusion and protection of
the movement serves a useful psychological need for the
individual. Basically the various groupings have little
concern for society, except for their demand for society's
conversion. As one psychologist well expressed, "Turning
everything over to Jesus is a great escape."[13]

While granting that a type of psychological need is
fulfilled for the devotee by the Jesus Movement, it is
tragic to see a grouping of people--gathered so frequently
from among the Blacks, women, and those of low socio-
economic status--who in the name of religion are basically
world denying, the polar opposite of the primary thrust
of the Judeo-Christian tradition. There is no glorious
affirmation of the celebration of the present. Instead
the emphasis is placed on ideas such as the burden of
sin coupled with the necessity of grace, the hope of salvation for some and the assurance of perdition for others,
the second coming, the escape from reality through glosso-
lalia, and the individual's escape into the antiquity of
the Bible apart from the Bible's contemporary message.
In sum, the movement is dominated by an excessively judg-
mental and escapist mentality; or, to use the statement
with which this discussion began, religious experience
may become a self-gratifying experience.

Second, religious experience may be misunderstood
by both the devotee and others with whom the devotee comes
in contact. The single factor best preventing such misunderstanding is education, for education both imparts
historical awareness and helps to clarify on rational
grounds where a particular religious body stands on

various issues. Secrecy and/or acting out of ignorance
can only encourage misunderstandings. It is difficult
for the individual approaching the Judeo-Christian tradition from a critical, analytical perspective to be misled
by emotionalism of the moment or the persuasive voice of
one who would sway a group for the fulfillment of personal
aspirations. Education is assuredly not the panacea to
answer all problems within the realm of religion nor should
religion ever be equated with rationalism, but education
can significantly enlarge perspectives and enable panoramic
outlooks which help to discourage narrow misunderstandings.

Third, the misunderstanding of religious experience
and its compulsion, especially when coupled with social-
political-economic factors, may lead to actions totally
incompatible with the religious tradition. Such actions
stand out in boldest relief when they are massive movements,
such as the Crusades or the Inquisition; and history records numerous instances of "Holy Wars." Even on the
individual scale, however, such incompatible actions are
unfortunately not uncommon, as murders "religiously" motivated. In such incidences an individual senses himself
compelled by God to be the protector of the faith through
the extermination of those who would "threaten" the faith.
We need not belabor the point, for we need only to keep
abreast of daily news to see numerous examples of acts
supposedly precipitated by religious conviction, yet the
acts are totally incompatible with the tenets of the
religious tradition.

Thus the social manifestations of religious affirmation are multiple, and we have touched on only some
ramifications. Religion is an all-pervasive entity; no
aspect of life is untouched by the individual's religious

conviction. This brief survey, therefore, is necessarily microscopic, focusing upon a portion, but a very small aspect of religious faith's social manifestation.

Conclusion

Comparatively ancient and modern man's views of the sacred have been investigated. That a differential exists is apparent; furthermore, it should be acknowledged that modern man probably never lives totally within his age. He frequently relapses into his ancestral past. Such relapse is occasioned by the inexorable ties which bind modern thought to its historic and/or mythic past. A return to the past, therefore, may occur unconsciously, as this relationship of past and present is affirmed anew, frequently within faith's cultic setting. Sometimes this is a nostalgic, purposeful return, however, as the present is rejected in preference for a more simple, less complicated existence. Such conscious rejection of the present is fraught with difficulties; and eventually the individual will be forced to confront his present, unless, of course, he becomes totally and irreversibly detached from reality. At that point, however, we refer to the individual as emotionally unstable or sick.

In terms of the four religious dimensions upon which attention has been focused--doctrinal, ritual, mythical, and social--these are four dimensions for investigation from among many shared characteristics of Judaism and Christianity which might have been chosen. While the four chosen can be supported as being among the most important, evaluations at this point leave a wide margin for individual judgment. Primarily one should be aware that Judaism and Christianity share many concerns, and the emphases in this Chapter have only begun the process of investigation.

VIII

RELIGION AND ACTION

Many factors provide actional motivation for both
the individual and the corporate body. As regards the
individual, one could argue, for example, the importance
of genetic influence or the perennial determinism-condi-
tioning question. Similarly, it is difficult, and frequently impossible, to stipulate precisely the one or
several factors precipitating a group action.

Acknowledging the influence of diverse factors, in
western culture religious associations are a primary
action motivator, regardless of the individual's personal
affirmation. When the tradition has thoroughly pervaded
the culture, as is true of Judeo-Christian thought in the
west, the individual and the group are influenced by a
pervasive cultural atmosphere which sets parameters regarding activities permitted or proscribed.

·   In the United States, and particularly in the South,
cultural sanctions set forth acceptable activities on
the "sabbath." Ironically, what many Christians designate the "sabbath" is not "sabbath" but the "first day
of the week." This not withstanding, the Hebrew scriptures have been interpreted to delimit activities on the
Christian day of worship. While this takes place, the
Hebrew sabbath is regularly desecrated. On the other
hand, in Israel the sabbath is ritually observed through
the closing of stores, public transportation's ceasing

to operate, as well as numerous other ways. What is acceptable is set by the cultural context.

Initially, investigation will focus on the Biblical text, seeking some assistance in formulating ethical decisions. This will then be pursued in some direct application of principle to problem.

Biblical Morality: Principle or Prescription

Most individuals agree that contemporary standards governing the moral decision making process are totally different from those used in Biblical times, either the period of ancient Israel or the early church. It is this assumption, however, which this Chapter questions.

Today the theme of "do your own thing" prevails. This viewpoint, however, is both closely akin to the Biblical perspective and encouraged by Biblical faith. The Priestly creation narrative enjoins humanity to be responsible, determining beings. This is the basic meaning of creation in the image of God (Genesis 1:26-27). Of all the creation, only man is created with the capability of responding to his Creator. Because he is capable of responding, he is responsible for his response. This is what it means to be created in God's image, and thus to avoid making moral decisions is a basic denial of one's essential humanity. This is true whether one retreats from the decision, falls back on prescribed rules, or permits someone else to make the decision. Any one of these reactions avoids human responsibility and thereby denies basic humanity.

Characteristically man desires to maintain his environment in a well-ordered state. As a result, strength asserts itself in the various areas of human involvement-- governmental, economic, military, and ethical. Of all these areas, the influences exerted in the ethical realm are the ones confronted in most subtle fashion.

Subtleties notwithstanding, however, we experience ethical coercion of various types continually. Certain types of actions are defined as acceptable, others totally unacceptable. During the Viet Nam crisis in this country, for example, many reacted negatively to the United States' involvement in that war. Dissident individuals were constantly harassed by those judging such reaction as unpatriotic or even anti-United States. Bumper stickers emerged which exhorted this nationalistic kerygma (proclamation)--"Your Country, Love It or Leave It." The Pauline statement in Romans 13:1 became a rallying point:

Let every person be subject to the governing authorities. For there is no authority except from God, and those that exist have been instituted by God.

It should be noted, however, that Paul wrote this letter when he still judged the Roman government to serve a useful function in the spread of the Christian Gospel, which, according to the Acts of the Apostles, it assuredly had. Might we guess Paul's reactions during his imprisonments under Roman guard at Caesarea and Rome, with the latter, if tradition be accurate, culminating with his death during the Neronian persecution of A.D. 64-65? One should also recall the caustic way in which some of the prophets criticized governmental authority, an Amos or a Jeremiah. These men recognized that because they loved their country they could not leave it! A divine imperative demanded their verbal judgment upon the contemporary situation. Society today cannot afford to lose this important insight of yesterday!

Harvey Cox, in The Secular City, spoke effectively to this issue. He interpreted the Biblical mindset as a powerful force toward secularization, "a historical process, almost certainly irreversible, in which society and culture are delivered from tutelage to religious control and closed metaphysical world views."[1] There is always a pull toward conformity, however, a trend to be drawn into the security of a closed system. Yet, as Cox so ably stated:

The man who has moved beyond tribal culture and its town or bourgeois afterglow knows that he must bear a burden the people of those eras never bore. He must live with the realization that the rules which guide his ethical life will seem just as outmoded to his descendants as some of his ancestors' practices now appear to him. No previous generation has had to live in the glaring light of this realization. Simple ethical certainty, of the sort once available to man, will never be possible again.[2]

This may seem to deny the efficacy of the Biblical thought pattern as a guide for ethical decision making, but it is actually an affirmation of Biblical thought. It denies only the prescription type ethical view which evolved as a perversion of the Biblical perspective. Cox's problem is with the perversion, not the record.

This fact is made clear in Cox's treatment of three specific areas. We will not attempt to relate the discussion, but the following encapsulates his concern: ". . . the disenchantment of nature begins with the Creation, the desacralization of politics with the Exodus, and the deconsecration of values with the Sinai Covenant . . . ."[3] Biblical thought is a liberating, freeing process, not an instrument of enslavement. The prescriptive mentality typical of the Puritan ethic, therefore, is more a perversion than a justified interpretation of Biblical thought. The same judgment is true for much of the western attitude toward ethics.

To understand both the Biblical view and the basis for the perversion, two important Biblical passages will be discussed: the Ten Commandments (Exodus 20:1-17) and the Sermon on the Mount (Matthew 5-7). In each passage, popular misunderstandings are evident. The Biblical mentality was actually freer than modern man has permitted it to be. The relativism characteristic of contemporary ethical thought coincides with Biblical thought, for both acknowledge the ethical agent as the responsible, determining actor.

A. The Ten Commandments

The Ten Commandments are found in two major but differing traditions in the Hebrew scriptures. Exodus 20:1-17 is generally regarded by scholars as the older form and is the one that is usually the referent point for discussion of the commandments. Deuteronomy 5:6-21 is a parallel tradition, although a comparison of the two reveals some important differences.

Terminology also differs. Ten Commandments is perhaps the most common description within Christendom, although Decalogue is also frequently used. Decalogue is a Greek-derivative word indicating Ten Words. The latter is the preferred designation within the Jewish community where the commandments are understood as having been originally brief, terse statements, usually called apodictic laws. When these laws are placed in the synagogue, therefore, they will be reduced to brief one-word formulations (a verb with the negative attached would be considered as one word in the Hebrew).

In Exodus 20:1, it is stated: "And God spoke all these words, saying . . . ." These are understood as the "words" of God, commandments derived from God. In antiquity, theophanies were common and nature was confronted as a "thou." Biblical man was convinced that he heard God speak, and he expressed this in terms of the objective data of voiced statement. Quite obviously, a modern individual could not and would not express this association in the same fashion. Only one who perceived nature as a thou, who affirmed theophanic experiences, and who accepted a three-tiered cosmological world view could have expressed this so.

The use of "law" has been avoided because of modern connotations. Western views of law are thoroughly colored by the Roman legal structure. In Hebrew the word usually translated as "law" is Torah. Torah also conveys the ideas of teaching and instruction, which clearly indicates that Torah does not necessarily convey that a specific act was or was not to be done. The "words" of God, understood as his Torah, provide the mechanism whereby relationship might be maintained between Yahweh and his elect people.

This thesis will now be tested from two different angles--the general view of Israel's covenant relationship, and some specific application to the Ten Words.

Israel's covenant with Yahweh was ratified in Exodus 24. A covenant ratification ceremony is portrayed, complete with an altar centerpiece, sacrifices, use of blood to bind the parties to the covenant, and the pledge of allegiance to "the book of the covenant" (24:7). Interestingly, however, what was included in this "book of the covenant" is not known. For historical reasons to be mentioned shortly, the Ten Words, at least as known today, are not to be judged a part of this "book of the covenant."

While one cannot prove the antiquity of Exodus 19:5-6, these verses convey the basic thrust of the covenant people. They were to be a "holy nation," with "holy" in Hebrew meaning something "cut out" or "separated." Israel was

198

indeed to be Yahweh's "own possession among all peoples," a privilege unlike that granted to any other people.

Characteristically in Biblical thought, however, privilege also carries with it responsibility. Thus they were to be not only his "holy nation" but also his "kingdom of priests." If a priest mediates between God and man, and if the entire nation be priestly, then this priestly role could and would be fulfilled only as Israel looked beyond herself. Her responsibility would be to serve as the mediator between Yahweh, the God of the covenant, and all men standing outside this covenant. Deutero-Isaiah, dated about 540 B.C. during the Babylonian Exile (597-539 B.C.), captured precisely this spirit in asserting that Israel's role was to be "a light to the nations" (Isaiah 42:6). "Nations" is the Hebrew word "goyim" and refers specifically to non-Israelite people. What Israel's role or responsibility was to be was not in question, but the way in which that role would be fulfilled was not specified. It is true that it is man's natural inclination to seek a clear focus on his responsibility, not only on what it is but how to fulfill it. Thus there was a tendency to firm up God's demands in written formulations, a tendency which rejected the vitality of the communicated word and which inevitably resulted in some stagnation within the people's thinking.[4] On the basis of the record itself, however, which affirms that these people emerged in a "word" relationship to Yahweh God, one should be careful in crystalizing too firmly and rigidly the nature of the divine demand upon them.[5]

Reading the Ten Words, one recognizes that a great deal of flexibility exists. The Words speak to both sacred and secular concerns, for the ancient recognized the inevitable association of these two categories of life. At least the first four commandments refer to the relationship between God and man. Man is to acknowledge that Yahweh indeed is God (number one, verse 2), that no other gods are to be worshipped (number two, verses 3-6), that the sacredness of the divine name must be recognized to place that name with its power beyond man's control (number three, verse 7), and that one day out of seven is to be set aside for the remembrance of the deity's actions in creation (number four, verses 8-11).[6] Word five (verse 12) may be seen either as focusing upon a God-man or man-man issue. It is traditionally interpreted in the latter fashion and indeed speaks meaningfully to the responsibility of children for parents in the Biblical sociological setting. This Word may also be interpreted in a God-man sense, for if one acknowledges God as the giver of all life, then proper respect for parents, the vehicles through whom life comes, is a way of ultimately expressing proper acknowledgment of God as source of life. If this view be taken, then the first five Words speak to the relationship of God and man.

The final five Words deal with the man-man relationship. Life must be acknowledged to come from God and thus the premeditated taking of human life is forbidden (Word six, verse 13). Human relationships constitute the basis for societal existence, and special care must be taken to maintain the fidelity of the marriage covenant, the essential societal relationship (number seven, verse 14). In the same sense, all things were held in trust for God, and thus any theft against man was in actuality theft against God (number eight, verse 15). Since all men were created by God, defamation by false witness demeaned all creation and the God of creation (number nine, verse 16). Finally, as a type of summary statement, the Words are capsuled in the final Word, namely, do not covet what belongs to your neighbors and the proper man-man relationship will be preserved (number ten, verse 17).

These are principles which governed the life of ancient Israel rather than a prescriptive ethic which narrowly delineated the proper reactions in all situations. For example, in the sixth Word, "you shall not kill" (verse 13), as usually translated, there appears to be a prescriptive statement. The word ratzaḥ, however, is more properly translated as "murder" or "slay." The sixth Word, therefore, refers not to just any killing but to murder with premeditation. When one looks carefully at the Biblical text, it is recognized that human need for a prescriptive ethic encouraged the delineation of certain situations in which capital punishment was prescribed, such as a priest's daughter who practiced prostitution being burned to death (Leviticus 21:9) or a girl guilty of harlotry being stoned to death (Deuteronomy 22:21). But these were reactions to specific situations, specificity deriving from principle. Exodus 20:13 simply affirms a basic principle about life, but specific reactions regarding capital punishment or actions in warfare were derived from the basic principle. Unfortunately, rather than maintaining a proper perspective whereby specificity situations become outline points A and B under the general principle, all related concepts tend to rise to the same level and the Biblical ethic becomes viewed in its entirety as a prescriptive ethic. This is not the intent of the Hebrew Torah, and it is only the later crystallization which has precipitated this misreading of the basic meaning of Torah.

This same type of development could be repeatedly demonstrated, but the point is clear--the ethic under which the Israelites operated was a non-prescriptive ethic. It was a morality based on principle, a lifestyle which is possible only in a living, dynamic, vital situation. Such a situation inevitably encourages continual clarification, and unfortunately clarification results in precedent and precedent too easily becomes the prescription--that binding force which removes the vitality of human ethical decision and which is the antithesis of ethical decision based on principle.[7]

B. The Sermon on the Mount

Matthew 5-7, the Matthean Sermon on the Mount, is generally accepted by scholars as a compilation of sayings by and/or attributed to Jesus by the editor-author of the Gospel. As compiled the Sermon emphasizes Jesus as a great teacher, the "new Moses," who is able to reinterpret the revered Law of Moses (see especially Matthew 5:21-48). With this view of Jesus, however, it was obviously assumed that the Law is open to interpretation, that it is not an absolutely closed system.[8]

The Sermon was a didactic address to believers rather than to the general public. The ideas expressed in the Beatitudes (5:3-12), in the salt and light parables (5: 13-16), and in the manifestations of Kingdom life (5:21-7:27) all presume the recipients of the message to be devotees. Again, however, a factor operates much akin to the Torah situation, namely that what we currently possess is a distillation of an oral teaching. Even in its present form, the Sermon begins by asserting: "And he opened his mouth and taught them, saying . . ." (5:2). Such teaching could not have been construed as inflexible legal axioms, but this is precisely the aura assumed by the teaching as it was placed into written form with the resultant veneration eventually associated with the written word. Such a reaction could only emerge in a cultural context where the vitality of the spoken word had been depreciated. Now authority was vested in the written word, and deviation from majority interpretation of that written word=Law became tantamount to heresy. Quite obviously, however, this developed reaction to the Sermon differed in its basic perspectives from that of one listening to the oral word of Jesus.

A good example of the legalistic accretion of the Sermon's teaching is seen in the use of the pericope (unit of tradition) dealing with divorce (5:31-32; see similar presentation in Matthew 19:9 and parallels in Mark 10:11-12 and Luke 16:18; for the purpose of reference, the relevant passages are given in outline form on the following page). In Christendom the divorce question has frequently been interpreted legalistically; and, in the process, the divorce-remarriage issue has become exceedingly divisive within the church.

According to Jewish law only the male could initiate divorce proceedings, although in Roman law either the male or the female could do so. While the Matthean and Lucan passages appear to support Jewish law, Mark 10:12 seems clearly to assume a Roman legal background. Whether Jesus actually agreed with the position of the Roman law or whether this was the perspective acceptable in the church at the time of Gospel compilations cannot now be known with certainty. If the latter be the case, to place the acceptable perspective on the lips of Jesus does no violence to the text since the church made no distinction between those words associated with the Jesus of history and the understandings however derived which were associated with the Christ of faith.[9]

In Judaism of the first Christian century, there was not uniform agreement as regards the necessary grounds for divorce. The followers of the great teacher Shammai were more conservative, judging that only a radical breach of the marriage bond justified divorce, something like adultery. On the other hand, the followers of the more

Matthew 5:31-32	Mark 10:11-12	Luke 16:18
"It was also said, 'Whoever divorces his wife, let him give her a certificate of divorce.' But I say to you that every one who divorces his wife, except on the ground of unchastity, makes her an adulteress; and whoever marries a divorced woman commits adultery." (See also Matthew 19:9.)	And he said to them, "Whoever divorces his wife, and marries another, commits adultery against her; and if she divorces her husband and marries another, she commits adultery."	"Everyone who divorces his wife and marries another commits adultery, and he who marries a woman divorced from her husband commits adultery."

Divorce-Remarriage Pericope

204

liberal teacher, Hillel, accepted less serious acts as justification for divorce. One possibility for interpreting Matthew 5:32 is to align Jesus with the followers of Shammai.

The background in the Hebrew scripture (Deuteronomy 24:1) is referred to in Matthew 5:31. This certificate of divorce was a clarification of the grounds for divorce. This was particularly important for the woman whose divorce was not precipitated by adultery, for apart from the certificate it could obviously be assumed that adultery was the rationale.

Reading carefully the passage, however, it is not divorce but remarriage which is denied. Divorce as a possibility is obviously left open.

When the passages are compared, it is evident that there is a major distinction between them, namely the exception clause found in Matthew 5:32--"except on the ground of unchastity." The interesting factor, therefore, and the clearest indication of the movement from principle to prescription, is the rationale for the inclusion of this clause.

Obviously the clause could be interpreted as the church's transforming a principle into a prescription. This would acknowledge that, as the church settled down to a recognized lengthy existence in the real world saturated with human problems, certain concessions had to be made to life as experienced. The church internally disrupted would not be able to survive, and such passages as this speak to the church's struggle for continuance.

The statement could also be read as a commentary on the Hebrew passage. Given the female's dependence on the male in the first-century culture, when a wife was separated from the home her options were few. She was fortunate if she still had family to provide for her; but prostitution was frequently the inevitable result, most particularly if she were rejected by her family because of already existent adultery. This exception clause, therefore, would be asserting that where the marriage had been terminated because of the wife's unfaithfulness the husband could not be held accountable for her later degenerate state.

Obviously this passage is open to numerous interpretations, although none of them remove the problem that remarriage is proscribed. Given the way the Gospels evolved, given the impossibility of knowing precisely the words of Jesus, the contemporary church must interpret cautiously the Gospels. There is another passage, however, which speaks rather pointedly to Jesus' attitudes:

And one of the scribes came up and heard them disputing with one another, and seeing that he answered them well, asked him, "Which commandment is the first of all?" Jesus answered, "The first is, 'Hear, O Israel: The Lord our God, the Lord is one; and you shall love the Lord your God with all your heart, and with all your soul, and with all your mind, and with all your strength.' The second is this, 'You shall love your neighbor as yourself.' There is no other commandment greater than these" (Mark 12:28-31).

These passages, derived from Deuteronomy 6:4 and Leviticus 19:18, demonstrate Jesus' relationship to Judaism. When it states, "You shall love," the verb is formed from the same root as agape. This is a particularly significant concept within Christendom, for it refers to self-giving love, where the love is expressed to the recipient apart from any concern for what returns to the giver. For the early church, there was only one clear example of agape,

206

namely the giving of the Christ by God. Nonetheless, all
of life is to be lived in the expectation of the realization of agape, this sense of openness, giving, and freedom.
Clearly this agape is not found isolated in this passage;
rather, agape is the motivating principle behind Jesus'
ministry and the church's life as it saw itself in the
ideal.

What is implied for the divorce question if it be
accepted that Jesus' life and ministry was governed by
the agape principle? Does this not assume at the same
time that people always took priority over precedent, that
law must give way to love? If this be the case, should
the church stand in the way where two individuals are
obviously incompatible? In like fashion, if an individual
be a gregarious type who happens to be divorced because
of circumstances over which the individual no longer has
control, should the church now stand in judgment and decree
that because one is divorced remarriage can never again
occur with the sanction of the church?

Jesus was motivated by agape, so too must the church
be so directed. When this thrust be lost from the church,
the church suddenly becomes a legalistic and prescriptive
institution where the life of the institution is judged
to take precedent over the life of the individual devotee.
At that point, the Gospel message has become so distorted
as to be almost totally lost!

Relativism in Ethical Decisions

The discussion thus far regarding both the Ten Commandments and the Sermon on the Mount affirms that when
the Judeo-Christian thought patterns are probed and understood a stance of relativism in ethical decision making
prevails. This assures the individual that personal autonomy will be preserved, that the power to effect decision

remains, and, equally as important, that the individual
is responsible for personal decisions. Unless the individual have such autonomy of action, actions are merely
measured against some externally imposed standard. Should
action fall short of the standard, the community responsible for the standard may, and usually will, impose certain sanctions upon the individual; yet the only criterion
for self-evaluation will be external community pressure,
not subjective ethical affirmation of proper action.

It has been suggested by Joseph Fletcher, among
others, that the individual must be responsible for personal action. He has argued further, however, that the
criterion for action must be the Christian view of _agape_,
that sense of love which seeks always the benefit of the
recipient without concern for what returns to the giver.[10]

While the situationist view has much to commend it,
how does a Jew relate to such a position? In the Hebrew
language there is a meaningful covenant word, _ḥesed_, best
translated as "covenant fidelity."[11] This word is best
witnessed in Israel's covenant relationship with Yahweh.
Yahweh elected the Hebrews from among all the peoples of
the earth (Exodus 19:5). As a result of this election
with its covenant, the Hebrews became Israel. Certain
responsibilities were laid upon Israel, responsibilities
often poorly maintained. Israel frequently was unfaith-
ful to the covenant, which should have precipitated Israel's judgment by Yahweh. This judgment potentially might
have resulted in the covenant's termination. Such was not
the case, however, for even though judgment did come Yahweh
consistently manifested _ḥesed_. It became Israel's conviction that only because of Yahweh's "covenant loyalty"
was the covenant preserved. Thus, it was incumbent upon
Israel to seek always to exercise _ḥesed_ in her relationships both with Yahweh and her neighbors.

In the Judeo-Christian tradition, therefore, a combined perspective to guide the situationist's seeking to make ethical decisions might be suggested, the hesed-agape view. One's relationships with his neighbors should be characterized by a covenant fidelity encompassed in love.

The Christian may relate to this, for the hesed perspective is an essential part of his tradition. While the Jew cannot view agape exactly as the Christian, the Jew may see agape defined in Yahweh's covenant fidelity as Israel and Yahweh have experienced covenant over these approximately three thousand years.

It is clear, however, that Yahwism-Judaism has not always been characterized by hesed and that agape has frequently been absent among Christians. This simply recognizes that the primary flaw in the situationist approach is the attempt to use a standard which man qua man cannot fulfill. Because of man's basic ego needs, man cannot be consistent in measuring his conduct against hesed-agape.

The example of pre-marital sex illustrates man's egocentricity. According to Judeo-Christian thought, a covenant association which binds all humanity together is the ubiquitous relationship of creatures to the Creator, Yahweh God. To treat a covenant creature as an object, as an "It" rather than a "Thou" to use Martin Buber's phraseology, is to reject the basic covenant relationship. It is in like fashion, from a strictly Christian perspective, a rejection of the agape thrust. In treating the individual as object rather than as person one indicates that the rationale for action is self-satisfaction. But is it not difficult in such a context for the individual(s) involved to have primary in their thoughts hesed and agape? If one grants this to be the case, then we might affirm that the hesed-agape principle is the ideal toward which one sets

his ethical intent; but one recognizes that intent and
action do not always correspond. The question then arises
as to how the individual might be assisted to achieve some
correspondence between affirmation and actualization.
This is not to deny the efficacy of the ḥesed-agape view,
but it is an acknowledgment of man's basic nature. Paul
expressed for Christian thought the problem when he stated:
"For I do not do the good I want, but the evil I do not
want is what I do" (Romans 7:19). This view was not
unique to Christianity, however, for late post-exilic
Judaism had recognized in man both an inclination to do
the good (yetzer hatov) and to do evil (yetzer hara').[12]
While Judaism did not accept cosmic dualism, since Yahweh's
monotheistic control was consistently asserted, these inclinations recognize man's psychological state. Obviously
problems have always attended the making of ethical decisions. Therefore, checks which can help in making
ethical decisions should be sought; but checks should
give direction without prescribing the action to be taken.

The life of the faith community lends assistance.
Over a lengthy period actions are evaluated in terms of
their results individually and corporately in the community's life. One uses this resource cautiously, however,
for it is characteristic of a community to propagate itself; and thus the community tends to become prescriptive
of actions to assure its continued viability. The individual whose resolutions differ from the community may become crushed under the weight of the community. In this
way the status quo of the community is preserved; and
serious questioning of moral rightness is discouraged or
eliminated, depending on the coercive power of the community.

A classic example of a community's strength would be

the approximate century between the theoretical "Emancipation Proclamation" and the practical civil rights legislation of the 1960's. The Black had all the prerogatives of first-class citizenship as a result of the Proclamation, but theory did not become practice until governmentally law demanded that the Black be accorded first-class citizenship. There were those in that interval who recognized the ethical impropriety of the double standard existent in the United States. There was little that the individual could do in the face of massive community prejudice, however, and thus the problem was eventually handled legally. Those who currently seek to correct historical wrongs of racial nature may still find themselves ostracized or threatened, but they at least now have the protection of federal law.

This one example simply affirms that life within community cannot be the final guide for action. Sadly the church, which by virtue of its affirmation should have been crusading for the dignity of all humanity, frequently stood as a prime deterrent to the recognized brotherhood of all men. Thus the community is instructive and frequently helpful, but community opinion/ directives must never supplant the individual's personal responsibility in the decision-making process. This the individual cannot abrogate to another.

Another source of assistance might be the crusading individual. Again, we recognize that ethical certainty is not discovered here. Adolf Hitler, crusader par excellence during the 1930's and 1940's, led Germany into a violent anti-Semitic era. This attitude, ultimately precipitating the deaths of six million Jews, was sick and demented. Needless to say, however, Hitler could not have been so successful had this view not been adopted or at least tolerated by countless thousands of people.

Fortunately the individual frequently serves as positive example. Martin Luther King, Jr., is a classic case where an individual mobilized a movement and sensitized thousands to the inequities of racial discrimination. In April 1963 King, as president of the Southern Christian Leadership Conference, participated in some non-violent demonstrations in Birmingham, Alabama. As a result, he was incarcerated in the Birmingham jail. A group of Birmingham clergymen issued an open letter which suggested that King's actions were "unwise" and "untimely." While he did not usually respond to such letters, King judged this letter worthy of response. His response, surely one of the classic documents in protest literature, has been reprinted in numerous anthologies and is also available as a separate reprint.[13] The letter demonstrates clearly that King was influenced by the thought of many people, among them Mahatma Gandhi, Jesus and the entire Judeo-Christian tradition, Georg Wilhelm Fredrich Hegel, Henry David Thoreau, Walter Rauschenbusch, and Reinhold Niebuhr. Coming to Birmingham by invitation of the local Southern Christian Leadership Conference affiliate to assist in a non-violent campaign if such were necessary (page 3), he stated: "Like Paul, I must constantly respond to the Macedonian call for aid" (page 3).

Having come to Birmingham, the non-violent campaign resulted in King's arrest. From his jail cell he responded to the clergymen responsible for the open letter noted above. He outlined the four basic steps necessary for an effective non-violent campaign:

1. Collection of facts to determine whether injustices are alive. 2. Negotiation. 3. Self-purification, and 4. Direct action (page 5).

Individually these steps were discussed, indicating how each had been followed as the decision was made to engage in the non-violent campaign.

King recognized both the majority's resistance to altering the status quo and the truth of Reinhold Niebuhr's conclusion that groups are more immoral in their actions than are individuals. As a result pressure must be brought if change is to be realized. Change results from "creative tension," whereby a community which has refused to negotiate the elimination of injustices is brought to realize the reality of existing injustices.

Having waited so long for justice, the time finally arrives when the oppressed must make judgments as to the justice of the law under which they live. Among other significant evaluative comments, King suggested that a just law is one which is equally binding on both the majority and the minority. Furthermore, an unjust law is one which the minority must obey but in the establishment of which they had no legal voice since they were restricted from exercising their vote (see pages 7-8).

Quite obviously existing law cannot be simply ignored. The rationale for non-violent resistance, therefore, is to force those capable of making adjustments in law, which changes would assure justice broadly, to be confronted with their responsibility. The one breaking the law is not devoid of responsibility, however, and King expressed two basic expectations of the one breaking an unjust law. The law must be broken "openly, lovingly" (page 9); and the individual breaking the law must be willing to accept the penalty for his action (page 9).

It is a basic tenet of Biblical thought that time is not a neutral entity, that time is filled with men's actions. King spoke eloquently to this concern. Referring to the White moderate church who judged King's actions

213

"untimely," King stated:

[There] is the strangely irrational notion that there is
something in the very flow of time that will inevitably
cure all ills. Actually time is neutral. It can be used
either destructively or constructively (page 11).

This letter is an intelligent and sensitive response
to concerns expressed by individuals more culturally conditioned than they could have realized. It is a letter
which exudes the hesed-agape thrust earlier discussed.
Indeed, it is a letter which could not conceivably have
been written apart from King's position within the Judeo-
Christian tradition. It is not only a classical representation of protest literature, therefore, it is also
an excellent example of how religious commitment influences an individual's lifestyle and further, how the
crusading individual influences the ethical decision-
making process for countless others.

This letter is characterized by a sense of openness
and concern, appealing for humanity's highest nature to
transcend its baser attitudes and inclinations. To be
sure, one can criticize King's methodology. Is it possible
to act in such a hesed-agape fashion in a basically volatile
society? How long can non-violent protest continue before
it becomes violent? Can a nation built upon violence understand non-violent protest? Can social change be effected
without violence? These are all valid questions, but they
do not remove the fact that King served as a type of prophetic, charismatic figure. He was that figure whom thousands, Black and White, emulated. While the United States
experienced some radical racial disruptions during the
mid- and latter-sixties after King's assassination, two
questions must be asked: Would we have experienced this

214

had he lived to see his cause to its conclusion? Would
the upheaval have been more radical had his temperate
voice not spoken earlier?

A third source of assistance is the individual's
commitment to a Judeo-Christian view of man. The person
confronting a difficult ethical decision must recognize
a basic Biblical injunction, namely that persons are always more important than principles. In asserting this
dictum, one does not denigrate at all the importance of
principles. It is easy, however, for the principle of
"sabbath observance" or "God helps those who help themselves" to ignore the human factors inevitably present
in ethical decisions. Responding to human need must always be the primary motivating factor. To achieve this
goal the individual must often struggle against social,
economic, and political pressures which constantly erode
the Judeo-Christian view of man.

The Expression of Civil Religion

In a national situation characterized essentially
by religious unity, the possibility exists of an alliance
of religious and political views so that both dimensions
gain added authority. In the United States, there is not
a single religious perspective in one sense, for there is
among Jews and Christians considerable diversity.[14] In
spite of this, there is a common heritage and affirmation
which draws the two communities together. Couple this
with the characteristic assimilative nature of United
States' society, and not even the constitutional safeguards protecting against the establishment of religion
have been sufficient to prevent the wedding of religious
and political concerns to form a type of national cult.
"Civil Religion" is the term usually applied to this

phenomenon, a designation first used by Jean Jacques Rousseau (1712-1778) in his book entitled The Social Contract. Such a structure has its clear affirmations-- the existence of God, the assurance of a better existence to come, the positive reward of virtue and the punishment of vice, and very importantly the exclusion of religious intolerance. Civil Religion cannot associate specifically with either Judaism or Christianity, for the affirmation of either would be a denial or a subjugation of the other. There must instead be an ideological assimilation of both, with the resultant phenomenon continually drawing upon the lowest common denominator(s) uniting both.

References to the supreme power, for example, must always be to God. To appeal to Jesus, Christ, or Moses as actor for God would hint too strongly of one faith view.

Where a religious tradition is shared, however, Civil Religious dogma may evolve a religio-political basis for common thought and action out of the nation's history.[15] For example, the movement from Europe to the new land becomes the new exodus, the national holidays (as Thanksgiving, July 4, and Memorial Day) become the holy days of the cult, while national leaders assume roles of historic/priestly character--men like George Washington, Thomas Jefferson, and Abraham Lincoln. The Presidents, as national high priests, continue to function within the cult as they appeal to the Almighty for sustenance and promise the assurances of the "New Frontiers" or the "Great Society."

When President Ford assumed office, he delivered an address to the joint Houses of Congress on August 12, 1974. Several quotations from his address clearly indicate that, in spite of the national trauma experienced as the Nixon government crumbled, the Civil Religion was still very much operative. In his opening remarks he asserted:

Nor will this be a formal report on the State of the
Union. God willing, I will have at least three more
chances to do that.

Near the conclusion of his speech, he stated:

So long as the peoples of the world have confidence in
our purposes and faith in our word, the age-old vision
of peace on earth will continue to grow brighter.

In his final remarks, the following was incorporated:

To the limits of my strength and ability, I will be the
President . . . of Christians, Jews, Moslems, Buddhists
and Atheists, if there really are any Atheists after what
we have all been through.
     Fellow-Americans, a final word:
     I want to be a good President.
     I need your help.
     We all need God's sure guidance.
     With it, nothing can stop the United States of
America.

Robert Bellah, discussing President Kennedy's inaugural
address, noted that similar references served as "book
ends" to the address, placing his remarks in a predeter-
mined contextual setting. Quite obviously, President
Ford, consciously or not, did precisely the same thing.
Indeed, in his desire to be President of all the people,
he extended religious tolerance to its broadest possible
interpretation, inclusive even of the "Atheists, if there
really are any Atheists . . . ." This type of statement

obviously correlates with the national cult, is sufficiently broad, but is yet protective of the cultic high
priest.

For the interpreter of Civil Religion, President
Carter poses an interesting problem. Since he is a pro-
claimed "born again" Christian and a member of a Southern
Baptist Church, one might conjecture that President Carter
would be inclined to intensify the "priestly" role of the
President. It came as a shock to many observers that, in
his acceptance speech at the Democratic Convention in New
York during the summer of 1976, Carter never mentioned
God's name. The inevitable question was whether Carter
was being true to his own nature in this speech.

During President Carter's inaugural address on
January 20, 1977, however, perhaps some clarification of
his position emerged. Avowedly influenced by the writings
of Reinhold Niebuhr, on record as opposing White House
worship services, and determined to attend worship services
at a local Baptist Church in Washington (which he did on
January 23, 1977, his first Sunday in office), Carter delivered an unusual inaugural address. Unlike the typical
"book end" use of "God" in presidential inaugural addresses,
Carter did not appeal to God or to the nation's faith in
God as the basis for a peaceful and productive period.
Instead, his primary reference to the Judeo-Christian
tradition came in the use of a passage taken from the
prophet Micah (6:8) at both the beginning and conclusion
of his address. Carter asserted that he had taken his
oath of office on a Bible earlier given him by his mother,
which Bible was open to the Micah passage which gave the
"timeless admonition" "to do justly, and to love mercy,
and to walk humbly with thy God." His second reference
to the Micah passage indicated his hope regarding people's
reflection upon his tenure when his time as President was

terminated: "That we had remembered the words of Micah
and renewed our search for humility, mercy, and justice
. . . ."

President Carter referred once to the need to "learn
together and laugh together and work together and pray
together . . . ." Near the end of his address he noted
that he hoped that when his time as President had concluded that "people might say . . . That we had torn down
the barriers that separated those of different race and
region and religion . . . ." Apart from these two explicit
citations, however, there were no other Biblical references.

Nonetheless, the humane themes of humility, mercy,
and justice dominated throughout the address as these quotations indicate:

Our commitment to human rights must be absolute, our laws
fair, our natural beauty preserved; the powerful must not
persecute the weak, and human dignity must be enhanced.

We will be ever vigilant and never vulnerable, and
we will fight our wars against poverty, ignorance and
injustice, for those are the enemies against which our
forces can be honorably marshalled.

The emphasis falls not on God's action but on the necessity for man to be about the task of establishing an
atmosphere conducive to the manifestation of humility,
mercy, and justice.   Indicative of Carter's emphases was
his full, complete, and unconditional pardon to all Viet
Nam draft evaders who had not been involved in any violent acts. Significantly, the pardon was issued on his
first full day in office (January 21, 1977).

President Carter's initial words and deeds are not
a renunciation of Civil Religion. The inaugural address

and the pardon may be seen as an advance in the understanding of Civil Religion, however. Concerns common to
both Judaism and Christianity are emphasized (humility,
mercy, and justice), but this is a more sophisticated
thrust than that generally manifest. Drawing on the best
understanding of the Judeo-Christian tradition, President
Carter has placed the emphasis on the importance of man's
rather than God's actions. This type of perspective correlates with the social justice theme of an Amos or the
forgiveness motif of the Gospels. It may well be that
at a later time, as one is able to reflect upon the
presidency of Jimmy Carter, it will be clear that the
nation saw the effects of religious affirmation in concern for and actions bringing about humility, mercy, and
justice while at the same time the nation heard very
little about God and religion.

Civil Religion has undoubtedly had positive effect
upon the nation in its concern for unity, tolerance,
openness, and other such virtues. Because of its assimilative nature, it has helped crystallize this land as truly
a meeting ground for diverse ideas and peoples.

One must not become so engrossed in the positive
virtues, however, that the potential for negative impact
be ignored. As noted earlier, Harvey Cox has commented
on the Biblical sources for secularization.[16] Defining
secularization as "the liberation of man from religious
and metaphysical tutelage, the turning of his attention
away from other worlds and toward this one" (page 15),
Cox judged Biblical thought to support such a process.
Specifically, he suggested the "desacralization of politics" to be tied to the Exodus of the Hebrews from Egypt
(page 15). He asserted that the Hebrews' departure from
Egypt was an act of "civil disobedience" against duly
constituted divine authority, for Egypt's ruler was

220

accorded divine status. This "deliverance of man out of
a sacral-political order and into history and social
change, out of religiously legitimated monarchs and into
a world where political leadership would be based on
power gained by the capacity to accomplish specific social
objectives" (pages 22-23) signaled the end to all sacral-
political rulers. Political authorities may attempt to
gather religious prestige and acceptance for their statements, but it is the obligation of the liberated individual within religious community to struggle continually
against such sacral-political establishment. Civil Religion always involves the specter of such establishment
becoming a reality, a possibility which came very near
to reality during the tenure of President Nixon. While
one acknowledges certain benefits to be derived from
Civil Religion, one always evaluates cautiously its advances. The question must always be phrased: with the
advances toward tolerance and openness, what freedoms
as an individual am I forfeiting? No more with Civil
Religion than with a prescriptive ethic may the individual abrogate to another his own responsibility in ethical
decision making.

Conclusion

Religious association, whether by affirmation or
acceptance, whether individually or corporately, is a
major factor in ethical decision making. While this need
not be a negative influence, the individual should at
least be conscious of this factor lest its potentially
negative effect be felt in subtle ways of which the individual is unaware.

Religious environment, apart from any direct association, also plays a significant role. This role can be
better understood, however, if the concrete demands of

the Judeo-Christian tradition upon the devotee be recognized. In this light, a grasp of the ḥesed-agape injunction is of vital significance. From this perspective individual actions may be measured, for one recognizes that by definition an ethical decision is never an isolated event.

As a practical manifestation of religion's joining with man's political concerns and aspirations, Civil Religion looms both as messiah of hope and as prophet of doom. Characteristic of man's experience, the role which historians accord Civil Religion will be determined by our use of the phenomenon. Will it truly move a nation toward increased tolerance and openness, or will it be only the vehicle by which narrow individuals manipulate people for their own ends? Will Civil Religion isolate the United States from other peoples who do not share precisely these faith-historic experiences, or will it be the ever-expanding platform upon which an international Civil Religion might be structured? Today's Civil Religion participants will determine the answers to these questions, but the ability to respond intelligently and creatively will largely be determined by the degree of religious sophistication which the broad spectrum of the populace brings to religious and political questions. Man determines whether he is free or bound, regardless of the type shackles he accepts!

IX

RELIGION AND THE INDIVIDUAL

Faith affirmation is ultimately individual. Whereas
both Judaism and Christianity have traditionally taught
that the continuing life of faith can be expressed only
in the nurturing sustenance of the community, the decision
for communal alignment and expression is ultimately individual choice and not made because of the circumstances
of birth. This is true even if one live in a situation
where national citizenship carries with it ecclesiastical
membership. A clear distinction demarks merely belonging
and affirming allegiance. Neither national birth nor
family association can supplant existential decision.

The ultimate to which the individual commits himself
has significant influence upon lifestyle. This is true
in both positive and negative fashion, depending on the
nature of the affirmation, as indicated by Jewish writings
such as Job and Ecclesiastes. The servant of Deutero-
Isaiah is also a classic example. Such influence did not
stop with the Judeo-Christian canonical period, however,
as some examples of more recent literature indicate.

Modern men, living in the openness of the scientific-
technological age, function most effectively when the parameters of existence are understood. Biblical man was
no different at this point, expressing his boundaries
through his creation and eschatological views. These
concepts, while expressed in ancient man's ideology and

223

terminology, continue to be meaningful for contemporary man.

Attention will be directed initially to the understanding of religion as a positive and negative contribution to lifestyle. The focus will fall specifically on the plight of the individual as expressed in various types of literature.

The Plight of the Individual in the Hebrew-Christian Experience

The book of Job is one of the most interesting writings of the Hebrew scriptures. Formulated perhaps 400 B.C. in its presently edited form, one cannot assign a singular author to the writing. At least the compiling author(s) was a sensitive individual who had agonized regarding the relationship of faith to life. Being a composite, an outline helps to clarify the book:

1. Chapters 1-2   Prose Prologue
2. Chapters 3-27   Poetry Dialogue
3. Chapter 28   Poem on Wisdom
4. Chapters 29-31   Job's Oath of Innocence
5. Chapters 32-37   The Speeches of Elihu
6. Chapters 38-41   The Divine Speeches
7. Chapter 42:1-6   Job's Submission
8. Chapter 42:7-17   Prose Epilogue

What reactions to life are expressed by the diverse characters in each of these literary sections?

1. Chapters 1-2: Prose Prologue

The Prologue is distinguished by its prose form, since the rest of the book, with the exception of the Epilogue, is written in poetry. The Prologue affirms that Job was truly committed to God, important since this provides the reader with vital information which Job's three "friends" (chapters 3-27) do not possess. Satan was exceedingly cynical regarding Job's true devotion to God, however, stating that if everyone prospered as Job then all would be pious. For Job, Satan says, piety pays!

After a brief introduction, in which God expressed his pride in Job (1:1-5), there are four scenes, one (1:6-12) and three (2:1-6) in heaven and two (1:13-22) and four (2:7-13) on earth. Job's situation continually deteriorated, until his suffering became practically unbearable. It should be noted at the outset that, while suffering plays such a major role in the story, the philosophical-theological problem of why the righteous must suffer is never addressed satisfactorily. The book explains that an individual may have a meaningful relationship with God even in the midst of suffering, a position directly counter to the deuteronomistic view of retribution. Thus the book vindicates the mutual trust of God and Job.

The Hebrew had no theater, and thus in their scriptures there are no examples of plays. Nonetheless, there was a dramatic instinct found among the Hebrews, especially the prophets--Isaiah's visual attempt to warn the people of Jerusalem by walking naked through the streets of Jerusalem (Isaiah 20), Jeremiah's use of a wooden and then an iron yoke to depict the inevitable enslavement of the people if they pursued their present policies (Jeremiah 27-28), and Ezekiel's frequent symbolic actions to express his message to the exiles (Ezekiel 4-5). Thus, while the theater was absent, the theatrical instinct was present. Of the Hebrew canonical writings, however, the book of Job most nearly corresponds to dramatic presentation. It is no wonder that Archibald MacLeish was able to develop the Jobian plot into his Pulitzer Prize play entitled JB.[1]

To this play, with its comparison and contrast to Job,
comment follows.

2. Chapters 3-27: Poetry Dialogue

Following a soliloquy by Job (chapter 3) where the
meaning of existence is questioned, this section incorporates three dialogues between Job and his "friends"--
Eliphaz, Bildad, and Zophar. The first dialogic cycle
(chapters 4-14) focuses on the justice of God, the second
(chapters 15-21) on the inevitable fate of the wicked,
while the third (chapters 22-27) concentrates on Job's
sinful condition. No resolution to Job's problem evolves
from these discussions, but each emphasizes Job's responsibility for his debased state (the typical deuteronomistic
position).

3. Chapter 28: Poem on Wisdom

This poem, which likely originated independently in
wisdom circles, is placed on the lips of Job. It is out
of place here since the type submission portrayed in the
poem only emerged later in the book's progression (the
divine speeches of chapters 38-41). Nonetheless, an important point is made in the poem, namely "that wisdom
far exceeds in value any precious material on or in the
earth, and is completely inaccessible to man except
through piety."[2]

4. Chapters 29-31: Job's Oath of Innocence

Job contrasted his happy past (chapter 29) with his
miserable present (chapter 30). Nonetheless, he continued
to maintain his innocence of wrongdoing. Thus, in chapter
31, he formulated sixteen oathes focusing on various religious and moral misdeeds, in each case affirming his
freedom from guilt. The impassioned plea of the individual

226

caught in the vise of overwhelming injustice rings out as
the appeal of "Everyman" caught in analogous situations.

5. Chapters 32-37: The Speeches of Elihu
      Elihu, a new character in the book, appears in this
section and is not mentioned again, not even in the Epilogue. While both Job and God speak briefly, it is Elihu
who does most of the talking in these chapters. He was
convinced that he could demonstrate Job's wrong to him,
even if everyone else had been unsuccessful! Elihu emphasized that suffering disciplined the individual, purg-
ing pride, Job's ultimate sin. In the total context, however, this disagrees with the Prologue, where the emphasis
focuses on Job's suffering to vindicate God's trust in
him. Regardless, the Elihu speeches could be eliminated
without doing harm to the book.

6. Chapters 38-41: The Divine Speeches
      Following a brief introduction (38:1-3), two divine
speeches are recorded, separated only by brief comment
from Job. In the first speech (38:4-40:2), the focus fell
on the wonders of creation. Job was rebuked because he
made wild and unfounded charges against God. His wrong
was ignorance. Job's response (40:3-5), while brief, was
all that was necessary--his concession to guilt. The second divine speech (40:6-41:34) affirmed that, whatever out-
ward conditions may seem to indicate, God is in control!
Even if the forces of evil seem to dominate, God is dominant over all situations.

7. Chapter 42:1-6: Job's Submission
      The book culminates with this section. Job has not
been vindicated, indeed outwardly everything remains as it
has been. Job affirms, however, that regardless of what

happens his faith in God is secure. The question of suffering has not been resolved; but the basic issue, the divine-human relationship, has been addressed effectively. It has been demonstrated that an individual may have a meaningful relationship with God even in the midst of suffering if the individual will humbly submit to God. While addressed in this wisdom writing in a fashion atypical for Hebrew canonical scriptures, the conclusion is quite typical. Man is finite; God is infinite. Man is the created; God is the creator. Man must submit to the sovereignty of God, even when man cannot or does not understand the factors precipitating his current condition.[3]

8. Chapter 42:7-17: Prose Epilogue

The Epilogue is one of the more difficult sections of the book because, if the editor wished to negate the deuteronomistic retributive view of rewards and punishments, this section does not correlate with his intention. As earlier indicated, this prose section depicts Job's restoration, as everything earlier taken from him was restored. It is possible that the editor, not having an expectation of afterlife, was compelled to depict such restoration so as not to call in question God's justice. Regardless, the conclusion obviously creates problems for the contemporary interpreter of the book.

The book of Job focuses on a Biblical theme, theodicy (justification of the ways of God), which neither Job nor any other Biblical writing adequately treats. Ancient men, like modern, knew the depths of despair when confronting apparent injustice. Acceptance of divine sovereignty was the typical Hebrew attitude, as exemplified in Job's response when he learned of both the loss of his worldly goods and the deaths of his children: "Naked I came from my

228

mother's womb, and naked shall I return; the LORD gave, and the LORD has taken away; blessed be the name of the LORD" (Job 1:21). Radical questioning of God's sovereignty was the exception rather than the rule. This notwithstanding, in the dialogue section of the book Job is depicted as just such an iconoclast:

Why dost thou not pardon my transgression
    and take away my iniquity?
For now I shall lie in the earth;
    thou wilt seek me, but I shall not be (7:21).

Thus, in the book of Job, two possible ways that faith's perspective leads one to react to life's problems are depicted. In the Prologue, in his ultimate submission (42:1-6), and in the Epilogue Job is depicted in the best of the Hebrew tradition, the individual absolutely submissive to God. Through the dialogue and the section where Job affirmed vehemently his innocence (chapters 29-31), however, Job is depicted more as the dissenter. This skeptical, questioning attitude is one of the views associated with the Biblical wisdom movement.[4]

The book of Ecclesiastes is, however, the primary Hebrew canonical writing exemplifying this overtly skeptical mood. Gerhard von Rad suggested that the book was the product of an individual who, in protest against traditional wisdom understandings, resigned himself to his "tragic existence."[5]

The spokesman in Ecclesiastes is designated Koheleth (1:1, English "Preacher"), and the author-compiler portrayed Solomon as author (1:1, 12). While this gave authority to the writing, Ecclesiastes is a post-exilic formulation dating perhaps from the third century B.C.

Its authorship, therefore, can only be designated as anonymous. Possibly the compiler's choice of Solomon was a conscious depiction of the central character as "a cosmopolite who had tasted fully of the world and known its satiation and weariness."[6] Solomon indeed was an individual who by tradition had tasted fully of life, and his reactions would demand an audience. If the wisest and wealthiest man in Israelite history found all of his multiple attainments to be unfulfilling, then surely no hope could be placed in the more limited achievements of others.

The book of Ecclesiastes is difficult to outline because of its lack of formal structure. This absence of structure characterized the period of the book's writing. Late in the post-exilic period, the earlier exuberance of the restoration community had receded because of pressing political and economic problems. While the problems were apparent, solutions were evasive. As expressed by Koheleth, regardless of the path pursued the end result was Hevel (1:2), emptiness!

Making this point, Koheleth pursued various objectives, seeking to infuse meaning into his meaningless existence. He sought the path of pleasure (2:1-11), but unfortunately he discovered that pleasure was a fleeting experience. Pleasure could not ultimately give meaning to life.

Perhaps wisdom (2:12-17), in the sense of learning, would satisfy. This, too, proved unsatisfactory. Ultimately the same fate awaits both the wise and the foolish, for both must confront death. Eventually both the wise and the foolish will pass from remembrance.

It may be that wealth (see interspersed in 2:18-6:12) would give life meaning. This too was rejected, for when an individual works diligently and accumulates great wealth he must at his death leave it to those who will probably use it unwisely (2:18-21). Even if this be not the case, the unjust courts might take the individual's hard-earned possessions (3:16), or wealth might precipitate jealousy among friends (4:4), or the individual will simply discover that the greater his wealth the more numerous the demands placed upon him (4:7-8; 5:11)! In summary, wealth cannot be the elixir for giving meaning to life.

Finally, is it possible that religious commitment (5:1-6) might offer the resolution to the problem? This also fails to satisfy for pragmatic reasons. Such an individual will make vows to God, but man frequently fails to keep his vows. Failure to abide by the vows will bring divine wrath, however, so it is really more advantageous not to make religious vows!

Thus, the response of Koheleth is that none of man's attempts will give meaning to life. He concludes as he began, therefore, with the affirmation that life is emptiness (12:8).[7] Such a conclusion leads many to evaluate Ecclesiastes as the most pessimistic writing in the Old Testament.

Gerhard von Rad suggested, however, that this may be too negative an evaluation of Ecclesiastes.[8] He noted that, even though Koheleth could find no satisfactory meaning to life, he nonetheless affirmed God's control of every event. One of the most familiar passages in Ecclesiastes expresses this conviction:

For everything there is a season,
And a time for every matter under heaven:
a time to be born, and a time to die;
a time to plant, and a time to pluck up what is planted;
a time to kill, and a time to heal;
a time to break down, and a time to build up;
a time to weep, and a time to laugh;
a time to mourn, and a time to dance;

a time to cast away stones, and a time to gather stones
    together;
a time to embrace, and a time to refrain from embracing;
a time to seek, and a time to lose;
a time to keep, and a time to cast away;
a time to rend, and a time to sew;
a time to keep silence, and a time to speak;
a time to love, and a time to hate;
a time for war, and a time for peace (3:1-8).

Koheleth recognized that man cannot by his own intelligent
reading understand his situation (9:11). Man must acknowledge that God determines "appropriate times" (3:14; 7:14).
Von Rad indicated that Koheleth's problem lies in this
juxtaposition. He acknowledges that God controls his
situation, but he cannot understand God's actions. Koheleth concludes, therefore, that the only possibility for
man is to hold himself open to any good which God grants
him. As a result, as man meshes with his environment,
even in life's most mundane aspects, he finds himself best
in accord with divine purpose:

There is nothing better for a man than that he should eat
and drink, and find enjoyment in his toil. This also, I
saw, is from the hand of God; for apart from him who can
eat or who can have enjoyment (2:24-25)?

The allegory found in 12:1-8 may be seen in this fashion,
for by its depiction of the deterioration of the body in
old age the individual is encouraged to appreciate and
enjoy youth as gift of God.

    Thus, typical of Israel's wisdom movement, Koheleth
could not find his succor in affirming the traditional
Lord of history in whose controlling, compelling goodness

absolute confidence for the future could be placed. As earlier indicated, he concluded where he began, on a note of pessimistic resignation (12:8), a position scandalous to the Hebrew mind.

In spite of this, either of two reactions to life are found in Koheleth. On the one hand, he is the skeptical, pessimistic individual who fails to discover any meaning in life. On the other hand, he is, while still skeptical and pessimistic, the individual who finds hope in a passive trust in the goodness and wisdom of God to provide for man's needs.

These two examples drawn from Israel's wisdom tradition, the books of Job and Ecclesiastes, give varying possibilities for the individual's reaction to life. Because of the composite nature of the writings, we can recover neither the "true" Job nor the "true" Koheleth. In both writings, however, we can discover possibilities for life affirming-confirming reactions. We recognize, however, that faith's reactions differently directed can also lead to life denying results. Both of these writings portray the positive and negative possibilities of faith's affirmation for the individual's reaction to life.

This same possibility for dual reaction is found in the servant poems of Deutero-Isaiah (Isaiah 42:1-4; 49:1-6; 50:4-11; and 52:13-53:12). This anonymous prophet of the Babylonian Exile expressed perhaps the most exalted portrayal of Israel's role found in the Hebrew scriptures. Earlier it had been customary to expect that serving God would lead to prosperity, whether on the part of the nation or the individual. Amos, in the eighth century, had countered this view with an emphasis on the responsibility and accountability which attends privilege (Amos 3:2). Nonetheless, this was a difficult concept for the elect people to comprehend fully and to assimilate into lifestyle.

The period of the Exile (597-539 B.C.), however, presented ideal circumstances for Deutero-Isaiah to approach this same problem, albeit with different emphases. Those individuals who were the most influential--politically, militarily, religiously, and economically--were the ones deported to Babylon by Nebuchadrezzar. It was difficult, however, to adjust to this new situation where self-determination had been stripped from them. Psalm 137 indicates the despondency of the exiles in this foreign setting:

By the waters of Babylon,
    there we sat down and wept,
    when we remembered Zion.
On the willows there
    we hung up our lyres.
For there our captors
    required of us songs,
and our tormentors, mirth, saying,
    "Sing us one of the songs of Zion!"
How shall we sing the LORD's song
    in a foreign land (137:1-4)?

As the mid-point of the sixth century passed, however, the possibility for renewed hope occurred for the exiles. Marching from north to south through the Mesopotamian Valley was Cyrus, king of the emerging Persian Empire. As the decade of the 540's passed, the realization that Cyrus would contest the Babylonian power became apparent. One who properly read historical events was Deutero-Isaiah, the prophet who referred to Cyrus as Yahweh's "anointed" (Isaiah 45:1). Cyrus would be Yahweh's instrument of release for the exiles.

But what is the future of these released peoples?

Deutero-Isaiah's interpretation focused on the released exiles as the servant of Yahweh. This was a new
perspective on Israel's role, the specific servanthood
commission, although the idea was earlier embodied in the
understanding that Israel as the covenant people was to
be a "kingdom of priests" (Exodus 19:6). Deutero-Isaiah
helped define what that commission involved.

The servant of Yahweh was patiently to spread Yahweh's
Torah (law, teaching) among the goyim ("nations," specifically non-Israelite peoples) for the purpose of establishing justice (42:1-4). The nation was to give itself
in the service of Yahweh, for it was only in this role
that Israel could find its own glorification (49:1-6).
Even though contemptuously treated by those confronted,
the servant nonetheless brought God's comfort to them
(50:4-11). But it was in the final poem (52:13-53:12)
that the full ramifications of servanthood became apparent. In giving himself, the servant encountered radical
persecution and ultimately death (53:3-9). An unexpected
dimension followed, however, namely that out of the suffering and death came glory (53:10-12). Thus, through a
circuitous and difficult route, the servant had accomplished Yahweh's purpose--many had been directed toward
righteousness.

It was this servant's garb that Deutero-Isaiah saw
prepared for Israel. Yet it should be expected that this
association would be assumed by an individual or a nation
with great reluctance. This role is one of ego-renuncia-
tion, and psychologically this is not man's predisposition,
either individually or collectively. Because the servant's
identity is unclear in the poems and because the role is
not one eagerly sought, Judaism has equated both the nation
and numerous individuals with the servant. Likewise,

traditional Christian understanding has interpreted Jesus in the role of the servant. Precisely who the servant was, however, is not so important as the commission it involved.

In terms of the individual's reaction to life, the servant motif has the potential for a positive and productive reaction. Few individuals can assume this role in healthy fashion, however, for it is easy for the role to become a psychological crutch for the individual which feeds his own neuroses. If assumed out of a sense of divine command and in response to sincere human compassion and concern, however, the servant motif offers one of Biblical literature's most instructive commentaries on relating to life with its problems and possibilities.

The Plight of the Individual in Recent Literature

Archibald MacLeish masterfully used the Jobian plot to depict the situation of an individual caught in similar context but in a modern setting. His play, JB, both won the Pulitzer Prize and enjoyed a long Broadway run in the late 1950's.

The Prologue to the play sets the context, informing the audience that purposefully the play is built upon the Biblical story of Job. Two circus vendors, Mr. Zuss and Nickles, emerge. They are obviously worn-out actors who still desire an audience. Thus, in the somberness of the near-deserted circus tent, their dialogue leads into the play as Mr. Zuss portrays God and Nickles Satan.

Two passages from the Prologue are helpful in orienting the direction and outlook of the play. At one point, as character determination is being discussed, Nickles has assumed that he will play Job. Mr. Zuss responds that this is not the role he envisions for Nickles. The dialogue proceeds as follows:

Nickles: You never thought of me for Job!
              What did you think of?
Mr. Zuss: Oh, there's always
              Someone playing Job.
Nickles: There must be
              Thousands! What's that got to do with it?
              Thousands--not with camels either:
              Millions and millions of mankind
              Burned, crushed, broken, mutilated,
              Slaughtered, and for what? For thinking!
              For walking round the world in the wrong
              Skin, the wrong-shaped noses, eyelids:
              Sleeping the wrong night wrong city--
              London, Dresden, Hiroshima.
              There never could have been so many
              Suffered more for less. But where do
              I come in?[9]

In the conversation that follows it was determined that
Nickles would play Satan. The important element, however,
is the slant this dialogue gives to the play. JB is not
a specific individual; rather, he stands for "Everyman"
caught in the injustices and inequities of life--"there's
always Someone playing Job."

     Once individual roles have been accepted, Mr. Zuss
and Nickles put on their masks and attempt to begin the
dialogue. Nickles, however, cannot suppress his laughter.
The attempt at the dialogue ceases, and Mr. Zuss scolds
Nickles for his irreverence. Nickles responds that the
Satanic eyes "see," to which Mr. Zuss asserts that such
eyes see every indecency, but why laugh at that? To this
Nickles replies:

237

                              It isn't
          That! It isn't that at all!
          They see the world. They do. They see it.
          From going to and fro in the earth,
          From walking up and down, they see it.
          I know what Hell is now--to see.
          Consciousness of consciousness . . . .[10]

This means not only that "Everyman" is Job/JB, but also
that man's existence is his own personal hell. "Consciousness of consciousness" is what distinguishes man from the
other animals. If man be man, therefore, he is confined
to his own hell!

     The Prologue not only sets the stage, informing the
observer that the play is patterned after the Biblical
Job, it also suggests radical differences from the Biblical mind. It has already been indicated that the ancient
Hebrew had no theater. Given the fact that a basic pre-
supposition of the Biblical mind was Yahweh's lordship
over and direction of history, we perhaps receive one clue
why the Biblical mind could not develop drama. Mr. Zuss
could portray God without problem, but no Hebrew could
ever assume that role for himself! Drama was impossible
for the Hebrew because neither the director nor the principal actor could be portrayed!

     In like fashion, the Hebrew affirmed man as God's
creation set in a cosmos created and sustained by God.
The Hebrew could never have reacted so negatively to life
as did Nickles. A homo-centric perspective has replaced
the Biblical theo-centric view. The loss of God's centrality, however, places man in a position of absolute
futility. The Hebrew wisdom literature has a similar
perspective in its view of God's inaccessibility, but
this led the Hebrew to recognize his dependence on the

                              238

"givenness" of God rather than pushing him into self-reliance. In JB, this recognition led instead to the conclusion that man's only hope, his ultimate recourse was his own humanity.

As Scene One opens, JB, a successful banker, and his wife, Sarah, stand with their five children--David, 13; Mary, 12; Jonathan, 10; Ruth, 8; and Rebecca, 6--around the Thanksgiving Day dinner table for a hurried grace before the meal. It is a joyous, festive occasion, and rightfully so it should be. The family prospers, enjoys good health, relates well to each other, and manifests a religious interest, however superficial the religious concern might be.[11]

As the play progresses, however, the Jobian format unfolds. David, now of military age, was killed in the army. JB and Sarah discover this, not through the usual channels, but through two drunken soldier-companions of their son who happen to stumble upon David's home. The parents sadly realize that their son's death was absolutely senseless, for his death occurred as he marched in a half-dazed state and stepped on a land mine. And then they had to discover his death in this fashion!

But tragedy had only begun to befall the family. Jonathan and Mary were killed in an automobile accident equally unnecessary, as a drunken youth in whose car they were passengers slammed into a viaduct at excessive speed. Four youngsters died, two of them their children!

The horror of Rebecca's death, the youngest, was overpowering. Her body was found in a lumberyard, attacked and killed by a psychopathic rapist! Can there be any reason to such a universe?

Only Ruth of the five children remained. But an explosion occurred in town, demolishing an entire block and ruining JB's business. That, however, was the lesser

239

consequence, for Ruth happened to be in the vicinity of the blast and was killed in the explosion.

Like Job, JB was confronted by three comforters--a psychiatrist, a politician, and a clergyman. Whereas Job's friends sought diligently to make Job assume his guilt, JB's friends refused to permit his accepting guilt. From their perspective authentic justice is lacking in the universe, and where all are guilty really none are guilty.

JB has now been completely stripped--his children, all of his possessions, and even his wife left him. She could not understand how JB could express any faith in God's goodness when her five innocent children were mercilessly killed. On top of everything else, JB's health had deteriorated so that he was offensive to behold!

As the play concludes, however, JB's illness has been healed and Sarah returned to him. In the closing lines, they are talking as they try to set straight the confusion of their home.

JB presents, however, a focus diametrically opposed to Job as regards reaction to life. For Job, even in the most incomprehensible moments, man's only hope is reliance upon God. Not so with JB. Ultimately JB affirms that final hope must be placed in himself. The final solution to man's predicament is to be found not in divine but in human love.

Richard Bach's fascinating story of <u>Jonathan Livingston Seagull</u> portrays another reaction to life. Jonathan's story more nearly parallels JB than Job, in terms of outlook, for it is basically humanistic. Jonathan, a seagull who forsakes the garbage scows and the traditional life of the seagull to pursue the fulness of his freedom in flight, assumes this capability to be accessible to every seagull. There is a strange juxtaposition of Jonathan

with Jesus. Jonathan is judged to be the Son of the Great
Gull, works "miracles," surrounds himself with disciples,
experiences a transfiguration event, attempts to instill
in others the recognition of the full life, and is subjected to a type of death-resurrection-return cycle. Like
Jesus, Jonathan was the one for others whose role led to
his being ostracized.

Nonetheless, one should not push excessively the comparison between Jonathan and Jesus. Jonathan's basic philosophy is that you can accomplish anything to which you
really set your determination:

Break the chains of your thought, and you break the chains
of your body, too . . . .[12]

We're free to go where we wish and to be what we are . .
. .[13]

Each seagull has unlimited ability which can be tapped
through the realization of self and the individual's potential:

Why is it . . . that the hardest thing in the world
is to convince a bird that he is free, and that he can
prove it for himself if he'd just spend a little time
practicing? Why should that be so hard?[14]

Recognizing his own potential, each individual is called
upon to assist his fellow to achieve the fulness of his
being:

You don't love hatred and evil, of course. You have to
practice and see the real gull, the good in every one of
them, and to help them see it in themselves. That's what

I mean by love. It's fun, when you get the knack of it.[15]

Thus, <u>Jonathan</u> <u>Livingston</u> <u>Seagull</u> moves along the
periphery of Judeo-Christian teaching and encourages a reaction to life that is at many points similar. Nonetheless,
the final motivation is basically a type of unbounded humanistic faith. Such a reaction to life is comforting, however, for it affirms that man's potential is never more than
barely touched and it assumes that the resources for continual enhancement forever reside within man. Regardless
of circumstances, therefore, man's potential is neither
absolutely fulfilled nor ultimately curtailed.

Albert Camus has been the subject of so many studies
that it is not our design to pursue such here. Because of
the impact of religious affirmation upon reaction to life,
however, Camus' principal character in <u>The</u> <u>Stranger</u>[16] is
of interest. In the novel, Meursault is portrayed as one
totally indifferent to everything in his existence except
the physical sensation of the moment. Only these circum-
stances/experiences are judged trustworthy. Apart from
these, life is essentially absurd and meaningless. To
respond as though life were meaningful would be inauthentic,
and thus Meursault refused to grieve at the death of his
mother for whom he thought death preferable or to show
remorse over having killed an Arab in the intense heat of
the scorching sun.

Because Meursault would not act according to society's
norm, however, he was convicted by this same society, condemned to die for the Arab's murder. While awaiting his
execution, he was visited by a priest.[17] The conversation,
broken by Meursault's thoughts, is interesting since Meursault, avowedly an atheist, exemplifies a self-control
absent in the theistic priest. The priest used every

psychological trick to coerce Meursault's expressing belief
in God, but Meursault refused to abandon his integrity. He
ends up resigned to but fully accepting his fate. Death
held no fear for Meursault; rather, he saw it as a time of
release, a thought not predicated on any afterlife concept.

Camus' novel is a classic study of presuppositional
influences upon the individual's reaction to life. In the
character of the priest, it makes the point painfully clear
that some religious affirmation is not necessarily better
than none!

One of the more intriguing novels of recent vintage
is Ken Kesey's One Flew Over the Cuckoo's Nest.[18] Like
Bach in Jonathan Livingston Seagull, Kesey's novel, whether
consciously or not, is thoroughly penetrated by symbols
and allusions clarified by reference to the Judeo-Christian
tradition. The primary character, rough and raucous Randle
Patrick McMurphy, is a Christ figure who assumes a suffering-
servant role which culminates in his death.

In the novel, McMurphy is met as a conniving figure
who feigned mental illness to gain admission to a mental
ward rather than work as a prison laborer. Upon his arrival,
he discovered a struggle being waged between Miss Ratched
(Big Nurse) and the inmates. Big Nurse sought virtually
to control the lives of the inmates, with little if any
attention being given to rehabilitation. McMurphy tried
to assist the inmates, initially as a type of game but later
in earnest, to be victorious over the domination of Big
Nurse and to become men in the process.

As the story unfolds, McMurphy gradually enabled the
men to recall their manhood, most notably a huge Indian who
was called Chief Bromden, who also serves as the narrator
in the novel. Bromden had been assumed deaf and dumb for
ten years, but soon after McMurphy's arrival he was speaking

again! A victory was in the making, but the "machine" (establishment) could not permit this. McMurphy was given shock treatments to subdue him; and, when these did not bring him under control, he was subjected to a lobotomy. When the swollen-faced McMurphy was brought back to the ward, the inmates could not believe at first that it was he. But Bromden knew. Thus, in the still of the night, Bromden suffocated McMurphy with a pillow because he knew that their fallen leader would not want to live as an example of what happened to an inmate who did not cooperate with the "machine." Then, recalling an early encouragement from McMurphy, Bromden picked up a heavy instrument control panel, threw it through a window, and escaped. He ran for hours, sensing the pulse of freedom and his manhood. Now he would return to his home, enabled once again to live among and relate to his fellows in a "normal" state. He was fully aware, however, that he was what he was because McMurphy had been among them!

Kesey[19] has portrayed some basic Biblical themes, such as the inviolate humanity of each individual. He has expressed excellently not only the way an individual fulfills a messianic role among his fellows but also how one may become messianic for his messiah (Bromden for McMurphy at the novel's conclusion). Kesey has also, however, given a masterful paradigm of the ways individuals relate to life. The inmates, prior to McMurphy's coming, had resigned themselves to a passive less-than-human existence. They were living under absolute domination, letting all decisions be made for them, exemplified perhaps best in Bromden who had become almost totally introverted. McMurphy had a dual reaction, beginning aggressively but then shrinking to passive cooperation briefly when he realized the full implications of his struggle. He could not let others make his decisions, however, and thus he reacted to the system with

a vengeance. He became truly a man for others, one who
realized the inevitability of his fate when he cut across
the status quo of the establishment. He lost himself in
the struggle, but truly he found not only himself but also
helped others to come to self-realization. While not a
"religious" writing, therefore, it is equally helpful to
the individual who seeks assistance in the age-old question
of how one relates to life. It portrays both the possibilities and the results of different courses of action,
while expressing vividly the impact of various reactions
to life in terms of the individual's quest for personhood.

These examples from recent literature are but some
of the possibilities which might be read. One cautiously
interprets such material, for "religious interpretations"
should not be imposed upon the material as normative when
not intended by the authors. Within the Judeo-Christian
communities, however, there has been a chauvinistic attitude assuming all "truth" to be embodied in the pages of
scripture. The earlier discussion of the origin and transmission of Jewish and Christian scriptures (Chapter II),
however, encourages us to realize the significance of the
human factor in these writings as well. Man as man is not
radically different, whether we view eighth-century B.C.
man or first- or twentieth-century A.D. man. He still encounters the same needs for fulfillment and self-realization,
and he still encounters diverse obstacles and frustrations
to these goals. Exactly what these obstacles and frustrations are may differ by content but remain rather static
in form. The radical difference lies in the presuppositions
with which problems are confronted. Non-religious literature may be helpfully evaluated, therefore, both to discern
varying presuppositions and their effects upon lifestyle.
Since religion involves the totality of the individual's

life, every avenue of assistance should be sought, whether
for personal assimilation or not is relatively unimportant.
An individual's faith affirmation can only be strengthened
as hammered out on the anvil of human experience!

The Radical Limits of Existence

As earlier indicated, man not only searches for the
limits of his existential situation, he also functions better under such an awareness. Obviously, only the present
is known; and, because of the variables influencing each
decision and action, the present is never fully known either.
Nonetheless, it is in the present that the individual stands
with some sense of certitude, aware both rationally and by
sensory experience of what surrounds him.

This same type of awareness is impossible for the
radical limits of existence, man's beginning (creation)
and end (eschatology). Whatever is posited about these
polarities of existence, therefore, must ultimately be in
the form of faith affirmation. This is equally true both
for modern man and for his ancient Biblical counterpart.

The creation affirmation asserts that the cosmos did
not just happen. There was an intelligent and purposeful
God responsible for the entire creative process. Such an
affirmation cannot be proved, obviously. Such faith expressions result from a lifestyle akin to that of the
Biblical wisdom writers, namely that the fear of God is the
beginning of wisdom.

Eschatological affirmations derive from the same type
of faith position. Just as creation thought is a projection
backward of faith's affirmation, so eschatological views
are faith's forward projections. Such expression is inevitably based on an understanding of God as creator, sustainer,
and fulfiller. It assumes that what God has brought into
being he brings to completion, thus eschatological

affirmation will express man's conviction regarding God's
aspirations for man and the cosmos. Eschatology is based
on a recognition that the present falls short of the divine
measure, that a morally perfect God aspires that his creation be even as he. It affirms that God finds unsatisfactory
the existence which man has fashioned for himself, man's
corruption of the good cosmos brought into being by divine
action. Thus, eschatological aspirations express both God's
displeasure with man's present condition and God's desire
to bring man into the relationship with the Creator for
which the creation was intended.

Even a cursory investigation of Biblical literature
reveals that creation and eschatology are two sides of the
same affirmation. The scriptural story begins with the
paradisiac account of Adam and Eve (Genesis 2-3), an existence made possible only by the creative power of Yahweh God.
Because of man's self-assertiveness (basic ego-centric
nature), however, the paradisiac relationship was soon
severed and man of his own volition was forced to spend his
existence in a situation characterized by difficulty, pain,
hardship, and reliance upon his own ingenuity. From that
point forward, the story chronicles the seeking God who
attempts to assist man in recovering the relationship earlier experienced--the Law, the prophets, priestly influences, and the Christian would say the Christ figure of
New Testament scriptures.

As one reads the final book of the New Testament, the
book of Revelation, this seeking theme is applied to eschatological hopes. It affirms apocalyptically that in the
imminent future the God of history will act in catastrophic
fashion to bring to conclusion the present age where the
powers of evil and corruption have such a death grip on
the entire cosmos. Out of this shaking of man's existence
there will emerge a new heaven and a new earth, and thus

in this eschatological anticipation history is affirmed
rather than denied. What God intended in creation will be
established, and the creature will live in perfect harmony
not only with his fellow creature but also with the Creator.
Thus, Genesis 2-3 and Revelation 21 stand as creation-escha-
tology book ends to the Biblical story. Attention will be
directed first to the Biblical creation affirmation and then
to some eschatological expressions.

In the Hebrew text, Genesis 1-3 actually incorporates
two different stories, Genesis 2:4b-3:24 deriving from the
Yahwist (tenth century) and Genesis 1:1-2:4a from the
Priestly writer (sixth century). Of these two, only the
Priestly narrative is truly a creation story, for the Yah-
wist account focuses more on the paradisiac situation.
The Yahwist story, therefore, is more anthropogonic, while
the Priestly account is truly cosmogonic.

While it is likely that creation theology was not
fully developed among the Israelites until the seventh
century, they had been assimilating and transforming materials associated with other cultures for centuries. Characteristically, however, the Hebrew purged what he absorbed
so that the end product could truly be called Israel's
affirmation. For example, the Mesopotamian creation mythology has Marduk, the god of Babylon, defeating the primeval
mother, Tiamat, and then splitting her body so that one
portion becomes the earth while the other is stretched out
as the heavens. This myth has analogous elements to the
Hebrew creation story, although quite consciously the
Hebrew creation view has been purged of polytheism. For
the Hebrew, the elements of creation could not be judged
as gods or semi-gods themselves, for they are merely the
stuff of creation used by God to formulate the created
order. Thus the Hebrews absorbed, even if in purified

fashion, and if somewhat reluctantly. Slowness to project
faith backward is indicated by a comparison of Deuteronomy
26:5-11, one of Israel's earliest creedal expressions which
begins with the migration into Egypt, and Nehemiah 9:6-31,
a post-exilic creedal expression which begins instead with
the affirmation of creation.

The Yahwist paradisiac story (Genesis 2:4b-3:24),
which evolved from the zenith of Solomon's reign, expressed
specific views regarding man which helped him understand
this limit of his existence. In an age of intense nationalism, the Yahwist was concerned that man not be overly
exalted. It was emphasized that man (adham) was formed
from the dust of the ground (adhamah) (Genesis 2:7). Lest
there be any confusion, it was emphasized "you are dust,/
and to dust you shall return" (3:19). Man is finite, and
there is nothing he can do to alter that basic finitude!

The Yahwist story clearly moves in the sociological
environment of Israel's early semi-nomadic existence. The
story began in a dust bowl, man was created from the dust,
and the mention of fish is conspicuously absent. The
writer was perhaps asserting personal conviction about the
type of environment in which relationship to Yahweh might
best be preserved.

Unique to the Yahwistic story is the fact that man
is created first and woman last. One must be cautious lest
he read excessively into this; but it is helpful to recall
that in Canaan the Israelites confronted the worship of the
god Baal, indigenous Canaanite storm-warrior-fertility god,
and Anat, his sister-consort. This was a sensual worship,
which presented almost insurmountable problems for the
Israelites. Since it was woman who first succumbed to
temptation and then led man astray in the Yahwistic account,
it is tempting to recognize in woman's secondary placement

the author's judgment on the evil potentialities of woman's
fertility function in the cultus.

In conjunction with woman's role, we should note the
priority accorded man. As the initial act of creation,
man assumed a collegial relationship with Yahweh in the
creative process. As Yahweh created each species, it was
brought to man for naming. This was a significant role,
given the Hebrew's view of the name as the embodiment of
the individual's personality.

A final word about Genesis 2:4b-3:24. The Israelites
obviously had difficulty understanding why his existence
should be so harsh if he were created and situated by Yahweh. This passage sought answers aetiologically. Why must
man work so diligently to eke out a living? Why does a
woman suffer in childbirth? Why do men and women sense a
shame before each other when naked? The answers given
are not scientific answers, but they were responses which
enabled the ancient Israelite to understand better the
parameters of existence and to relate thereby more effectively to life.

The Priestly creation account, Genesis 1:1-2:4a, derives from the Babylonian Exile era; and the self-esteem
of the Israelite was considerably weakened when compared
to the tenth century. A people in Exile need encouragement,
and this was precisely the role of the Priestly writer.
Only here in the Hebrew scriptures is man asserted to have
been created in the image of God (Genesis 1:26-27), thereby
affirming that the species (male and female) is created
uniquely capable of responding to God. In typical Biblical
perspective, privilege carries responsibility. Because
mankind is capable of responding to God, the individual
is responsible for the response made to God.

This reciprocal relationship of privilege and

responsibility was one of the factors of Israel's existence which the people were never permitted to forget. Most especially the prophets constantly reminded of this fact, as we hear Amos:

You only have I known
   of all the families of the earth;
therefore I will punish you
   for all your iniquities (Amos 3:2).

One of the principal differences between the Priestly and Yahwistic accounts is that the former is a timed account, being fitted into seven days. This structure gave particular sanction to the sabbath, thereby assisting the Israelites in grasping another parameter of their existence.

Both accounts are preserved as a testimony to the vitality of Israelite thought. Widely separated chronologically and culturally distinct with the Yahwistic semi-nomadic thrust and the Priestly agrarian emphasis, the accounts complement each other's views of man. Whereas the Yahwist tends to portray man in a lesser position, the Priestly view counters this with an exaltation of man. Beyond this theological thrust, the differential in sociological setting earlier noted is also helpful in understanding Israel's thought pattern.

But what about creation for modern man? It is obvious that the Biblical affirmations regarding creation cannot be modern man's unless the latter accepts the Bible in its own milieu rather than trying to make the Bible a modern scientific document. If one recognizes that Biblical man affirmed the "who" standing behind the process rather than the "how" of creation, then one finds meaning in the Biblical affirmations. "Who" relates to faith's inquiry as

does "how" to the scientific question. The Biblical writers never sought to respond to the "how." As pre-scientists,
they could not have responded had they desired. There can
be, therefore, no conflict between science and religion unless we misguidely address questions to the Biblical text
which it was not formulated to answer.

    If the Biblical creation material be permitted to stand
in its own context, then modern man is free to postulate
any scientific creation views that reason justifies. But
modern man must be cautious lest he attach too much certitude to what is affirmed, for even our scientific theories
regarding the beginnings of our universe/earth fall short
of absolute verification. One must not permit theory or
hypothesis to become confused with fully substantiated fact.
Thus, even modern man, in spite of his scientific and technological achievements, is still at points where the Biblical man was--to speak of creation is ultimately to rely
upon faith's affirmation. This recognition is not intended
to detract from modern scientific achievements. It is a
reminder, however, that one should be cautious to evaluate
differing types of "knowledge." It is an admonition, furthermore, that one expression modality is not automatically su-
perior to another. Frequently "conclusions" have definite
faith orientation. Rather than creating a false illusion
of modern man's radical supremacy over Biblical man, one
needs to recognize the shared kinship of modernity and
antiquity.

    As earlier indicated, eschatology--the understanding
of the end which gives meaning to all time separating the
now from the then--is faith's projection into the unknown
future. As a Biblical concept, eschatology is predicated
upon several assumptions.

    First, the understanding that Yahweh is the creator

God affirms not only Yahweh's responsibility for the cosmos' existence but also his concern for the cosmos' future. Yahweh God is credited with creation, conservation, and consummation.

Second, Biblical man accepted Yahweh as the Lord of history. As such, Yahweh could never be satisfied with the corruptions of the historical process nor with the perversions to which man gives himself. As Lord of history, Yahweh will sit in the role of judge over the wrongs of history and will act to right man's corruptions.

Third, Israel affirmed Yahweh as the acting God, a view covenantally oriented. In the covenant (suzerainty) relationship with Yahweh, it was accepted that the Hebrews were offered covenant with Yahweh on the basis of the deity's prior activity on their behalf (Exodus 20:2). Israel's conviction was that God would act in the future as he had acted in the past.

Fourth, Israel accepted Yahweh as a continually searching God. This affirmation was built upon past activity, for Israel recognized that the God of the covenant constantly sought to manifest his purposes among men and to bring into fulfillment his created cosmos.

These assumptions, plus others which could be discussed, encouraged eschatological thinking. Inevitably thought development progressed along several differing lines at the same time, however.

In Israelite thought, God's creation of the cosmos expressed the cosmos' goodness. The Priestly writer, relaying God's activities during the days of creation, asserted that, having finished the creative process, God evaluated: "And God saw everything that he had made, and behold, it was very good" (Genesis 1:31). Internalization of this judgment meant that the Hebrew focused his attention on this life rather than on the future. There was no desire to escape life, nor was physical existence seen as bondage. Life was given by God, was therefore good, and was to be lived to the full.

Nonetheless, man's desire for permanence inevitably expressed itself. During the patriarchal period, attention focused on the offspring, with the first-born male child especially important to propagate the father's name and bloodline. On the analogy of the Mesopotamian Arallu, the Biblical concept of Sheol developed. This was a sub-terranean abode for all of the dead, totally apart from any ethical factor. It was not a destiny to be anticipated, as loss of personal identity and the possibility of Yahweh's absence were both fears associated with Sheol.

The prophets developed the "day of Yahweh" as an eschatological concept. The day of Yahweh was originally conceived as a time of judgment upon the enemies of Yahweh's people, reinterpreted by Amos to include also the judgment of Israel-Judah, but post-exilically reverted to only judgment upon the enemies.

Apocalypticism arose in the period roughly 200 B.C. to A.D. 200. This thought pattern evolved during a period of military, economic, political, and religious oppression. When the situation became so corrupt that it was assumed that not even God could bring the glorious future out of this evil present, cataclysmic judgment by God was seen as the only hope. This anticipation could not be discussed openly, however, during a period of persecution. The message was conveyed to the faithful, therefore, in written form and in a purposefully cryptic style, in such fashion as to exhort continued faithfulness and to give assurance that Yahweh's decisive action is imminent. In the Hebrew scriptures, the book of Daniel is the best representation of this literary genre, while in the New Testament the book of Revelation is the prime example.

Apocalyptic thinking is perhaps the sharpest eschatological link between the Old and New Testaments. The anticipated kingdom of God, expressed by Jesus in both word and deed, awaits the coming of God's designated figure for its completion. Jesus seems to have been influenced by this thought pattern, and most assuredly Paul was. Both resurrection affirmation and son-of-man eschatological views have their roots in apocalyptic thought.

This brief survey, inadequate as a summary of Jewish-Christian thought, is sufficient to clarify that eschatological thought was built upon faith affirmations and developed in both Jewish and Christian circles. As faith's projection forward, one cannot judge the thought right or wrong, true or false. One can only survey the material, recognize the presuppositions, and seek to relate the meaning to a contemporary setting.

While normally used with religious connotations, eschatology does not necessarily restrict itself to religious applications. Broadly speaking, whenever a vision for the future colors activities between "now" and "then," that thought assumes eschatological overtones. John F. Kennedy's "New Frontier" or Lyndon B. Johnson's "Great Society" both held out such anticipation for the future and thereby motivated conduct in the present. We should also recall the earlier discussion of civil religion (Chapter VIII) where Biblical motifs are used to influence sociopolitical actions and ambitions. This might present no problems at all, but it could lead not only to radical perversions of the particular faith structure's thought pattern but also to an abuse of religious affirmation to fulfill personal or national ambitions. The public must ever be on guard to prevent the exploitation of commonly held ideas by religious charlatans and political opportunists. This is particularly important in the realm of eschatology since man by nature wants so desperately to believe that a better day is coming.

Conclusion

Universal to the experience of mankind is the fact that life frequently seems harsh and abrasive, frustrating of aspirations rather than being conducive to fulfillment. Also common to mankind's experience, however, is the demand to determine personal reactions to life. It is this decision-making process which lifts man above the other animals with whom he shares earth space. Were man simply to be buffeted about by life's encounters, he would in essence be reacting at a point less than his basic humanity.

The materials investigated have been viewed only briefly. It is not assumed that any writing used has been developed as thoroughly as possible. What is apparent, however, is that both Biblical and non-Biblical writings offer valuable assistance to the individual determining reactions to life's problems and possibilities.

From the survey of materials included, two primary conclusions may be expressed. One, presuppostions doubtlessly differ for the Biblical and non-Biblical writers, but regardless of presuppositions the focus may often be analogous. For example, the author of the servant poems in Deutero-Isaiah and Ken Kesey write out of radically differing backgrounds and presuppositions. The role for the servant and McMurphy are analogous, however, as are the results of having assumed the role. Second, even for writers not overtly motivated by religious thought at all, the cultural background of western existence frequently so permeates the product that the plot and characters would be unintelligible apart from an awareness of western culture. JB is much more emphatic because of some knowledge of the book of Job. Jonathan Livingston Seagull is filled

with a wealth of meaning for the individual having some
awareness of the Judeo-Christian tradition. In like fashion, The Stranger strikes the reader so vividly not only
because of the strength of its plot and characters but also
because of its primary character's deviation from Judeo-
Christian expectation of the individual. The book would
not be nearly so powerful apart from this contrast.

Recognizing the harsh blows often struck by life, the
individual needs every assistance he can muster in responding to life so as to affirm and confirm his own humanity.
Biblical materials are an obvious resource, but the individual of Judeo-Christian orientation should never assume
that his assistance possibilities are restricted to the
Bible. As an analytical, determining being, the individual
must respond to life; and any reactions to life, whether
in agreement or not with one's personal presuppositions,
help to clarify and refine one's responses. Being human
involves existential decisions, and fallible creatures that
we are we need every resource at our disposal to make such
decisions creatively and effectively.

In the context of this Chapter, we have suggested
that individuals operate most creatively and effectively
when the parameters of existence are recognized, even if
not understood fully. Biblical man expressed his outer
limits in terms of creation and eschatology; and, however
these phenomena be stated, they were affirmed to be directed
solely by God. Because God is both beginning and end, man
cannot ultimately determine either his genesis or his demise or destiny, as the case may be.

This does not relegate man's actions to relative
unimportance, however, for Biblical man did recognize that
God, regardless of his ultimate sovereignty as Lord of
history, was influenced (but not determined) by the course
of man's actions. Thus, man attempted to direct his actions

257

so as to orient himself toward God's purposes and goals for history as understood by man.

There is a danger in this, namely that man sometimes structures his actions to live primarily for the future, whether historical or suprahistorical, rather than for the present. Assuredly this was the error of the medieval church. It has been our emphasis, however, that this is one of the helpful corrections which Christianity can draw from Judaism, for the latter has almost consistently recognized the importance of man's present orientation.

Modern man may understand his existential parameters differently from Biblical man, but nonetheless the affirmations embedded in Biblical thought can be helpful starting points for modern man as he seeks to comprehend his own limitations. Biblical man's recognition of his humanity and the limitations of his finitude still stand as helpful correctives to an undue exaltation of man's potential. However one understands the concept of God, and few today accept fully the ancient Biblical views, it is axiomatic that the surest path to failure in dealing with our own humanity is absolute reliance upon that humanity with its inexorable "progress" orientation.

So where does one go from here? That is the individual's choice. The plight of the individual in both Biblical and non-Biblical literature is his inability to escape from the limitations of his own humanity. How one deals with this is personal decision, and therein lies the blessing and bane of being human. All things considered, however, who would want the situation to be different?

Conclusions have been formulated with each Chapter, and it would not be helpful to reiterate these statements. More constructively, some bases for positions taken will be emphasized with some indication of implications deriving therefrom.

Pivotal to the investigation has been a view of religion characterized by breadth and depth, affirming man's responsible nature and God's depth of being which expands beyond the anthropomorphisms of Biblical thought. Religion has been recognized as a pivotal aspect of an individual's existence, conditioning his reactions to all aspects of life.

Basic to the investigation is acknowledgment that religious language is necessarily symbolic and mythical. On the one hand, this means that literalization of Biblical literature/thought is both a refusal to take the material seriously and an automatic hindrance to depth understanding. On the other hand, this necessarily indicates that two individuals seeking to communicate regarding religious truths must first clarify the presuppositions with which each approaches the subject. Until presuppositions are at least understood, there can never be agreement on issues. Presuppositional agreement does not guarantee consensus, but apart from such there can be no agreement, or perhaps even helpful dialogue.

Given the unlimited possibilities for seeking and interpreting religious truths, religious dogmatism is the characteristic of either the uninformed or the domineering. This does not mean, however, that all opinions are equally valid. Certainly any judgment must be held up to the critical evaluative scrutiny which is informed by every available historical-literary investigative tool. Breadth of awareness of the Judeo-Christian tradition impresses one with the flexibility and openness of the tradition rather than its inflexibility and narrowness. One should always be cautious of the individual overly enthusiastic to make others in his own image!

Significant emphasis has been given to history. In part this has been done because Judaism and Christianity are both historically oriented faith structures, not just existing historically but taking history seriously. It is also the case, however, that a study of history opens windows into men's minds, demonstrating clearly the altruistic activities to which man might rise as well as the sheer demonic potential of his actions. One cannot study history with any seriousness and come away either totally dejected by man's irreversible baseness or exalted by man's unerring human compassion and concern. History helps us to recognize and to accept man for his multifaceted humanity.

During this study many traditional ideas have been questioned. Tradition should not be discarded simply because it is tradition, but any individual should be willing to rethink heritage. When one truly fulfills one's destiny as homo sapiens, perhaps only one thing is certain, namely that a human is a thinking, reasoning being. If one accepts as normative the passive transmission of tradition apart from existential involvement, in essence one denies a basic and vital aspect of humanity.

Deutero-Isaiah expressed in painful clarity the concept of the "suffering servant," which Christianity has applied to Jesus as "the man for others." If one would find the ultimate meaning of human existence, it will be discovered as concepts such as that of the "suffering servant" are assimilated to personal lifestyle, as Deutero-Isaiah enjoined Israel and as church tradition has encouraged the Christian. Ego-renouncing roles are difficult to assume, however, for just as renunciation of ego-centric value systems is recognized as the demand upon the individual so the individual is aware that the result which can be expected is community rejection and perhaps persecution.

Western culture has a glorious past and can supposedly anticipate a continued future development. In terms of moral sensitivity, however, one wonders about the future. For example, so long as the majority of participants in western culture were unaware of the atrocious treatment of Jews by Christians throughout the church's history, this repression did not act so much as a cancer upon western culture. Is it possible for western culture to continue to be eaten away from within by anti-Semitism and still survive? In western culture we must reach the point where we react to individuals as persons, not as Jews or Christians, Black or White, male or female. Unless we can accept the integrity of the "other" or "thou" confronted, regardless of race, creed, or color, one wonders how long before the moral decay will begin to show serious impact on western culture.

It is perhaps true, however, that before the relationship of Christians and Jews can be addressed effectively Christianity needs to do some internal self-evaluation. Christians need to make peace among themselves, recognizing and accepting their differences. While fortunately the problem has been somewhat alleviated, the individual chauvinistic attitudes of various Christian denominations of an

261

earlier period created almost insurmountable problems on
mission fields. For the individual who was not Christian,
it was practically unfathomable why four or five different
Christian churches were established in a given locale as
if the churches were "contesting" for the non-Christian
folk. One cannot claim, however, that the age of ecumen-
icity has arrived!

With the recent emphasis on Indian affairs, we are
discovering that a similar confusion and uncertainty existed
also among the Indians. The Nez Percé tribe, located in
the northwest, was confronted in 1873 with the possibility
of establishing schools on their land; but Chief Joseph
rejected the offer on the basis that schools would lead
to churches. The Chief explained his objection to establishing churches as follows:

"They will teach us to quarrel about God," Joseph said.
"We do not want to learn that. We may quarrel with men
sometimes about things on this earth, but we never quarrel
about God. We do not want to learn that."[1]

Christians must learn that all Christians seek the same
objectives and that persons are not to be contested; persons are to be affirmed and confirmed.

Religious conviction is a factor in an individual's
ethical decision making. While this has probably been
sufficiently discussed, let it be noted only that religious
conviction may lead either to a humanizing ethic or to a
radically repressive ethic. Persons who have experienced
the liberation of the Judeo-Christian tradition must ever
be on guard lest an attempt to establish a prescriptive,
regulative ethic be successful. Establishment of such an
ethic negates a part of each individual's humanity who falls
subject to such legislated morality.

In the United States, commonly shared Judeo-Christian traditions have encouraged a union of religious and political concerns and aspirations. If held in proper balance, this joining of cultural experiences can serve to enhance human achievement. Unfortunately, however, this union potentially may be used for exploitation by persons who do not possess stellar ethical scruples! The primary check on the assimilation must derive from those who recognize the potentially oppressive nature of a divinely legitimated political structure.

Each individual existentially faces the reality of old age, sickness, and death in solitary fashion. Regardless, he can receive encouragement, sustenance, and even guidance from both Biblical and non-Biblical materials. The individual is assisted simply by recognizing that his situation is not unique, that all humanity shares a common plight deriving from their finitude. This recognition need not lead to despair, indeed it may encourage authentic encounter with life's potentials. At best it leads to a recognition that the individual does largely determine what he encounters and the nature of the experience. Defeatism, therefore, is probably the least defensible reaction. Defeatism breeds despair, but an enthusiastic encounter with life which is determined to draw from life's possibilities the fulness of human experience will be rewarded with an affirmation of one's essential humanity.

We conclude as we began, with the working definition of religion which has guided our pursuit:

Religion is affirmation or acceptance on the part of an individual and/or community of an ultimate commitment which affects the totality of lifestyle (beliefs, emotions, and actions), which ultimate commitment serves to encourage meaningful relationship(s) with a transcendent presence

and/or man, to assist the individual's integration into
his existential situation, and to enable the individual
and/or community to find meaning in/for his/their existence.

<u>NOTES</u>

<u>Excerpt</u> <u>from</u> NATHAN THE WISE

1. Gotthold Ephraim Lessing, <u>Nathan</u> <u>the</u> <u>Wise</u>, trans. Bayard Quincy Morgan (New York: Frederick Ungar Publishing Co., 1955), p. 118 (Act IV, Scene 7, lines 144-147).

<u>Introduction</u>

1. Edward Cell, ed., <u>Religion</u> <u>and</u> <u>Western</u> <u>Culture</u> (New York: Abingdon Press, 1967), p. 7. This anthology is an excellent collection of readings focusing on theories relating religion and culture.

2. Christopher Dawson, <u>Religion</u> <u>and</u> <u>the</u> <u>Rise</u> <u>of</u> <u>Western</u> <u>Culture</u> (Garden City, New York: Doubleday & Company, Inc., 1958), p. 15.

3. Dawson, <u>Religion</u> <u>and</u> <u>the</u> <u>Rise</u> <u>of</u> <u>Western</u> <u>Culture</u>, p. 14.

4. Dawson, <u>Religion</u> <u>and</u> <u>the</u> <u>Rise</u> <u>of</u> <u>Western</u> <u>Culture</u>, p. 22.

<u>I. What is Religion?</u>

1. Paul Tillich, <u>Christianity</u> <u>and</u> <u>the</u> <u>Encounter</u> <u>of</u> <u>the</u> <u>World</u> <u>Religions</u> (New York: Columbia University Press, 1963), pp. 4-5.

2. Spokesman-author in the book of Ecclesiastes.

3. See Luther H. Harshbarger and John A. Mourant, <u>Judaism</u> <u>and</u> <u>Christianity</u> (Boston: Allyn and Bacon, Inc.,

1968), pp. 11-13.

4. Monasticism has always been foreign to Judaism.

5. Kenneth Scott Latourette, A History of Christianity (New York: Harper & Brothers, 1953), p. 222; see also broader coverage pp. 217, 221-235.

6. Some refer to this as the amphictyony, as characteristic in the Greek City States.

7. Published by Harper & Brothers in the "Religious Perspectives" Series and edited by Ruth Nanda Anshen in 1961. The book was also released as a Harper Torchbook in 1965.

8. In Proverbs 28:20, for example, what we today might be inclined to call a "religious man" was designated as a "faithful man."

9. F. D. Gealy, "Religion," The Interpreter's Dictionary of the Bible, ed. G. A. Buttrick (New York: Abingdon Press, 1962), IV, 32.

10. Transition initiated with the Babylonian Exile, which is dated 597-539 B.C.

11. This passage, designated the Shema in Hebrew tradition, is the single most important passage for Judaism. The Shema is constituted of three parts: Deuteronomy 6:4-9 and 11:13-21; Numbers 15:37-41.

12. This translation follows the suggestion of the late H. H. Rowley in The Re-Discovery of the Old Testament (Philadelphia: The Westminster Press, 1946), p. 156.

13. John A. T. Robinson's Chapter "Worldly Holiness" in Honest to God (Philadelphia: The Westminster Press, 1963), pp. 84-104, is an excellent statement of this problem.

14. Sigmund Freud, The Future of an Illusion, trans. W. D. Robson-Scott, rev. and ed. James Strachey (New York: Doubleday & Company, Inc., 1964), p. 78. See also pp. 77-79.

15. The process of scriptural evolution, transmission, and canonization is discussed in Chapter II.

16. <u>Revolt</u> <u>Against</u> <u>the</u> <u>Faithful</u>, by Robert S. Alley (New York: J. B. Lippincott Company, 1970), pp. 21-39, gives a good approach to Jesus as interpreter of scripture.

II. The <u>Hebrew-Christian</u> <u>Scriptures</u>: <u>Origin</u> <u>and</u> <u>Trans-mission</u>

1. See Sigmund Freud, <u>The</u> <u>Future</u> <u>of</u> <u>an</u> <u>Illusion</u>, trans. W. D. Robson-Scott, rev. and ed. James Strachey (New York: Doubleday & Company, Inc., 1964).

2. Quite obviously Protestant Christians have not so interpreted the passage. The thrust of the passage has been diverted more toward that of a faith prototype, plus there is considerable questioning of the historicity of the passage on the part of Protestant Christian scholars. It should be noted that the doctrine of papal infallibility was enunciated by the First Vatican Council in 1870.

3. It is interesting to note that the Protestant Reformation had as a chief concern the opening of scripture to all men. Quite unexpectedly, however, this opening process has resulted in Biblical critical methodologies which have in many circles had the effect of questioning the importance of the scriptures.

4. One should recognize that the historical-critical approach has had little effect in the more traditional Jewish circles (Orthodox Jews and many Conservative Jews) or in the more conservative Christian groups.

5. See Chapter III for a discussion of Biblical criticism.

6. The differences between these two accounts are not to be ignored, for it is not as though Matthew and Luke stand uniformly together to refute the Gospel of John. They

differ in the annunciation procedure, the role of Joseph, the visitors to the birthplace, the home of Mary and Joseph, and the genealogies. For a brief but effective treatment, see Francis Wright Beare, The Earliest Records of Jesus (New York: Abingdon Press, 1962), pp. 29-36.

7. We will regularly use the rubric of Hebrew and Greek manuscripts/scriptures to refer to the Old Testament and New Testament texts. With the exception of minor Aramaic sections, the Jewish scriptures are exclusively found in the Hebrew materials, while the Christian scriptures include both the Jewish Hebrew materials plus those Greek specifically Christian writings. One must recognize that the Jew might be justifiably offended by the designations "Old Testament" and "New Testament," for such designations obviously smack of Christian chauvinism.

8. See John Bright, A History of Israel, sec. ed. (Philadelphia: The Westminster Press, 1972), p. 289, who states a child "presumably to the royal house."

9. See Johannes P. E. Pedersen, Israel, Its Life and Culture, III-IV, trans. Miss Annie I. Fausbøll (London: Oxford University Press, 1940), p. 555.

10. Also designated as the Pentateuch ("the five scrolls"), the Law (one of the meanings of the Hebrew word Torah), and the Five Books of Moses.

11. The division of Samuel and Kings into two books each was a later action.

12. The Book of the Twelve is composed of the shorter prophetic writings beginning with Hosea and concluding with Malachi. Although these are often called the "Minor Prophets," this is an unfortunate designation. The distinction between the writings comprising the Book of the Twelve and the three larger prophetic writings must be understood as quantitative rather than qualitative.

13. Included in this account is only a skeletal

description of some of the more important steps in the process.

14. See The New Testament (Garden City, N.Y.: Double-day & Company, Inc., 1956), especially the "Preface," pp. vii-x.

III. The Biblical Text: Encounter with Modernity

1. Kendrick Grobel, "Biblical Criticism," The Interpreter's Dictionary of the Bible, ed. G. A. Buttrick (New York: Abingdon Press, 1962), I, 411. See entire article, pp. 407-413, plus S. J. De Vries, "Biblical Criticism, History of," The Interpreter's Dictionary of the Bible, ed. G. A. Buttrick (New York: Abingdon Press, 1962), I, 413-418.

2. When the vowels were added in the sixth and seventh centuries, the sacredness of the divine name had caused it to cease being pronounced centuries earlier. As a result, no one knew how to pronounce the sacred tetragrammaton. The Masoretes, who were responsible for "pointing" (adding the vowels) the text, assumed a close association between the word substituted for the sacred name, Adonai (My Lord), and the word itself. Thus the consonants of the sacred name and the vowels of Adonai were conjoined to create the medieval hybrid, Jehovah.

3. Some would see either editing by other "J" editors or indications of other sources in this material.

4. The view of Deuteronomy's emergence and transmission is essentially that of Gerhard von Rad, Studies in Deuteronomy, trans. David Stalker, "Studies in Biblical Theology," No. 9 (London: SCM Press, Ltd., 1953).

5. This analysis agrees with that of J. Coert Rylaarsdam, "The Book of Exodus" (Introduction and Exegesis), The Interpreter's Bible, ed. G. A. Buttrick

(Nashville: Abingdon Press, 1952), I, 903, except that I have assigned vs. 33 entirely to J and all of vs. 35 to P for clarity.

6. The word "Synoptic" derives from root words meaning "to view alike" and refers to the way the first three Gospels follow a common outline, record so many similar events and sayings, and frequently preserve verbatim accounts of Jesus' actions and words.

7. See the article "Biblical Criticism, History of" by S. J. De Vries in The Interpreter's Dictionary of the Bible, I, especially pp. 415 and 417.

8. An excellent although brief introduction to the problems of Mark's Gospel may be found in D. E. Nineham, Saint Mark, "The Pelican Gospel Commentaries," ed. D. E. Nineham (Baltimore: Penguin Books, 1963).

9. The student would find helpful the brief but perceptive analysis by Wayne G. Rollins, The Gospels: Portraits of Christ (Philadelphia: The Westminster Press, 1963).

10. See Rudolf Bultmann, The History of the Synoptic Tradition, trans. John Marsh (New York: Harper & Row, 1963). Of major importance see also Martin Dibelius, From Tradition to Gospel, trans. and rev. Bertram Lee Wolf (New York: Charles Scribner's Sons, 1935).

11. Matthew 4:1-11 and Luke 4:1-13 considerably expanded the Marcan temptation narrative by incorporation of Q material.

12. It should be noted that this pericope also might be classified as a pronouncement story just as the earlier classified miracle story (Mark 3:1-5) might be used to depict the controversy story.

IV. Yahwism-Judaism: A Faith Within History

1. See "Canaanites," by A. Haldar, in The Interpreter's Dictionary of the Bible, ed. G. A. Buttrick (New York: Abingdon Press, 1962), I, 494-498.

2. Jeremiah 52:28-30 clarifies that there actually were three deportation occasions--597, 587, and 582 B.C.

3. Monolatry refers to the consistent worship of one god while acknowledging the existence of other gods.

4. See R. B. Y. Scott, "Palestine, Climate of," The Interpreter's Dictionary of the Bible, ed. G. A. Buttrick (New York: Abingdon Press, 1962), III, 623. See pp. 621-626.

5. One of the better descriptions of Palestinian topography and geography is found in The Westminster Historical Atlas to the Bible, rev. ed., by George Ernest Wright and Floyd Vivian Filson (Philadelphia: The Westminster Press, 1956), pp. 17-20.

6. C. C. McCown, "Palestine, Geography of," The Interpreter's Dictionary of the Bible, ed. G. A. Buttrick (New York: Abingdon Press, 1962), III, 633. See entire article, pp. 626-639.

7. Most altitudinal indications are drawn from the topographal map found in Wright and Filson, The Westminster Historical Atlas to the Bible, rev. ed., p. 21.

8. Recall that in the Hebrew canon they are the "Former Prophets."

9. One cannot determine from our present vantage point whether the Priestly, Deuteronomic, or Chronicler author(s) should be spoken of singularly or in the plural. It is likely, however, that in each case it was a community of writers who did the recording.

10. See as one example Otto Eissfeldt, The Old Testament, trans. Peter R. Ackroyd (Oxford: Basil Blackwell, 1965), pp. 191-199, for discussion of the "Lay source,"

or L, which he judges the earliest source.

11. See the author's discussion of this, "The Priests and Cultic Concerns," pp. 128-163, in The Religion and Culture of Israel (Washington, D.C.: University Press of America, 1977).

12. B. W. Anderson, "Creation," The Interpreter's Dictionary of the Bible, ed. G. A. Buttrick (New York: Abingdon Press, 1962), I, 727.

13. Walther Eichrodt, Theology of the Old Testament, I, trans. J. A. Baker (Philadelphia: The Westminster Press, 1961), p. 218.

14. See Eichrodt, Theology of the Old Testament, I, 218-220.

15. See the author's "Israel's Sine Qua Non: The Exodus Event," in The Religion and Culture of Israel, pp. 51-76.

16. Israelites is a proper term once the covenant has been ratified.

17. See Eissfeldt, The Old Testament, pp. 241-248, for a good summary of the arguments on both sides of this issue.

18. Eissfeldt, The Old Testament, p. 299.

19. Originally the dual books of Samuel and Kings were one book each.

20. It should be noted that the books of Samuel have two distinct traditions embedded. One of these, the Early or Saul Source as exemplified in 1 Samuel 9:1-10:16; 11: 1-15; 13:1-7a; and 13:15b-14:52 indicates that Samuel willingly anointed Saul as king. The Late or Samuel Source as exemplified by 1 Samuel 8:1-22; 10:17-27; 12:1-25; and 15:1-35 indicates to the contrary that Samuel very reluctantly went along with this desire of the people, doing so only after being so instructed by Yahweh and warning the people of their folly. According to the Samuel Source,

there ultimately developed a complete breach in relationship between Saul and Samuel.

21. The deuteronomistic editors chronicle this period
in an interesting if difficult fashion. The editors move
Judah to a certain point, then reach back and pick up Israel
and move Israel past Judah, then back to Judah, etc. This
constant shifting from Judah to Israel makes difficult one's
maintaining historical perspective.

22. Eissfeldt, The Old Testament, p. 531. See also
Martin Noth, The History of Israel, rev. ed., trans. P. R.
Ackroyd (New York: Harper and Row, Publishers, 1960), p.
356.

23. Eissfeldt, The Old Testament, p. 535. See discussion of these features, pp. 535-538.

24. While the Deuteronomic History does give material
relative to the pre-exilic prophets, the exilic prophets
(Ezekiel and Deutero-Isaiah) fall beyond its purview. In
like fashion the post-exilic prophets demand separate reading. The wisdom writings (Job, Ecclesiastes, and Proverbs)
provide insight into another aspect of Hebrew life.

V. Religious and Intellectual Currents in Early Christianity

1. See the selections from Josephus on the Pharisees,
Sadducees, and Essenes in C. K. Barrett, ed., The New Testa-
ment Background: Selected Documents (New York: Harper &
Row, Publishers, 1961), pp. 124-127.

2. See J. A. Sanders, "Dispersion," The Interpreter's
Dictionary of the Bible, ed. G. A. Buttrick (New York:
Abingdon Press, 1962), I, 855.

3. See G. Ernest Wright and Reginald H. Fuller, The
Book of the Acts of God (New York: Doubleday & Company,
Inc., 1960), p. 223.

4. Paul's Letter to the Colossians indicates a problem with Christian gnosticism, while the Fourth Gospel's Prologue was quite possibly formulated partially to combat the gnostic heresy.

5. This is probably better explained by the hypostatization of the divine Word in post-exilic thought. See the author's The Religion and Culture of Israel (Washington, D.C.: University Press of America, 1977), pp. 175-179, and notes.

6. See James L. Price, Interpreting the New Testament (New York: Holt, Rinehart, and Winston, Inc., 1961), pp. 318-321; and Donald J. Selby, Toward the Understanding of St. Paul (Englewood Cliffs, N.J.: Prentice-Hall, Inc., 1962), pp. 94-98.

7. See Chapter II, pp. 27-31. See also Gordon C. Oxtoby, Prediction and Fulfillment in the Bible (Philadelphia: Westminster Press, 1966).

8. The New Testament is not of singular witness on this point. John 10:22, for example, records that Jesus bestowed the Holy Spirit on the day of his resurrection.

9. See Chapter VI for further comment regarding the widening breach between Judaism and Christianity.

10. Several good books dealing with the diversity of church order in the New Testament are Oscar Cullman, The Early Church, ed. A. J. B. Higgins (Philadelphia: The Westminster Press, 1966), and Edward Schweizer, Church Order in the New Testament, trans. Frank Clarke, "Studies in Biblical Theology," No. 32, ed. C. F. D. Moule, et al. (London: SCM Press, Ltd., 1961). Also instructive regarding the distinctive development of first-century Judaism and Christianity is Martin Buber's Two Types of Faith, trans. Norman P. Goldhawk (New York: Harper & Row, Publishers, 1961).

11. John A. T. Robinson, in The Body, "Studies in

Biblical Theology," No. 5, ed. C. F. D. Moule, et al.
(London: SCM Press, Ltd., 1952), pp. 81-82, suggests that
Paul's thought should be understood in terms of the church
rather than in an individualistic manner.

12. Two Types of Faith, p. 99.

13. Three good books dealing with the development of
messianic thought are Sigmund Mowinckel, He That Cometh,
trans. G. W. Anderson (New York: Abingdon Press, 1956);
Joseph Klausner, The Messianic Idea in Israel, trans. W. F.
Stinespring (New York: Macmillan, 1955); and Helmer Ringgren, The Messiah in the Old Testament (Naperville, Ill.:
Alec R. Allenson, Inc., 1956).

14. See Dialogue: In Search of Jewish/Christian
Understanding by Rabbi Jack D. Spiro and the Reverend John
S. Spong (New York: The Seabury Press, 1975), to which I
contributed the Prologue, p. 78. Dialogue records the
exchanges between Rabbi Spiro and Mr. Spong as the two
congregations met for interfaith dialogue.

15. Trans. Ronald Gregor Smith, 2nd. ed. (New York:
Charles Scribner's Sons, 1958).

16. The section in John A. T. Robinson's Honest to
God (Philadelphia: The Westminster Press, 1963), pp. 64-
83, continues to be a readable and helpful statement on
Christology which is sensitively formulated. A more con-
servative view may be found in D. M. Baillie's God was in
Christ (New York: Charles Scribner's Sons, 1948). Baillie's
approach might be compared with Reginald H. Fuller's The
Foundations of New Testament Christology (New York: Charles
Scribner's Sons, 1965), or John A. T. Robinson's The Human
Face of God (Philadelphia: The Westminster Press, 1973).

17. Rudolf Bultmann's Primitive Christianity, trans.
R. H. Fuller (New York: The World Publishing Company,
1956), is a helpful summary of these diverse influences.

18. An example of the vitality discovered in continual

investigation is found in Martin Buber's explanation of
one step in the deification process as Jesus of Nazareth
became increasingly a divine figure in the life of the
church. He notes that the Jews found credible the idea of
communal resurrection, but not individual resurrection.
This made difficult Jewish acceptance of Jesus' resurrection
as proclaimed in the church. On the other hand, the Greeks
found incredible mass resurrection but could accept individual resurrection: "for them resurrection is an affair
of the gods of the Mysteries and their kind--one only needs
to make the Christ the God-man to make him credible to
them" (Two Types of Faith, pp. 100-101).

VI. Jews and Christians in Historical Perspective

1. Much of the data in the present Chapter is included in Dialogue: In Search of Jewish/Christian Understanding by John Shelby Spong and Jack Daniel Spiro (New
York: Seabury Press, 1975), in my Prologue entitled
"Shalom: Faith's Quest, Man's Hope."

2. In the following material I have been influenced
by numerous Jewish historians. Particular indebtedness
is expressed to the late Cecil Roth, A History of the Jews,
rev. ed. (New York: Schocken Books, 1970), for the clarity
and thoroughness of his presentation.

3. See Chapter II.

4. The excellent volume by Martin Buber, Two Types
of Faith, trans. Norman P. Goldhawk (New York: Harper &
Row, Publishers, 1961) is recommended as a Jewish interpretation of the widening breach developing between early
Christianity and Judaism.

5. See Chapter V.

6. See Bo Reicke, The Epistles of James, Peter, and
Jude, The Anchor Bible (Garden City, New York: Doubleday &

Company, Inc., 1964), XXXVII, pp. XIX-XX.

7. Jakob J. Petuchowski, "The Jewish-Christian Dialogue," Jewish Spectator (March-April, 1965), pp. 8-9.

8. See Kenneth Scott Latourette, A History of Christianity (New York: Harper & Brothers, 1953), pp. 91-93.

9. From The Book of Common Prayer (New York: The Seabury Press, 1953), pp. 15-16. Of prime importance is the adoption of the term homoousion, "of the same substance," to indicate the unity of Father and Son. See The Early Christian Fathers, ed. and trans. Henry Bettenson (New York: Oxford University Press, 1956), pp. 33-37.

10. Fuller quotation found in Roland de Corneille, Christians and Jews (New York: Harper & Row, Publishers, 1966), pp. 20-21. See also Gregory Baum, The Jews and the Gospel (Westminster, Maryland: The Newman Press, 1961), p. 6.

11. One should recognize as well that the nature of Judaism encouraged communal development, but this characteristic should not be used to excuse the land restriction.

12. Roth, A History of the Jews, p. 194.

13. A grouping of sixty-three books of legal, ethical, and historical writings edited in the religious academies of Babylon during the fifth and sixth centuries. The Talmud is revered second only to the Torah in Judaism.

14. Roth, A History of the Jews, pp. 195-197. See also de Corneille, Christians and Jews, p. 24.

15. Roth, A History of the Jews, p. 191.

16. In The Documents of Vatican II, under the general editorship of Walter M. Abbott, S.J. (New York: Corpus Books, 1966), p. 667, n. 28, it is stated: "In four of their seventy canonical enactments, the Fathers of the Fourth Lateran Council (1215 A.D.) dealt with the Jews: Christian princes must watch lest Jews enact too high

interest of Christian debtors; baptized Jews may not observe Jewish customs; Jews may not appear in public during
Easter week; Jews must give tithes on their houses and
other property to the Church and pay a yearly tax at Easter;
no Christian prince may give an office to a Jew under pain
of excommunication; Jews must wear a distinctive dress from
their twelfth year to distinguish them from Christians.
If there was anti-Semitism in these laws, it is here repu-
diated by the Second Vatican Council ("at any time and from
any source")" [underlining added].

17. The Jews had been forced out of southern Spain
as early as 1172.

18. Leo Trepp, Judaism (Belmont, California: Dickenson Publishing Co., Inc., 1966), p. 209.

19. Quoted in de Corneille, Christians and Jews, pp.
36-37.

20. de Corneille, Christians and Jews, pp. 34-35.

21. See Roth, A History of the Jews, Chapter 25, for
an excellent description of "Life in the Ghetto."

22. de Corneille, Christians and Jews, p. 39.

23. Trepp, Judaism, pp. 55-56.

24. Roth, A History of the Jews, p. 392. See also
Bernard J. Bamberger, The Story of Judaism, Third, Augmented
edition (New York: Schocken Books, 1970), p. 396.

25. See James Parkes, A History of the Jewish People
(Baltimore: Penguin Books, Inc., 1964), p. 217.

26. Two examples of dialogue which have occurred with
positive result may be read in the earlier mentioned Dia-
logue: In Search of Jewish/Christian Understanding and
Roland de Corneille, Christians and Jews (Toronto, Canada).
Jewish-Christian Dialogues by Leonard Swidler and Marc H.
Tanenbaum (Washington, D.C.: National Council of Catholic
Men and National Council of Catholic Women, 1966) is an
excellent study booklet prepared especially to aid and

encourage dialogue between Jewish and Catholic groups.
Orthodox and Conservative Jews generally reject any type
of religious dialogue. In a still operative resolution
adopted at the Union of Orthodox Jewish Congregations of
America Convention in 1966, it is stated: "The recent
Vatican Council of the Roman Catholic Church produced a
declaration dealing with the Jews and the canard of deicide.
The Jewish people must be deeply disappointed that there
remained in this declaration a gratuitous undercurrent of
absolution and a complete absence of any open and frank
acknowledgment by the church of her historic guilt for
the unspeakable atrocities committed by her adherents,
under the provocation of the deicide thesis, against the
Jewish people . . . The Jewish people must reject . . .
any endeavor to become engaged in dialogues concerning
our faith and its theological foundations . . . ." In
similar fashion, The National Jewish Community Relations
Advisory Council serves in an advisory role to the various
denominations and agencies of Jewry on diverse issues. On
the subject of ecumenism and the Jews guidelines were set
forth in the Joint Program Plan for 1972-1973 and reaffirmed
in the Joint Program Plan for 1974-1975. Among the statements is the following: "We deem inimical any proposal
that would seek to blur fundamental differences between
Judaism and Christianity. Certainly, Jewish participation
in any council arrangement that seeks to deal in matters
of theology or religious thought is to be avoided." Generally, social dialogue is possible; but religious dialogue
is an option only between Christians and Reform Jewish bodies.

    27. On October 28, 1965, the Second Vatican Council
deplored the persecution of the Jews historically and officially recognized the fact that the Jews should not be held
accountable for the death of Jesus--see Abbott, The Documents of Vatican II, pp. 663-667. Such steps as this must

be initiated by Christendom, but it must also be recognized that such theoretical affirmations must be followed by more concrete actions which affirm in practice the brotherhood of Christians and Jews as worshippers of the one God.

VII. Religion in Cultural Experience

1. New York: Charles Scribner's Sons, 1969, pp. 6-12.

2. See two classic works: Rudolf Otto, The Idea of the Holy, trans. John W. Harvey (New York: Oxford University Press, 1958); and Mircea Eliade, The Sacred and the Profane, trans. Willard R. Trask (New York: Harper and Brothers, 1961).

3. Eliade, The Sacred and the Profane, pp. 11-12.

4. Eliade, The Sacred and the Profane, p. 14.

5. Kenneth Scott Latourette, A History of Christianity (New York: Harper & Brothers, Publishers, 1953), pp. 135-136.

6. See Latourette, A History of Christianity, pp. 135-136; and Williston Walker, A History of the Christian Church, rev. ed. (New York: Charles Scribner's, 1959), pp. 54-55.

7. Brevard S. Childs, Myth and Reality in the Old Testament, "Studies in Biblical Theology," No. 27 (London: SCM Press, Ltd., 1960), pp. 29-30.

8. See Frank E. Eakin, Jr., The Religion and Culture of Israel (Washington, D.C.: University Press of America, 1977), pp. 208-221.

9. Two good books on symbol are Philip E. Wheelwright, The Burning Fountain, rev. ed. (Bloomington: Indiana University Press, 1968); and Paul Ricoeur, The Symbolism of Evil, trans. Emerson Buchanan, in "Religious Perspectives," ed. Ruth Nanda Anshen, vol. 17 (New York: Harper & Row, Publishers, 1967).

10. Martin Buber, in Two Types of Faith (New York: Harper & Row, Publishers, 1961), trans. Norman P. Goldhawk,

p. 99, makes the interesting suggestion that probably the earliest affirmation of the Christians was the ascension rather than the resurrection.

11. The implications of the social perspective will be discussed further in Chapters VIII and IX.

12. See especially Lowell D. Streiker, The Jesus Trip (New York: Abingdon Press, 1971); William G. McLoughlin, "Is There a Third Force in Christendom?" in Religion in America, ed. William G. McLoughlin and Robert N. Bellah (Boston: Beacon Press, 1966), pp. 45-72; Robert Coles, "God and the Rural Poor," Psychology Today (January 1972), pp. 33-40; and Michael McFadden, The Jesus Revolution (New York: Harper & Row, Publishers, 1972).

13. McFadden, The Jesus Revolution, p. 201.

VIII. Religion and Action

1. Harvey Cox, The Secular City, rev. ed. (New York: The Macmillan Company, 1966), p. 18. See Daniel Callahan, ed., The Secular City Debate (New York: The Macmillan Company, 1966).

2. Cox, The Secular City, rev. ed., p. 27.

3. Cox, The Secular City, rev. ed., pp. 15, 19-32 for discussion.

4. See Chapter II for some of this process.

5. A conscious distinction must be made in attempting to separate Israel's earliest commission from her understood role as eventually developed and set forth in written formulation.

6. Deuteronomy 5:12-15 suggests that the basis for this remembrance is Yahweh's freeing act as the Hebrews were delivered from Egypt. Since creation theology is generally understood as a rather late development in Israelite thought, many scholars would agree that the rationale based

on the Egyptian experience should be judged the earlier
basis for sabbath observance. Regardless, most scholars
would agree that the developed, sophisticated sabbath
observance met in the Bible is a relatively late development in Israelite thought; and, however early one would
wish to push its development, it is questionable (although
not impossible) that it was a practice among them during
the semi-nomadic period.

7. I have discussed the Ten Words in greater detail
in The Religion and Culture of Israel (Washington, D.C.:
University Press of America, 1977), pp. 67-74.

8. See discussion in Chapter I.

9. See F. W. Beare, The Earliest Records of Jesus
(New York: Abingdon Press, 1962), pp. 18-22.

10. See Joseph Fletcher, Situation Ethics: The New
Morality (Philadelphia: The Westminster Press, 1966). On
the basis of an earlier statement by Fletcher, the position
was supported by John A. T. Robinson in Honest to God
(Philadelphia: The Westminster Press, 1963), describing
Fletcher's view as the "most consistent statement I know"
(p. 116). See also Harvey Cox, ed., The Situation Ethics
Debate (Philadelphia: The Westminster Press, 1968); John
C. Bennett, et al., Storm Over Ethics (United Church Press:
The Bethany Press, 1967); and Robert L. Cunningham, ed.,
Situationism and the New Morality (New York: Appleton-
Century-Crofts, Meredith Corporation, 1970).

11. Nelson Glueck did an excellent study entitled
Ḥesed in the Bible, trans. Alfred Gottschalk, introduction
Gerald A. Larue, ed. Elias L. Epstein (Cincinnati: The
Hebrew Union College Press, 1967).

12. This is clearly evident in the Dead Sea Scrolls.
See J. T. Milik, Ten Years of Discovery in the Wilderness
of Judaea, trans. J. Strugnell, "Studies in Biblical Theology," No. 26 (Naperville, Ill.: Alec R. Allenson, Inc.,

1959), pp. 118-119. The thought continues in rabbinical literature.

13. The letter sent to Martin Luther King, Jr., by the eight Alabama clergymen, his classic response, plus his "I Have a Dream" address delivered at the Lincoln Memorial during the March on Washington, August 28, 1963, is available inexpensively in pamphlet form from the Fellowship of Reconciliation, Box 271, Nyack, New York. Quotations from the Birmingham Jail letter are taken from this Fellowship publication.

14. Quite obviously there are representatives of many other religious bodies as well; but here the focus is only on the major religious bodies, namely Judaism and Christianity. See the helpful contribution by Will Herberg, Protestant-Catholic-Jew, rev. ed. (Garden City, New York: Doubleday & Company, Inc., 1960).

15. An excellent statement of this phenomenon is found in the article entitled "Civil Religion in America" by Robert N. Bellah which first appeared in Daedalus (Winter, 1967), pp. 1-21. This article has been reprinted in numerous anthologies. More recently see Robert N. Bellah, The Broken Covenant (New York: The Seabury Press, 1975). See also Conrad Cherry, ed., God's New Israel (Englewood Cliffs, New Jersey: Prentice-Hall, Inc., 1971); and Russell E. Richey and Donald G. Jones, eds., American Civil Religion (New York: Harper & Row, Publishers, 1974), see pp. 273-278 for bibliography.

16. See Cox, The Secular City, rev. ed., pp. 15-32.

IX. Religion and the Individual

1. Boston: Houghton Mifflin Company, 1956.

2. Marvin Pope, Job, in The Anchor Bible, ed. by William Foxwell Albright and David Noel Freedman (Garden

City, New York: Doubleday & Company, Inc., 1965), vol. 15, p. xviii.

3. The reader is encouraged to see the author's The Religion and Culture of Israel (Washington, D.C.: University Press of America, 1977), pp. 164-181, where the wisdom movement in Israel and some of its characteristics are discussed.

4. See R. B. Y. Scott, "Priesthood, Prophecy, Wisdom, and the Knowledge of God," Journal of Biblical Literature, LXXX (1961), 11, who distinguishes between two streams of Hebrew wisdom thinking, one which was "conservative, conventional, confident, worldly-wise, and didactic"--book of Proverbs, Job's friends--the "other current is radical, heterodox, skeptical . . ."--Job, final editors compiling book of Job, and Ecclesiastes.

5. Gerhard von Rad, Old Testament Theology, I, trans. D. M. G. Stalker (London: Oliver and Boyd, 1962), pp. 454-459.

6. Norman K. Gottwald, A Light to the Nations (New York: Harper & Brothers, Publishers, 1959), p. 486.

7. It is generally agreed that 12:9-14 is a later postscript to the book which helped to bring the writing more into orthodox conformity.

8. See discussion by Gerhard von Rad, Wisdom in Israel, trans. James D. Martin (New York: Abingdon Press, 1972), pp. 227-232.

9. Archibald MacLeish, JB (Boston: Houghton Mifflin Company, 1956), p. 12.

10. MacLeish, JB, p. 22.

11. In light of the discussion of "Civil Religion" in Chapter VIII, it is significant that MacLeish has depicted this ritual around a civil religious focus rather than in association with either a specifically Jewish or Christian commemoration.

12. Richard Bach, photographs by Russell Munson, Jonathan Livingston Seagull (New York: Macmillan Publishing Co., Inc., 1970), p. 77.

13. Bach, Jonathan Livingston Seagull, p. 77.

14. Bach, Jonathan Livingston Seagull, pp. 90-91.

15. Bach, Jonathan Livingston Seagull, p. 91.

16. See The Stranger, trans. Stuart Gilbert (New York: Vintage Books, 1942).

17. Camus, The Stranger, pp. 144-153.

18. New York: The Viking Press, Inc., 1962.

19. See Tom Wolfe, The Electric Kool-Aid Acid Test (New York: Bantam Books, Inc., 1969), for interesting and helpful material regarding Kesey.

Postscript

1. Dee Brown, Bury My Heart at Wounded Knee (New York: Holt, Rinehart & Winston, 1970), p. 318.

SELECTED BIBLIOGRAPHY

The areas listed below indicate additional readings
helpful in specific areas. These selections do not cover
every topic discussed in the book, nor are these choices
intended to do more than direct the individual to materials
which will be both enlightening and instructive of additional bibliographical resources. Attention should also
be given to the Notes for each Chapter.

Religion and Culture

Allport, Gordon W., The Individual and His Religion. New
    York: The Macmillan Company, 1950.

Capps, Walter H., Ways of Understanding Religion. New
    York: The Macmillan Company, 1972.

Cell, Edward, ed., Religion and Western Culture. New York:
    Abingdon Press, 1967.

Dawson, Christopher, Religion and the Rise of Western Cul-
    ture. Garden City, New York: Doubleday & Company, Inc.,
    1958.

Johnson, Roger A., et al., Critical Issues in Modern Reli-
    gion. Englewood Cliffs, New Jersey: Prentice-Hall,
    Inc., 1973.

Monk, Robert C., et al., Exploring Religious Meaning. Engle-
    wood Cliffs, New Jersey: Prentice-Hall, Inc., 1973.

Needleman, Jacob, et al., Religion for a New Generation.
    New York: The Macmillan Company, 1973.

Newman, William M., The Social Meanings of Religion.

Chicago: Rand McNally College Publishing Company, 1974.

Smart, Ninian, The Religious Experience of Mankind, second
edition. New York: Charles Scribner's Sons, 1976.

Streng, Frederick J., Understanding Religious Life, second
edition. Belmont, California: Dickenson Publishing
Company, Inc., 1976.

_____, et al., Ways of Being Religious. Englewood
Cliffs, New Jersey: Prentice-Hall, Inc., 1973.

Tillich, Paul, The Future of Religions. New York: Harper
& Row, Publishers, 1966.

_____, What is Religion? New York: Harper & Row,
Publishers, 1969.

Tremmel, William Calloley, Religion: What Is It? New York:
Holt, Rinehart and Winston, 1976.

Whitehead, Alfred North, Religion in the Making. New York:
The New American Library, Inc., 1960.

Biblical Study Background

Anderson, Bernhard W., Understanding the Old Testament,
third edition. Englewood Cliffs, New Jersey: Prentice-
Hall, Inc., 1975.

Barr, James, The Bible in the Modern World. New York:
Harper & Row, Publishers, Inc., 1973.

Bratton, Fred Gladstone, A History of the Bible. Boston:
Beacon Press, 1959.

Colwell, Ernest Cadman, The Study of the Bible, rev. ed.
Chicago: The University of Chicago Press, 1976.

Connick, C. Milo, The Message and Meaning of the Bible.
Belmont, California: Dickenson Publishing Company,
Inc., 1965.

Davidson, Robert, and A. R. C. Leaney, The Pelican Guide
to Modern Theology, Volume 3 (Biblical Criticism).
Baltimore, Maryland: Penguin Books, Inc., 1970.

Eissfeldt, Otto, The Old Testament, trans. Peter R. Ackroyd.
    Oxford: Basil Blackwell, 1965.

Feine, Paul, and Johannes Behm, Introduction to the New
    Testament, fourteenth revised edition, ed. Werner Georg
    Kümmel, trans. A. J. Mattill, Jr. New York: Abingdon
    Press, 1966.

Flanders, Henry Jackson, Jr., and Bruce C. Cresson, Intro-
    duction to the Bible. New York: The Ronald Press Com-
    pany, 1973.

Gottwald, Norman K., A Light to the Nations. New York:
    Harper & Brothers, Publishers, 1959.

Grant, Robert M., A Short History of the Interpretation of
    the Bible, revised edition. New York: The Macmillan
    Company, 1963.

Hayes, John H., Introduction to the Bible. Philadelphia:
    The Westminster Press, 1971.

Kee, Howard Clark, Franklin W. Young, and Karlfried Froeh-
    lich, Understanding the New Testament, third edition.
    Englewood Cliffs, New Jersey: Prentice-Hall, Inc., 1973.

Lindblom, J., The Bible: A Modern Understanding, trans.
    Eric H. Wahlstrom. Philadelphia: Fortress Press, 1973.

Price, James L., Interpreting the New Testament. New York:
    Holt, Rinehart and Winston, 1961.

Wright, G. Ernest, and Reginald H. Fuller, The Book of the
    Acts of God. Garden City, New York: Doubleday & Com-
    pany, Inc., 1957.

Hebrew History and Religion

Bright, John, A History of Israel, second edition. Phil-
    adelphia: The Westminster Press, 1972.

Eakin, Frank E., Jr., The Religion and Culture of Israel.
    Washington, D.C.: University Press of America, 1977.

Eichrodt, Walther, Theology of the Old Testament, 2 volumes,

trans. J. A. Baker. Philadelphia: The Westminster
Press, 1961, 1967.

Kaufmann, Yehezkel, The Religion of Israel, trans. and
abridged Moshe Greenberg. Chicago: The University of
Chicago Press, 1960.

Noth, Martin, The History of Israel, revised edition, trans.
P. R. Ackroyd. New York: Harper & Row, Publishers,
1960.

Ringgren, Helmer, Israelite Religion, trans. David E. Green.
Philadelphia: Fortress Press, 1966.

von Rad, Gerhard, Old Testament Theology, 2 volumes, trans.
D. M. G. Stalker. London: Oliver and Boyd, 1962, 1965.

Vriezen, Th. C., The Religion of Ancient Israel, trans.
Hubert Hoskins. Philadelphia: The Westminster Press,
1967.

Jewish History

Bamberger, Bernard J., The Story of Judaism, third, augmented edition. New York: Schocken Books, 1970.

Grayzel, Solomon, A History of the Jews, revised edition.
New York: The New American Library, Inc., 1968.

Margolis, Max L., and Alexander Marx, A History of the
Jewish People. New York: Atheneum, 1972.

Parkes, James, A History of the Jewish People. Baltimore:
Penguin Books, Inc., 1964.

Roth, Cecil, A History of the Jews, revised edition. New
York: Schocken Books, 1970.

Sachar, Abram Leon, A History of the Jews, fifth edition,
revised and enlarged. New York: Alfred A. Knopf, 1967.

Christian History and Thought

Bultmann, Rudolf, Theology of the New Testament, 2 volumes,

trans. Kendrick Grobel. New York: Charles Scribner's
Sons, 1951-1955.

Conzelmann, Hans, An Outline of the Theology of the New
Testament, trans. John Bowden. New York: Harper & Row,
Publishers, Inc., 1969.

Grant, Frederick C., An Introduction to New Testament
Thought. New York: Abingdon-Cokesbury Press, 1950.

Harnack, Adolf, The Mission and Expansion of Christianity
in the First Three Centuries, trans. and ed. James
Moffatt. New York: Harper Torchbook, 1962.

Hordern, William, A Layman's Guide to Protestant Theology,
revised edition. New York: The Macmillan Company, 1968.

Latourette, Kenneth Scott, A History of Christianity. New
York: Harper & Brothers, Publishers, 1953.

Macquarrie, John, Principles of Christian Theology, second
edition. New York: Charles Scribner's Sons, 1977.

_____, The Scope of Demythologizing. London: SCM
Press, 1960.

Marty, Martin E., A Short History of Christianity. New
York: The World Publishing Company, 1959.

Petry, Ray C. (I), and Clyde L. Manschreck (II), eds.,
A History of Christianity, 2 volumes. Englewood Cliffs,
New Jersey: Prentice-Hall, Inc., 1962-1964.

Scott, William A., Historical Protestantism: An Historical
Introduction to Protestant Theology. Englewood Cliffs,
New Jersey: Prentice-Hall, Inc., 1971.

Spurrier, William A., Guide to the Christian Faith. New
York: Charles Scribner's Sons, 1952.

Tillich, Paul, A History of Christian Thought, ed. Carl E.
Braaten. New York: Simon and Schuster, 1967.

_____, Systematic Theology, 3 volumes. Chicago:
The University of Chicago Press, 1951-1963.

Walker, Williston, A History of the Christian Church, revised edition. New York: Charles Scribner's Sons, 1959.

Anti-Semitism

Arendt, Hannah, Antisemitism. New York: Harcourt, Brace & World, Inc., 1951.

Dawidowicz, Lucy S., The War Against the Jews, 1933-1945. New York: Holt, Rinehart and Winston, 1975.

de Corneille, Roland, Christians and Jews. New York: Harper & Row, Publishers, 1966.

Eckardt, A. Roy, Your People, My People. New York: Quadrangle, 1974.

Flannery, Edward H., The Anguish of the Jews. New York: The Macmillan Company, 1965.

Kirsch, Paul J., We Christians and Jews. Philadelphia: Fortress Press, 1975.

Littell, Franklin H., The Crucifixion of the Jews. New York: Harper & Row, 1975.

Parkes, James, Anti-Semitism. Chicago: Quadrangle Books, 1963.

Poliakov, Leon, The History of Anti-Semitism, trans. Richard Howard. New York: Schocken Books, 1974.

Ruether, Rosemary, Faith and Fratricide. New York: The Seabury Press, Inc., 1974.

Spong, John Shelby, and Jack Daniel Spiro, Dialogue: In Search of Jewish/Christian Understanding. New York: The Seabury Press, Inc., 1975.

Commentaries

The Abingdon Bible Commentary, ed. F. C. Eiselen, Edwin Lewis, and D. G. Downey. New York: The Abingdon Press, 1929.

The Anchor Bible, ed. W. F. Albright and D. N. Freedman. Garden City, New York: Doubleday & Company, Inc., 1964 onwards.

The International Critical Commentary (not completed to

date, changing editorial board).

The Interpreter's Bible, 12 volumes, ed. G. A. Buttrick.
New York: Abingdon Press, 1952-1957.

The Layman's Bible Commentary, 25 volumes, ed. Balmer H.
Kelley. Richmond: John Knox Press, 1959-1964.

Neil, William, Harper's Bible Commentary. New York:
Harper and Row, 1963.

Peake's Commentary on the Bible, rev. ed. Matthew Black
and H. H. Rowley. New York: Thomas Nelson and Sons,
Ltd., 1962.

Torch Bible Commentaries, ed. J. Marsh and C. A. Richardson.
London: SCM Press, 1952 onwards.

Dictionaries

Buttrick, G. A., ed., The Interpreter's Dictionary of the
Bible, 4 volumes. New York: Abingdon Press, 1962.
Supplementary Volume, ed. Keith Crim, 1976.

Hastings, James, ed., Dictionary of the Bible, rev. ed.
F. C. Grant and H. H. Rowley. New York: Charles
Scribner's Sons, 1963.

Miller, Madeleine S., and J. Lane Miller, et al., Harper's
Bible Dictionary. New York: Harper and Brothers, 1952.

THE CANON OF HEBREW SCRIPTURE

Below are found the Hebrew canonical writings arranged according to the Hebrew and English translation systems. The Hebrew canon consists of twenty-four writings, while the Protestant canon by assessing differently the same material counts thirty-nine writings. The Roman Catholic Church still includes the fourteen apocryphal writings in its canon, thus constituting a canon of fifty-three books.

The divisions of the Hebrew canon are listed as accepted within Judaism. There are three specific sections: Torah, Nebi'im, and Kethubim. On the other hand, the divisions listed with the English translation are not ecclesiastically decreed but rather are divisions as popularly understood.

The English arrangement has juxtaposed improperly certain writings (as 1-2 Chronicles with 1-2 Samuel and 1-2 Kings, Ruth with Judges, and Daniel with the prophets, among others), has made more difficult the dating of material (as with Ruth), and has confused literary type (as Daniel with the prophets). This rearrangement resulted from the organizational tendencies of the Septuagintal translators, but it serves little useful purpose presently. The English translations would be clearer, both in terms of literary type and as regards the date of an individual book's writing, were the arrangement of the Hebrew canon to be followed.

For further comment, the reader is referred especially to Chapter II. The listing of the canonical arrangements with division headings and the number of books included in each section follows:

Hebrew	English
<u>Torah</u> (Law) (5)	<u>Law</u> (5)
Genesis	Genesis
Exodus	Exodus
Leviticus	Leviticus
Numbers	Numbers
Deuteronomy	Deuteronomy
<u>Nebi'im</u> (Prophets) (8)	<u>History</u> (12)
<u>Former</u> <u>Prophets</u> (4)	Joshua
Joshua	Judges
Judges	Ruth
Samuel	1-2 Samuel
Kings	1-2 Kings
<u>Latter</u> <u>Prophets</u> (4)	1-2 Chronicles
Isaiah	Ezra
Jeremiah	Nehemiah
Ezekiel	Esther
The Book of the Twelve	<u>Poetry</u> <u>and</u> <u>Wisdom</u> (5)
Hosea	Job
Joel	Psalms
Amos	Proverbs
Obadiah	Ecclesiastes
Jonah	Song of Songs
Micah	<u>Prophecy</u> (17)
Nahum	Isaiah
Habakkuk	Jeremiah
Zephaniah	Lamentations
Haggai	Ezekiel
Zechariah	Daniel
Malachi	Hosea
	Joel

<u>Kethubim</u> (Writings) (11)

Psalms
Job
Proverbs
Ruth
Song of Songs
Ecclesiastes
Lamentations
Esther
Daniel
Ezra-Nehemiah
Chronicles

Amos
Obadiah
Jonah
Micah
Nahum
Habakkuk
Zephaniah
Haggai
Zechariah
Malachi

CHRONOLOGICAL SURVEY

The dates included in the survey are primarily those specifically mentioned or at least alluded to in the various Chapters. On occasion dates are indicated to give a sense of relative events even when not discussed in the text. The reader would find helpful studies which treat in greater depth the individual periods of history, both Biblical and non-Biblical.

	Mesopotamia	Canaan	Egypt
3000			Pre-Dynastic
			1st Dynasty (ca. 3000)
2500	Sumerian City States (ca. 2800-2360)		
	Empire of Akkad (ca. 2360-2180)		Old Kingdom (ca. 2700-2200)
2000	Sumerian Renaissance (Ur III, ca. 2060-1950)		First Intermediate Period (ca. 2200-2000)
	Assyria (ca. 1950-605)		Middle Kingdom (ca. 1991-1778)
	Babylon (ca. 1830-1530)	Abraham-Sarah	Second Intermediate Period (ca. 1778-1570)
	Hammurabi (ca. 1728-1686)	Isaac-Rebekah	Hyksos (ca. 1720-1570)
		Jacob-Leah/Rachel	Hebrews enter Egypt
		12 sons	

	Mesopotamia	Canaan	Egypt
1500			New Kingdom (1570-1100)
			Seti I (1309-1290)
			Rameses II (1290-1224)
			EXODUS--MOSES
1250		Israelite Settlement	
		(1250-1020)	
		Joshua-Judges	
1000		United Monarchy	
		(1020-922)	
		Saul (1020-1000)	
		David (1000-961)	
		Solomon (961-922)	
		Yahwist	
		Divided Monarchy (922-597)	
		Judah (922-597)	Israel (922-722/721)
		Rehoboam (922-915)	Jeroboam I (922-901)
		Jehoshaphat (873-849)	Omri (876-869)
	Assyria		Ahab (869-850)
850	Shalmaneser III (853)		(Elijah)
			Elohist(?)

297

	Assyria	Judah	Israel
		Jehoram (849-842)	
		Ahaziah (842)	Jehu (842-815)
		Athaliah (842-837)	(Elisha)
800		Jehoash (837-800)	Jeroboam II (786-746)
750		Uzziah (783-742)	(Amos)
		(Isaiah)	(Hosea)
	Tiglath-Pileser III	Jotham (742-735)	Elohist (?)
	Shalmaneser V		Hoshea (732-721)
	Sargon II	Ahaz (735-715)	Fall of Samaria (722/721)
700	Sennacherib	Hezekiah (715-687)	
650		Manasseh (687-642)	
		Amon (642-640)	
		Josiah (640-609)	
		(Jeremiah)	
		(Zephaniah)	
		(Nahum)	
	Babylonia	Deuteronomic Reform (622)	
	Nabopolasser (626-605)	Deuteronomistic Material	
	(Fall of Nineveh, 612)		
	Nebuchadrezzar (605-562)	Jehoahaz (609)	

	Babylonia	Judah	Persia
600	Battle of Carchemish (605)	Jehoiakim (609-598)	
		(Habakkuk)	
		Zedekiah (597-587)	
		Fall of Jerusalem (597/587)	
		Babylonian Exile	
		First Deportation (597)	
		(Ezekiel)	
		Second Deportation (587)	
		Third Deportation (582)	
		Deuteronomic Editors	Persia
		Priestly Material	
	Amel-marduk (562-560)		Cyrus (550-530)
	Neriglissar (560-556)		
550	Nabonidus (556-539)		
	Belshazzar	(Deutero-Isaiah)	
	Persia conquers Babylon (539)		
	Cyrus' Edict (538)	Post-Exilic Israel	
		Return, Zerubbabel (538)	
		Work begun on Temple (538)	
		Temple completed (520-515)	
500			Cambyses (530-522)
			Darius I (522-486)

Post-Exilic Israel
(Haggai-Zechariah)
(Trito-Isaiah)
(Obadiah)
(Malachi)
(Joel)

Nehemiah (445, 432)

Ezra (398)

Psalter (400-100)

Persia
Xerxes (486-465)

Artaxerxes (465-424)
Xerxes II (423)
Darius II (423-404)
Artaxerxes II (404-358)
Artaxerxes III (358-338)
Arses (338-336)
Darius III (336-331)

Greece
Alexander the Great (336-323)

Successor States:
Antigonus: Asia Minor
Lysimachus: Thrace
Seleucus: Babylonia, Syria
Cassander: Macedonia
Ptolemy: Egypt, Palestine

450

400

350

300

	Post-Exilic Israel	The Seleucids
300	Chronicler	
250	Septuagint (ca. 275–100)	
	Wisdom Literature	
	Jonah-Ruth-Esther	
200	Israel transferred to Seleucid control (198)	Antiochus III (223–187)
		Seleucus IV (187–175)
	Profanation of Temple (168)	Antiochus IV, Epiphanes (175–163)
	Central thrust of Maccabean Revolt (168–164)	
	Book of Daniel	
	Purification of Temple (Hanukkah, 165/164)	
150	Jews exempted from Seleucid taxation (142)	
	Termination of Seleucid authority (129)	

Jewish-Christian Interaction

From this point all dates will be listed sequentially.
Pompey of Rome conquered the Hasmonean Kingdom in 63 B.C.,
setting the stage for the emergence of the Christian movement within a Greco-Roman environment. Once the church
was born, a course of Jewish-Christian interaction was
inevitably set. The relationship was so consistent,
whether for blessing or bane, that significant events for
one community almost invariably have at least ripple effects
on the other. No attempt will be made, therefore, to clas-
sify these listings either as Jewish or as Christian.

10 (?)	Birth of Paul
7-6 (?)	Birth of Jesus
30 (?)	Crucifixion of Jesus
47-56	Paul's Three Missionary Journeys
50	Jerusalem Conference
64/65	Death of Paul
66-73	Jewish revolt against Rome
	Fall of Jerusalem, 70
	Fall of Masada, 73
ca. 90	Jamnia, determination of Hebrew canon
132-135	Bar Kokhba revolt
200	Mishnah
ca. 200	Muratorian Canon (Rome)
306-337	Constantine, Emperor of Rome
	Adoption of Christianity, 312
	Edict of Milan, 313
	Decree regarding Jews, 329
325	Council of Nicaea
363	Council of Laodicea
367	Easter letter of Athanasius
393	Council of Hippo
397	Council of Carthage

410	Fall of Rome
451	Council of Chalcedon
ca. 500	Completion of Babylonian Talmud
570-632	Mohammed
590-604	Pope Gregory the Great
600's	Beginning of Muslim conquests
633	Fourth Council of Toledo
655	Ninth Council of Toledo
800	Charlemagne crowned Emperor
1054	Schism between East and West
1088-1099	Pope Urban II
1096-1291	Crusades
1135-1204	Moses Maimonides
1179	Third Lateran Council
1215	Fourth Lateran Council
1242	Papal Bull (Pope Gregory IX)
1278	Papal Decree (Pope Nicholas III)
1290	Jews expelled from England
1309	Jews expelled from France
RENAISSANCE	Fourteenth, fifteenth, and sixteenth centuries
1380, 1397	John Wyclif's translations
1453	Printing Press
1480	Spanish Inquisition
1492	Jews expelled from Spain
1496	Jews expelled from Portugal
1516	Ghetto introduced at Venice
1517	Luther's "Ninety-five Theses"
1520	Excommunication of Luther
REFORMATION	Sixteenth Century
1525, 1529	William Tyndale's translations
1534	Henry VIII, separation from Rome
1546	Council of Trent
1553	Talmud burning in Rome
1555	Papal Bull (Pope Paul IV)

1582, 1609-1610	Rheims-Douay translation
1611	King James Bible
1654	Jews settle in New Amsterdam
1655	Jews readmitted to England
1760	Death of Baal Shem Tov (Hasidic founder)
1775-1783	American Revolution
1786	Death of Moses Mendelssohn
1789	Inauguration of George Washington
1789	French Revolution
1791	United States constitutional guarantee of religious freedom
1861-1865	War Between the States
1896	Theodor Herzl published The Jewish State
1897	Modern Zionist movement founded at Basel, Switzerland
1909	Tel-Aviv founded
1917	Balfour Declaration
1920-1948	Palestine controlled by Britain (League of Nations mandate)
1933	Adolf Hitler came to power
1935	Nuremberg Laws, Jews lose rights
1938	Synagogues in Germany burned (November 9)
1942	"Final Solution" to "Jewish Problem" adopted by Third Reich
1946	Revised Standard Version, New Testament
1947	Dead Sea Scrolls, initial discoveries
1948	State of Israel proclaimed (May 14)
1952	Revised Standard Version, Old Testament
1956	Israeli war with Egypt-Syria
1957	Revised Standard Version, Apocrypha
1961	New English Bible, New Testament
1962-1965	Vatican Council II
1967	Six-Day War (June 5-10) with Egypt-Syria-Jordan

1970	New English Bible, Old Testament and Apocrypha
1973	Yom Kippur War with Egypt-Syria

INDEXES

Index of Authors

306

307

Index of Biblical Passages

Index of Subjects

Abel, 90

Abiathar, 66

Abimelech, 96

Abraham, 53, 55, 57, 86, 90, 91, 109

Adam, 57

Adar, 114, 115

Adham, 249

Adonai, 269

Adoptionism, 120

Agape, 143, 206-207, 208, 209

Ahab, 56, 98, 99

Ahasuerus, 113

Ahaz, 28, 99

Ai, 24, 70

Alexander the Great, 101

American Standard Version, 40, 42

Ammon, 82

Amos, 76, 99, 195, 233

Amphictyony, 96, 266

Ananias, 125

Anat, 249

Antioch, 123, 129

Anti-Semitism, impact on western culture, 261

Apocalypticism, 32-33, 36, 140-141, 254

Apostles, Acts of, 123

Apostles Creed, 173-175

Aqabah, Gulf of, 83

Aqiba, Rabbi, 150

Arabah, 78

Arabian Desert, 83

Arallu, 254

Arius, 151

Ark of the Covenant, 96

Armageddon, 81

Asa, 94

Ascension, 133, 184, 185

Asheroth, 94

Asphaltitis, Lake, 78

Assyria, 55, 56, 74, 85, 100, 110

Athaliah, 99

Athanasius, 34

Athens, 121

Auschwitz, 164

Authority, 20-23

Baal, 94, 99, 249

Babylonia, 74, 85, 100

Babylonian Exile, 56-57, 74, 75, 109

Balaam, 110

Balak, 110

Balfour Declaration, 165

Baptism, 125-127

Bar Kokhba, 150

Barnabas, 125

Bashan, 82

Bathsheba, 101

Beer-Sheba, 77, 80, 82, 83

317

existence, 246-252
Theology, 89
Yahwist, 249-250
Cromwell, Sir Thomas, 39
Crucifixion, 65
Crusades, 145, 156-157, 191
Cyrus, 138, 234

Dachau, 164
Dagon, 180
Dan, 77
Daniel, book of, 254
David, 66, 73, 97, 101, 139
Day of Yahweh, 254
Dead Sea, 77, 79
Debir, 82
Deborah, 96
Decalogue, 197
Deicide, 156
Deity (see "God"):
    Anthropomorphism (E), 54-55
    Anthropomorphism (J), 54
Deliverers, 96
Demiurge, 174
Deutero-Isaiah, 109, 138, 199,
    223, 233-236, 256, 260
Deuteronomic history (see
    "Biblical histories")
Deuteronomic Reformation, 94,
    100
Deuteronomic source (see "Pen-
    tateuchal sources (D)")
Divorce, 203-207
Docetism, 119-120

Documentary hypothesis
    (see "Biblical criti-
    cism" and "Pentateuch"),
    50-58, 84
Dome of the Rock, 84
Domitian, 8, 117, 148
Dreyfus, Alfred, 146

Ebal, Mount, 56, 82
Ecclesiastes, book of, 223,
    229-233
    Plight of individual,
        229-233
    Solomon, 230
Edom, 73, 82
Edward I, 158
Egypt, 74, 83
Eichmann, Adolf, 164
Eilat, 79
Ein Gev, 78
El Shaddai, 57
Elihu, 224, 227
Elijah, 56, 98, 133
Eliphaz, 226
Elohim, 54
Elohist (see "Pentateuchal
    sources (E)")
Emancipation Proclamation,
    211
Emmaus, 133, 134, 183
Emperor Cult, 116-117, 148
Enoch, 133
Ephraim, 54
Epicureanism, 121

Omri, 94, 98
One Flew Over the Cuckoo's
   Nest, 243-245
Oral transmission (Gospels),
   65

Palestine, 73, 74, 83-84
Papacy and Peter, 21-22
Papal infallibility, 267
Parable, 68
Parker, Archbishop, 39
Passion Narrative, 125, 130
Passover, 128, 148
   Crucifixion, 59
   Gospel's dating, 60
   Matzah, 157
Paul, 107, 109, 115, 116, 123,
   129, 135, 144, 149, 195
Paul IV, 161
Pekah, 27
Pentateuch, 50, 85
Pentateuch, Samaritan, 85
Pentateuchal sources, 51-58
   Babylonian Exile, 57
   D, 55-57
   Diagram, 52
   E, 54-55
   J, 51-54
   P, 57-58
Pentecost, 9, 128, 139
Pericope, 65
Persia, 112
Peter, 128, 139
Pharisees, 63, 64, 67-68,

106-107, 144
   Paul, 107
   Resurrection, 107
   Scripture, 106-107
   Synagogues, 106
Philip, 125
Philip the Fair, 159
Philistines, 24, 73
Pilate, 67
Pilpul, 160
Plague, hail, 58
Plain, Maritime, 80
Plain, Philistine, 80
Plenary (see "Inspiration")
Pogroms, 157
Poore, Bishop, 176
Presuppositions, impor-
   tance of, 259
Priestly duties, 88
Priestly history (see "Bib-
   lical histories")
Priestly sources (see
   "Pentateuchal sources
   (P)")
Pronouncement story, 65-66
Prophets:
   Faith, 11-12
   Minor, 268
Protestant Reformation,
   47-48, 160, 267
Protestantism and Biblical
   authority, 22
Providence, divine, 53
Purim, 26, 182

324

326

About the Author

Frank E. Eakin, Jr.,
Professor of Religion at
the University of Richmond,
has been associated with
the University since 1966, having taught earlier at Duke
University and Wake Forest University. He received his
B.A. from the University of Richmond (1958), B.D. from
Southern Baptist Theological Seminary (1961), and Ph.D.
in Biblical Studies (Old Testament emphasis) from Duke
University (1964). His earlier publications include The
Religion and Culture of Israel (Allyn and Bacon, Inc.,
1971; University Press of America, 1977); "Spiritual Ob-
duracy and Parable Purpose" in The Use of the Old Testa-
ment in the New and Other Essays: Studies in Honor of
William Franklin Stinespring (Duke University Press, 1972);
"Zephaniah" in The Broadman Bible Commentary, VII (Broad-
man Press, 1972); "Shalom: Faith's Quest, Man's Hope" in
Dialogue: In Search of Jewish/Christian Understanding
(The Seabury Press, 1975); and articles in Jewish Spectator, Journal of Biblical Literature, Perspectives in
Religious Studies, and Review and Expositor.